BEST REGARDS TO AIDA

BEST REGARDS TO AIDA

The Defeats and Victories of a Music Man on Two Continents

by

HANS · W · HEINSHEIMER

Alfred · A · Knopf: New York

19 68

THIS IS A BORZOI BOOK
PUBLISHED BY ALFRED A. KNOPF, INC.

FIRST EDITION

 Published in the United States by Alfred A. Knopf, Inc., New York, N.Y., and simultaneously in Canada by Random House of Canada Limited, Toronto. Distributed by Random House, Inc., New York, N.Y.

Library of Congress Catalog Card Number: 68-23964

Chapter XI was originally published by Doubleday & Company, Inc., as part of *Menagerie in F Sharp*, copyright 1947 by H. W. Heinsheimer.
Chapter XIV was originally published in the October issue of *Tomorrow* under the title "Béla Bartók: A Personal Memoir," copyright 1949 by Garrett Publications, Inc.
Chapter XVI was originally published by *Saturday Review* as "The Saga of Schweitzer's Bach Edition" in the Philharmonic Hall Program for October 1965.
Chapter XV and Chapter XVI are based in part on the files on Albert Schweitzer and Arnold Schoenberg in the archives of G. Schirmer, Inc.

Manufactured in the United States of America

"I had the good fortune to have been in my twenties in the twenties."

Aaron Copland on a television program, 1967.

ILLUSTRATIONS

Following page 118

BEST REGARDS TO AIDA

On a Friday afternoon in the spring of 1923 Professor Honiger of the Law Faculty of Freiburg handed me my doctor's diploma. He didn't look very happy. He was, it seemed, unimpressed, and rightly so, with my thesis, and suspicious that I had no intention ever to become a judge in Untergrundersheim or a lawyer in Oberheimersgrund. He just felt in his erudite bones that no sooner had I shaken his limp and slightly critical hand and pocketed my diploma than I would be rushing to the station to take a train to Vienna. The diploma would never be framed. Because the following Monday I was to become a Volontär, an apprentice, in the most interesting, colorful, and imaginative music-publishing house in Europe. I was lost to the law forever.

Today, rapidly and happily approaching threescore and ten, I am still at it. I loved my job with Universal Edition in Vienna—a marvelously universal name for an enterprise thinking truly universally. They published Bruckner and Mahler, Schönberg and Strauss, and soon after I had stepped off the train and begun working for them I found myself closely associated with most of the composers of the explosive post-World War I, pre-World War II generation—most of them men of my own age. I would have stayed in Vienna forever and would never have given up my job with Universal if Adolf Hitler hadn't, rather urgently, asked me to do so.

And I loved my job with the New York branch of Boosey & Hawkes of London and would have stayed in it forever if Ralph Hawkes hadn't fired me after my book *Menagerie in F Sharp* had been published. He wanted a worker, not a writer, and told me so—it was again a Friday afternoon—in no uncertain terms. Hawkes, just like the fellow who was in the first place responsible for my working for him, had a little black mustache and he, too, was a great conqueror, much more successful, however, and more persevering. He established beachheads in Australia, invaded South Africa and Canada, and put his satraps in charge of German and French branches. His weapons, as mild as powerful, consisted mainly of the copyrights of *Rosenkavalier*, *Sacre du Printemps*, *Colonel Bogey*, and *Mikrokosmos*. I again had a wonderful time, serving as a general in his tuneful army. But came a Friday afternoon, and I had to surrender my commission and be, a little unceremoniously, returned to civilian life.

By then it was too late. I had become an incurable, enthusiastic addict to music publishing, and it was only what I expected from fate when it turned out that Hawkes had fired me straight into the outstretched arms of G. Schirmer, Inc., of New York. Undoubtedly more to spite Hawkes than to please me, G. Schirmer, who had been in the music-publishing business since 1861, longer than any other music publisher in America and therefore should know what they were doing, considered it chic to hire a worker who was also a writer. They made their point most elegantly: soon after I had started working in a dingy corner of the old Schirmer Building on 43rd Street, I was called up to the cloudless sunlight of the board room on the seventh floor, just being readied for a director's meeting. In the slightly faded elegance, so awe-inspiring to the newcomer, beneath the portraits of Gustav I, Gustave II, and Gustave III, my new boss, flanked on one side by a samovar whose origin and purpose remained for ever unknown and on the other by two spotty mirrors left there by a dance studio that once, in times of stress, had been permitted to be a tenant on the fifth floor, I saw, next to pad, pencil, and cigars, a copy of my book *Menagerie in F Sharp* in front of every empty chair. The boss himself—clean-shaven, no little black mustache this time—was standing in the door, smilingly pointing a well-fed finger at the flatteringly adorned table.

The books, I found out a little later, had not been purchased: they had been borrowed from the Schirmer store, whither they were returned after the director's meeting. But it was a brief moment of glory, cherished forever.

Gustave III, alas, has since joined II and I and the Schirmer store is now a church, the Chapel of St. Christopher—a most appropriate transformation: nothing ever made more money for the house of Schirmer than the musical setting by Albert Hay Malotte of *The Lord's Prayer.*

After fifty years of occupancy we left the old place without tears, as we moved to a sparkling airline building, the very symbol of a new age. All the old taboos were left behind. Enormous tubs filled with papers, uselessly kept for generations but still, sinister, fear-inspiring guardians of the past silently watching over every one of our days, were carted away to destruction. Rows of sacred wooden trays, filled with little cards carrying forgotten symbols and meaningless numbers, were dumped irreverently despite the tearful protestations of their vestal guardians. We left behind manuscripts that had been pushed by successions of editors to the bottom of the pile, frayed dictionaries of 1891, pictures of composers whose unidentifiable faces had been forgotten and of cousins whose names had never been known.

A large room was discovered on the sixth floor which nobody had known was there. When the door was forced with trepidation, the room turned out, to everybody's disappointment, not to contain the bloody remains of beautiful young wives murdered by music-publishing bluebeards, but rows after rows of peaceful Canadian copyright certificates.

Nobody knew who had brought them there or what their purpose was. They, too, were carted away and were never seen again or missed.

We moved uptown, away from the memories of the past, bringing along only the golden samovar and the spotted mirrors as remembrances of the director's room and the pleasant, if fleeting, memories it held for me. Only once in a while we drift back from our streamlined, air-conditioned lives, back into the quiet Chapel of St. Christopher, which had been the Schirmer store for fifty years and is now crowded with lunch-hour worshippers as it was once crowded by lunch-hour shoppers. We are a little embarrassed and look around before we enter to see whether, perhaps, one of our colleagues had the same thought—and if we spot one of them (they all come back from time to time and they all look around to see that they are alone) we make believe that we have some business at the Emigrant Savings Bank across the street or, if it's too late to cross over, we hide in the shiny new elevator to the fifth floor, now the offices of a stockbroker—Mammon and Prayer still under the same roof.

After we have made sure that we are unobserved, we enter the chapel, greeted by rows of flickering candles burning brightly in their racks where the gaily colored covers of sheet music, burning brightly in the morning sun, used to greet us when we arrived for work. There, to the right where an old man kneels in absorption, was the book department, where I could see from the corner of my eye the oh, so slowly shrinking stack of my book when I crossed the store.

To the left, the curtain of the confessional swallows up the pale face of a woman, her troubled head covered by a kerchief. Right there Gustave III used to perch, having descended from the presidential splendor of his seventh-floor office to sell musical toys. There he is again surrounded by dogs that play nursery rhymes and rabbits wheezing folk songs, hugely enjoying himself holding a tiger, singing "Beautiful Dreamer" over his head so that the crowd can admire it and him—and then being grandiosely pleased when an irate customer, dissatisfied with his salesmanship, asks for his name and number so that he may write a letter of complaint to the president of the firm, Mr. Gustave Schirmer III.

And here, through the flicker of the candles, floating on the wings of the hymn fervently sung by the worshippers, here come the members of the board of directors, just descended from their ghost-gray Rolls-Royces now cruising aimlessly around the block, waiting for the tiny, creaky elevator that isn't here any more to take them up to the director's room that isn't there any more, to leaf, a little surprised and really not very interested, through my book that isn't here any more. I, myself, have almost forgotten that it ever was here. In the new streamlined surroundings, freed from the little white cards of the past, we are happily, excitingly, busy around the clock. Every day brings new challenges. There is no time to think about an old book.

But people wouldn't let me forget it. It seems that there is no finer Christmas gift, no more desirable addition to a library, no more indispensable present for a young man or woman entering or leaving school than a book that is out of print. Everybody suddenly wants it. As the only editions of *Menagerie in F Sharp* still available were in Hebrew and in German, and as few of the petitioners were Germans and not very many were Hebrews, there was little I could do to help.

As time passed, I myself got a little restless. Perhaps an author whose work has once adorned the director's table will never be at ease again. Thus, when the chance came to visit my *Menagerie* again and to revise, augment, cut, improve, or mess it up to my heart's delight, I hadn't to be pushed too hard. Maybe, I thought, some of those who wanted a book of mine which they *couldn't* get would not be deterred by the fact that now there would be one they *could* get. Of course, those who still prefer the original will have to learn Hebrew or German.

It's a wonderful experience to revisit a book written some twenty years before, and to do so not on a sentimental, perhaps slightly sad journey into the past, but with an invigorating contract from a publisher and with the assurance of resurrection to inspire, cajole, encourage, and urge you on. Soon things begin to fall into place. Some of the things you thought and said prove still valid. Some, quite a few, are dated. Some of your predictions came true. Others didn't. And so much has happened since—new faces, new events, new trends, new evaluations: the visit soon carries you far beyond the familiar precincts and you wander among new surroundings, new scenery, many different people.

Where to begin? As I step back to take a look at the landscape, filled with figures, colors, and events, crowded and full of surprises and discoveries like a Brueghelian canvas—there, look, right here is a tall, bearded man, sparkling eyes under a wide-brimmed hat, an erect figure, kindly but very much in command. It is Emil Hertzka, head of Universal Edition in Wien. As a student I had met him during a vacation trip at the house of my uncle in Vienna. He had told me—just to be nice to the uncle, I suppose, and not with any serious intention ever to have me on the premises—that he was always looking for eager young men. I was eager. I was young. I was never the same again. Everything during the final two years of my education for the bar was blighted by the magic spell his careless words had produced, and even my thesis, scorned and marked with a very ordinary *cum laude* by Professor Honiger, had been on some obscure subject of musical copyright—the only aspect of the law that still held any interest for me.

But now the train was speeding through the night: Munich—Salzburg—Vienna at last. I had a letter from Hertzka in my pocket: one of his eager young men had just called it quits. A desk and a secretary had been left behind. If I wanted to try my luck at a token salary, both would be mine Monday morning.

Monday came at last—and what an entry into a new life! The offices of Universal Edition were on the second floor of the Musikverein, the most beautiful musical building I had ever set foot in. Its tradition-soaked walls housed the golden splendor and the matchless acoustics of the Grosser Musikvereinsaal, the famous concert hall in which the Vienna Philharmonic Orchestra gave its Sunday morning concerts, and the beautifully proportioned Kleine Musikvereinsaal, where chamber music concerts and recitals took place.

On the second floor was the home of the library of the K.K. (the Kaiserlich-Königlich Double Eagle was still holding its protective imperial wings over the republican door) Gesellschaft der Musikfreunde, a treasure house of manuscripts, books, and rare musical prints presided over by a white-bearded savant with an angelic face under a black skullcap who had been a close friend of Brahms and whose name, musically melting on the tongue, was Eusebius Mandyczewski. My office was to be directly below the manuscripts of the "Unfinished" Symphony, a dozen or two symphonies by Joseph Haydn, and more Beethoven string quartets than any other apprentice in the music-publishing business ever worked beneath. As I ascended the stone stairs to my new job, I trod reverently: they were worn by the steps of Gustav Mahler, Anton Bruckner, and Richard Strauss. And when I finally sat down at the little desk and got my eyes off the little Viennese secretary, I looked at the baroque columns and the green-golden cupola of the Karlskirche. I had a choice among Fischer von Erlach, the Rasumovsky quartets, and Fräulein Mizzi.

This was the setting for my first day in the music business.

Among the hues of ancient gold, patinaed copper, and white-bearded savants, Emil Hertzka, my boss, was only a rent-paying tenant. Patina wasn't for him. He was the most progressive, the most daring music publisher in Europe and if I had thought of Beethoven, Bruckner, and Brahms while ascending the stairs in the morning, I was already thinking of Bartók, Berg, and Busoni when I descended them after my first day at work. There couldn't have been a more seductive introducer than Emil Hertzka to the world of new music for an eager young man who had just filed his law diploma away and was ready to assign his soul to any Mephistopheles who would guide him to the Walpurgisnacht that was to be his destiny.

Hertzka, a remarkable, unique figure in the international world of music publishing, had come into it in the most remarkable way. Universal Edition had been founded around the turn of the century by a group of Viennese who thought that a new, a green and purple, edition of the classics—another set of Beethoven sonatas, Bertini etudes, Well-Tempered Claviers—could successfully compete with such long established editions as the green Peters, the gray Breitkopf, and the yellow Schirmer. It couldn't. After six years they had a catalogue of 1,550 titles, a large stock, and very little business. One of the directors knew a man who had made good in the textile business: Hertzka was put in charge of Universal to rescue what there was to be rescued or, if need be, to liquidate the mess. Instead, he built one of the leading publishing houses in the world.

He didn't try to sell more Chopin waltzes or Hanon exercises. He didn't invest in paper: he began, at once, to invest in people. During the first year of his administration he made exclusive publication contracts with Gustav Mahler, Arnold Schönberg, and Franz Schreker (who, today, is all but forgotten but for many years was a terrific success and moneymaker for the firm). Universal had already bought the rights in most of the important tone poems by Richard Strauss from a small publisher in Strauss's home town, Munich. They found out later that he had not even bothered to invest the one-dollar registration fee for an American copyright for *Till Eulenspiegel, Tod und Verklärung*, and *Don Juan*, thus abandoning them, irrevocably, to a shameful public-domain life in the United States—but they were still nice properties in the rest of the world. Hertzka added to them the symphonies by Anton Bruckner, which he bought from two small publishers who, once, had acquired them from the composer for the Austrian equivalent of peanuts. The deal also brought him a nice, old-fashioned music store, owned by one of them, located appealingly, if a little darkly, under the arcades of the Vienna Opera House.

By the time I ambled in, the remarkable refugee from the textile business also had contracts with a plethora of composers from all over the world—among them Béla Bartók, Alban Berg, Leoš Janáček, Zoltán Kodály, Ernst Krenek, Karol Szymanowski, Darius Milhaud, Francesco Malipiero, Alfredo Casella, Anton von Webern, and Kurt Weill. This was to be my teacher, this was my Mephistopheles.

That such an enterprise, dedicated almost exclusively to the discovery, the encouragement, and the promotion—worldwide, ruthless, and victorious—of new composers and new, often far-out musical ideas should be organized and successfully carried out in Vienna of all places adds a special twist to the Hertzka miracle. On the surface, it seems a logical choice: Vienna and music are almost synonyms. But as one looks a little closer, the Hertzka concept was essentially foreign to a city which has an Eroica Road and a Mahler Strasse and whose Schubert House is a must on the tourist circuit, but which has not been the birthplace of a really significant new opera since *The Marriage of Figaro* (withdrawn after a few performances), *The Magic Flute*, *Cosí fan tutte*, and *Fidelio*. Of the operas of Richard Strauss, almost an adopted son of the city, head of the Vienna Opera for many years and owner of a splendid villa given to him by the Vienna city council, only one, *Die Frau ohne Schatten*, was baptized with Danube water, and a work such as *Salome* was permitted to disgrace the hallowed boards of the famous Vienna Opera House only thirteen years after its first performance in Dresden: the Austrian *première* of that scandalous work had to be given in the provincial city of Graz, where the opera was produced a few months after the Dresden performance with Gustav Mahler, Alban Berg, Arnold Schoenberg, Alexander von Zemlinsky, and many other composers and musicians from Vienna in the audience.

Richard Wagner tried hard and stubbornly to bestow on Vienna the honor of being the first place to produce *Tristan*. After seventy-seven rehearsals the work was dropped as unperformable, and it took twenty years after the Munich *première* for the opera to reach Vienna. Even first performances in German of great international successes were almost never given there. *La Bohème* came to Vienna seven years after its world *première*. *Tosca* had its first German performance in Dresden, *Madama Butterfly* in Berlin, Charpentier's *Louise* in Elberfeld, *Pelléas* in Frankfurt. Of all the lasting successes of the nineteenth century, only *Carmen* seems to have been heard in Vienna (after its original production in Paris) before it got anywhere else. For sticklers—Viennese sticklers—I hasten to add that the world *première* of *Martha* did take place in Vienna on November 25, 1847, and pleased the Viennese so much that thirty-five years later Flotow celebrated his seventieth birthday by attending the 500th performance of his opera as an *Ehrengast*. Oh yes, Weber's *Euryanthe* of overture fame was first produced in Vienna and Massenet's *Werther* had its world *première à* l'Opera Imperial de Vienne *le 16 février* 1892, almost a year before the first performance in Paris.

Or take the case of Gustav Mahler, for many years the city's most celebrated operatic director, married to one of the city's most celebrated beauties—Mahler, who seems as close to Vienna as a composer can get to a city. Of his nine symphonies, only one, the Ninth, had its *première* performance there. And that was, of course, a posthumous première: the Viennese love dead composers. After Mahler had himself presided over the first performances of Numbers 1 to 8 in Budapest, Berlin, Krefeld, Munich, Cologne, Prague, and Essen—a veritable array of un-Mahlerian names—Bruno Walter conducted the world *premières* of the Ninth and of the *Lied von der Erde* in Vienna—in honor of a great departed. And where did the Viennese composer's Ernst Krenek's world success *Jonny spielt auf* originate? In Leipzig. And the Viennese Korngold's *Tote Stadt* and other works of his that made the international circuit and brought honor and money to his native city? In Hamburg, Munich, and Cologne.

As for Alban Berg, I don't know of an Alban Berg Strasse or Alban Berg Platzerl in Vienna yet—but they will get around to it. In the meantime, he got an *Ehrengrab*, an honorary tomb, from the city when he died. While he was alive, he had to find a German conductor, Hermann Scherchen, to introduce three fragments from *Wozzeck* at a music festival in Germany where Erich Kleiber—another Viennese who had to gather his laurels abroad—heard them and decided to produce the opera, in Berlin. *Wozzeck* came to Vienna four years after its sensational debut in Berlin—the birthplace and the home of its composer was the twelfth European city to produce the work. And even after Berg had received a prize from his native city (in 1930) and was resting in his *Ehrengrab* (since 1935), nobody in Vienna touched his second opera, *Lulu:* we had to travel all the way to Zürich, to hear the work there, for the first time, in 1937. In the ensuing years, *Lulu* was, of course, no suitable fare for the Vienna of the Anschluss. Only several years after the de-Anschlussization, in 1949, was the work heard in concert form, and only in 1962, twenty-seven years after the composer's death, was the opera finally staged at the famous Theater an der Wien, once the birthplace of *Die Zauberflöte* and now, at last, a worthy frame for Berg's posthumous masterpiece, proudly produced as part of the Viennese Festwochen and a smashing success, an American Lulu, the talk of the town and of Europe.

In post-World War I Vienna, modern music was rarely heard outside of the Society for Private Musical Performances, founded and ruled by Arnold Schoenberg—or, as he then spelled his name, Schönberg. Its performances were strictly for members only. Guests (foreign visitors excepted) were not admitted. Members were obligated under the bylaws to abstain from applause (or from showing their disapproval) and especially from writing or inspiring criticisms, notices, or discussions of the performances in the press. Musical works were to benefit solely through good performances and through the effect made by the music itself. "Propaganda," the original declaration, written by Alban Berg, stated, "for works and their composers is not the aim of the Society. No school of music is to receive preference, and only the worthless shall be excluded: for the rest, all modern music—from that of Mahler and Strauss to the newest, which practically never or, at most, rarely is heard, will be performed."

The newest music, never or at most rarely heard in public performances, was, of course, the music of what is now known as the Viennese school of contemporary music. What could be more ironic than to recall that this music, celebrated today and, in fact, of great and lasting influence on the music of our time, could be performed only clandestinely in the very city that gave it its name. And even so, the Society could not sustain itself for very long. Schönberg, who had tried in vain to obtain a position as a teacher at the Vienna Conservatory ("Maybe the director of the Conservatory could be made to understand who I am and how lacking in talent they would be if they took anyone else as long as they could have me. And, unfortunately, I can be had!"), moved to Berlin, where he was given a master class at the Academy. Alban Berg lived—in every sense of the word—on the periphery of Vienna. Anton Webern, considered a serious-minded, shruggingly tolerated screwball, was permitted to make a bare living as conductor of the Workers Concerts organized by the Socialist Party. We always went to hear them, to pay homage to their thin, bespectacled conductor, whose stooped, slightly clumsy, professorial movements, his face deeply buried in the score, had only one purpose: to serve the music. My most poignant memory of this unique man is a performance of Mahler's Eighth Symphony. As the audience rose in applause, he lifted, not without difficulty, the huge, heavy score over his head. The work, not the conductor, was to be applauded. I have often thought of that gesture of proud modesty, never encountered again.

This was the Vienna the apprentice entered. As an abode, of course, it was paradise. Hertzka lived in a sprawling house in Kaasgraben. The composer Egon Wellesz, the conductor Alexander von Zemlinsky, writers, architects, and horticulturists were his neighbors, and he had a garden full of fruit trees and flowers where once in a while there were parties for visiting composers and where, right at the beginning of my career, I made the *faux pas* of bringing along Fräulein Mizzi. She was, at once, removed from the scene at Universal, leaving me with nothing but Fischer von Erlach and the Beethoven quartets as solace. I myself lived in a small, dark, furnished room—but we all breathed the lovely Viennese air, could sit under the trees along the avenues in front of the coffeehouses and dip wonderfully crisp crescents in proverbial coffee. If there was no Schönberg or Stravinsky at night, there were the lilacs in the parks and the winegardens with *schrammel* music, schmaltz directly from heaven.

For an eager young and for a forever eager old man, however, the most important feature of Vienna was the railroad stations from which one could leave for where the action was: the Westbahnhof to Salzburg, Munich, Paris, London, perhaps even to New York; the Südbahn for the music festivals in Venice and Barcelona, for Zagreb, Milan, Rome —ah, and the Nordbahn, only a few hours to Brno, the home of Leoš Janáček and many of his exciting *premières*, or to Prague, where a German and a Czech opera house competed in productions of new works. Then there was the speedy Arpad to Budapest or a bus to Bratislava, where an enterprising director had made the local opera house a show place for new music.

But the train more frequented than any other was the sleeper special, leaving Vienna at night and putting you down at Berlin's Anhalter Bahnhof in the refreshing breeze of an early morning. After a few draws of the *Berliner Luft*, *Schrammels* and coffeehouses, crescents, flowers, and Fräulein Mizzi were forgotten. Your heart beat faster as you stepped from the station.

II

How can i describe the Berlin of that era to anyone who did not see it, did not feel its impact, did not smell its air, did not once get drawn into the whirlpool of its bubbling, boiling intellectual life? No visit to the new Berlin of today will even faintly mirror its past. Perhaps the only people who can appreciate what it was like, without being able to draw from their own nostalgic memories, are the New Yorkers of today. New York strikes you with a force very similar to the one Berlin overpowered you with. Even the air seems the same, the invigorating air that sweeps in from the ocean and the woods and the not-too-distant mountains and makes people walk and think and act faster, helps to breed big and daring and sometimes wild and fantastic thoughts, and changes the slow-moving Southerner and the sun-spoiled Westerner into real New Yorkers almost overnight—just as the air of Berlin, sweeping in from the pine woods and the lakes and across the plains from the not-too-distant sea, changed slow-moving Austrians and sun-spoiled Italians, Russians and Poles, Frenchmen and Hungarians, and the Germans from all four corners of their land and made them into Berliners.

What a city it was, that Berlin, wedged in between the end of one world war and the sudden descent of the dark ages that preceded the second one—given fifteen years only to develop what Alfred Kerr, its chief drama critic, once called the Periclean Age of German arts and letters. Fifteen short years—or even less when allowance is made for a little reorientation after the collapse of the imperial order and for a little time lost at the other end of the rainbow, when the shadows had already begun to lengthen and you got into the habit of looking over your shoulder to see where the sun had suddenly gone. Ten years, then, twelve perhaps. But what years, what people, what a time!

It was a time of youth and a city of youth. November 1918 had put a sudden end to everything that was old. The old empire had vanished, the old conceptions, the old conventions, the old traditions, and the old people. A new generation of writers, composers, directors, painters, barely in their twenties, returned from the war and, faced with a new order of things, found themselves not in oppressed opposition but in actual command. One of them, Walter Hasenclever, wrote on the manuscript of his play *Der Sohn* ("The Son") (a son who, of course, murdered his father): "This play intends to change the world." Ernst Gläser's *Jahrgang 1902* ("Vintage 1902") was the most talked about, the most typical novel of the era. The young soldiers, back from the war, met under huge banners, proclaiming "*Nie wieder Krieg*"—never again war. The young musicians, looking into a new, exciting future, changed a single letter in the proclamation that was to be so short-lived and soon would be high treason, and proclaimed, "*Nie wieder Grieg*."

And Berlin opened its arms wide to everything that was new, young, daring, different. Almost overnight it became the center of the postwar intellectual life of Germany, perhaps of Europe. Censorship had been abolished by the new German republic. The Prussian Ministry of Culture and the city government of Berlin were driven by an almost frantic desire to wipe out the philosophies of the imperial past.

Soon three important teachers of musical composition had settled in Berlin. Ferruccio Busoni—half Italian, half German—became head of the master class in composition at the Academy of the Fine Arts, and when he died in 1924, only Arnold Schönberg sufficed to fill his place. Franz

Schreker, teacher and composer, was called in to become head of the Music Academy, leaving a tired, politically troubled Vienna that rapidly yielded much of its talent to the drawing power of Berlin. Around these magnetic teachers a whole generation of young composers came to study in Berlin, live in Berlin, and soon settle and produce in Berlin. Ernst Krenek, Karol Rathaus, Ernst Toch, Hanns Eisler came from Vienna. Alois Hába, protagonist of quarter-tone music, came from Prague. Wladimir Vogel and Boris Blacher came from Russia, Louis Gruenberg, Edgar Varèse, and George Antheil from America.

Kurt Weill, short, bespectacled, already balding as a very young man, eager to learn, to hear, to absorb, came from Dessau, a middle-sized German town which soon after became the home of the Bauhaus, the high temple of modern architecture. At twenty-one, Weill, a pupil of Busoni, was paying tribute to his new home town by writing his *Berliner Symphonie*. Like him, everybody was nineteen, twenty, or perhaps twenty-five years old. At thirty they had to be celebrities. At thirty-five they were suspect spokesmen of the older generation. At forty they were a Herr Professor, a Herr Generalmusikdirektor, a Master—or forgotten.

It was the same everywhere—in the theaters, in the opera houses, in the night clubs and cabarets, in the government-operated radio, where Hans Flesch, brother-in-law of Paul Hindemith, had full authority to produce the most up-to-date musical and dramatic fare in a set-up that had never heard of a rating, and where he soon attracted writers, composers, and top performers to make the Berlin radio a sparkling mirror of the time. Hermann Scherchen, a native Berliner who had returned from a Russian PW camp, conducted concerts devoted to new music and founded *Melos*, a magazine for modern music which is still in existence to this day.

Erich Kleiber was thirty-three years old when he was made head of the State Opera Unter den Linden, taking over from the old guard and at once toppling the imperial traditions of the house. In 1925, two years after his appointment, he made history with the world *première* of *Wozzeck* by Alban Berg, who had to come to Berlin to hear his work performed just as Darius Milhaud and Paul Claudel would come from Paris a few years later, to have their *Christophe Colomb* performed for the first time by Kleiber and his team.

The State Opera Unter den Linden was only one of three opera houses in that fabulous postwar (or prewar), that fabulous between-war Berlin. They were all operating for ten months of the year. One of them was heavily subsidized by the City of Berlin, two were supported by the Prussian State (which also rebuilt Kleiber's Opera Unter den Linden to the tune of almost three million dollars and heavily subsidized the State Theater of Drama at the Gendarmenmarkt). They had brilliant casts and brilliant conductors and competed with each other with only slightly veiled ferocity.

The second State Opera was founded in 1927 and closed again under the pressure of the onrushing reaction in 1931, but its four hectic, embattled, crazily wonderful years are not forgotten. It occupied a house that originally had been the home of a glorified beergarden, founded in 1844 by a certain Kroll. Berliners never learned to call the new opera house by its official name, the Opera at the Square of the Republic—it remained the Kroll Opera even when it served, after the Reichstag fire of 1933, as the home for the Nazi Parliament and later became rubble in the Berlin holocaust. Otto Klemperer, the forty-two-year-old Silesian giant who had been a prominent German conductor since, at the recommendation of Gustav Mahler, he had obtained a leading position at the age of twenty-two, was called from Wiesbaden (another Prussian State Theater) to become the uncompromising leader of the new house. Every performance was rehearsed to the very last drop of energy left in any of the participants—the singers were not even permitted to sing with half voice during rehearsals, and it is reported that a leading tenor, when urged again and again by the merciless Klemperer to SING, stepped to the footlights and said, *sotto voce:* "I have only two high B's left, Herr Klemperer. Do you want to hear them now or tonight at the performance?"

Klemperer's directors and stage designers were recruited not only from the world of opera but also from the drama and the arts. His repertory offered a provocative mixture of contemporary works (among them the world *première* of Hindemith's *Neues vom Tage*, the German *première* of Janáček's *From the House of the Dead*, and the rarely performed operas by Stravinsky), standard operas in nonstandard productions and the exhumation of forgotten works by the masters, such as Verdi's *Luisa Miller* and Smetana's *The Kiss*, most of which, however, had to be buried again, hastily and discreetly. The unorthodox style of most of these productions was not always appreciated by the old-timers, still entrenched in the Prussian Ministry of Culture, nor were they much to the taste of many of the subscribers who, rather than endure *Neues vom Tage*, Schönberg's *Erwartung*, or a *Hoffmann* à la Bauhaus, painted by Moholy-Nagy, sneaked over to one of the more conservative opera houses to hear *Tiefland* or *Der Waffenschmied* the way they and their ancestors had been accustomed to hear and see opera. When *Fidelio* was produced in the abstract, cool, uncompromising Kroll style, a Berlin paper headlined its report "Fidelio on the rocks." A revolutionary production of *The Flying Dutchman* was a sacrilegious shocker. A Dutchman without beard, Senta in blue pull-over, heavy skirt, and a fiery red wig, chorus girls without pigtails, and no spinning wheels—the morning of the first performance the Berlin chief of police called in person to announce to Klemperer's first lieutenant, Hans Curjel, that demonstrations were planned for the evening. Curjel laughed—but at night fifty detectives mingled with the unruly audience, arrests were made as an intermission feature, and Curjel didn't laugh any more. Siegfried Wagner, not suspecting that he was nursing in Wahnfried a little boy, Wieland, who would soon out-Klemper Klemperer by shaving off *all* of grandfather's beards, summed up his impressions of the controversial *Dutchman* with a word that soon would ring through Berlin and Germany and would finally sweep clear across the border Klemperer and everything he and his Kroll Opera stood for: *Kulturbolschewismus.*

At the City Opera House—another large house, another large cast, another brilliant repertoire—still another firebrand was in command: Carl Ebert, who had brought with him a group of brilliant young men, the stage director Rabenalt, the painter Reinking, the wonderful stage designer Caspar Neher, who also wrote the libretto for a Kurt Weill opera, *Die Bürgschaft,* which had its world *première* there. I still remember its haunting music and a scene in the fog, the foggiest fog ever produced in an opera house. Neher, like Bert Brecht, came from Augsburg, a medium-sized ancient town in Bavaria, and like Brecht, he always kept his slightly provincial, slow Bavarian speech—two more out-of-towners who had been absorbed by the miraculous city, had helped to make it miraculous, and always kept that little aura of strangeness, of a touch of their home town in their speech and their dress and in their habits of life. But they *were* Berliners, just like all the other writers and musicians, the stage designers from Greece, the conductors from Poland, the publishers from Russia, playwrights from Budapest, composers from Spain and Italy, pianists from Latvia and Switzerland, and Professor Paul Hindemith from Frankfurt, who, too, moved to Berlin to become a teacher at the Music Academy in 1927, at the age of thirty-two.

The reservoir of available talent was inexhaustible—and it was constantly enlarged by visitors from all over the world. Habima and the Moscow Art Theater of Stanislavski came on regular visits, fertilizing the conceptions of directors and actors. The Folies-Bergère came from Paris and brought Josephine Baker to Berlin—and Berlin's women were never the same again. Jack Hilton came from London. Paul Whiteman brought *Rhapsody in Blue* from New York. If one looks over the names of the actors, singers, stage designers, and directors constantly employed in some thirty theaters throughout the city, the list is as dazzling as today's star-studded marquees of New York, London, and Hollywood. "Whenever we discover a young actor, a fine singer, a promising director, he goes to Berlin," complained the manager of a (not so very) provincial German theater in 1928. "If we have a success, Berlin at once adopts it as its own. Berlin has the greatest arsenal of talent—and twenty-five newspapers which have it in their power to make and to break a man, a play, a whole era."

Head of the Philharmonic Orchestra was, of course, the one German musician worthy to head the Philharmonic Orchestra of the supermetropolis: Wilhelm Furtwängler. He had succeeded, in 1922, Arthur Nikisch, himself the successor of Hans von Bülow and Richard Strauss. Glancing through the chronicle of the Furtwängler era one senses here, too, the blending of many important creative forces. Alternating with Furtwängler, and each bringing his own contributions to the air of Berlin, were Fritz Busch, Otto Klemperer, Bruno Walter, Thomas Beecham, Serge Koussevitzky, Erich Kleiber, Ernest Ansermet, Dimitri Mitropoulos (whose name, in the chronicle, is followed by the word Athens), Carl Schuricht—and, a firm policy, composers conducting their own works—Stravinsky, Busoni, Glazunov, Respighi, Ravel, Schreker, Korngold. Other composers—Bartók, for instance, Prokofiev, Casella, Rachmaninoff—appeared as soloists performing their works. During a week of Austrian music, in 1923, Alban Berg, Arnold Schönberg, Anton von Webern, and Alexander von Zemlinsky shared the podium, conducting their own music.

What Kleiber was at Unter den Linden, Klemperer was at Kroll (where he also conducted regular concerts: "I consider this of prime importance, because I am convinced that an opera orchestra will play opera much more beautifully if they are trained, at the same time, to play symphonic music."), Carl Ebert at the City Opera, and Furtwängler at the Philharmonic, Leopold Jessner, Erwin Piscator, and Max Reinhardt were in the flowering field of drama. Leopold Jessner was called to Berlin from the German hinterland (now the Polish hinterland, far, far behind the new frontier) to take over the Prussian State Theater—to democratize the court theater of Kaiser Wilhelm. When he opened the house at the Gendarmenmarkt in September, 1919, with a performance of Schiller's *Wilhelm Tell*, with Albert Bassermann as Tell and Fritz Kortner as Gessler—staged in a startling, revolutionary style that brought home the revolutionary power of the drama to a public made thoroughly receptive to its impact by the political events of the very recent past and the still unsettled turmoil of the present—Alfred Kerr wrote the next morning: "Yesterday, for the first time, the former Royal Theater was really royal."

Erwin Piscator carried the new conception of a stage without painted scenery—without attempted illusion—to its very extreme. He had started out as a political, far-to-the-left producer and director, taking his plays into the smoky beer-halls and assembly places of the workers' districts. Soon he staged fantastic productions in the Volksbühne, a theater founded and maintained by the labor unions of Berlin, which bought most of the tickets for their members. They were all sold at one price, and the locations were drawn from an urn as one entered the house, a modern amphitheater without balconies, built at the outskirts of the city among tenement houses and factories. Later, Piscator had his own theater where he performed *The Good Soldier Schweik* with the unforgettable Max Pallenberg in a grandiose, nightmarish stage design by George Grosz, and where in 1927 he reached the culminating point of his hectic career with the play *Hoppla, wir leben* by Ernst Toller, one of the many strange talents of the German theater, who burned shortly, brightly, meteorlike, through this incredible, meteorlike period, soon to be extinguished and to disappear.

Hoppla, wir leben was the story of a fighter in the revolution of 1918 who spent eight years in an insane asylum. Released, he found himself facing the realities of a Germany of 1927, so very different from the dreams and the ideals he had been hoping and fighting for. The play was acted in a huge, two-story construction of iron tubes with the use of motion pictures, loudspeakers, translucent screens, a very elaborate system of lights, and even an audible projection of the heartbeat of an aviator crossing the ocean. An elegant, bejeweled public paid up to $25 for a seat to mingle with students and workers at the opening of the play, whose closing words were: "There are only two chances left—to hang oneself or to change the world." One segment of the audience began to sing the "*Internationale*" after the final curtain had come down, while the other half called for their chauffeurs to be taken to the Adlon Hotel for supper or to one of the many cabarets—the spacious Cabaret of the Comedians, the subterranean Katakombe, The Blue Angel, Sound and Smoke, or, simply, Megalomania—where they could eat *Gulaschsuppe*, listen to the brilliant couplets of Friedrich Holländer, Rudolf Nelson, or Mischa Spoljansky, and hear famous *conferenciers* debunk their world in even more acid, more unafraid, more prophetic and yet smilingly shrugged-off words.

Not everything, of course, was vibrating with the undertones of doom. There were lavish musicals from America, Vienna, and Budapest, beautiful dancers wearing barely a handkerchief, fabulous revues. There was the greatest of all continental stage successes, *The White Horse Inn.* There was Max Reinhardt, restlessly commuting among Vienna, Salzburg, New York, and Berlin, running his world-famous productions in four different theaters in Berlin, among them his "Theater of the 5000," the Grosses Schauspielhaus, a combination of Madison Square Garden, Radio City Music Hall, and St. Patrick's Cathedral. It had been a circus before Reinhardt converted it into a theater, and it never quite lost the smell of the circus, either symbolically or literally.

There were the Brothers Rotter, running a string of theaters throughout the city as if the Shuberts of New York had been anticipated in Berlin. There was Marlene Dietrich. There was Lotte Lenya. There, facing the most preposterous landmark of imperial Berlin, the Gedächtniskirche, was the Romanische Café, abode of countless painters, writers, musicians, newspapermen, philosophers, and assorted intellectual hangers-on from all over the world.

And there were the most wonderful little revues along the Kurfürstendamm—who will forget the wit, the bitter satire, the music, the superb acting that went into a show such as *Es liegt in der Luft* ("It Is in the Air")? The air—the biting, exciting, exotic, erotic air, the prickly, inspired, inspiring air—was, of course, the air of Berlin.

The man who wrote this and many other wonderful shows was one of the masters of the craft, Marcellus Schiffer, who went on from there (before killing himself) to write the libretto for Hindemith's *Neues vom Tage*, filled with a cynicism that already knew that all this was not to last long, that already the shadows were drawing longer, and that the thunder, barely drowned out by the music, was growing louder as the clock ticked on. It is reported that among the spectators at Klemperer's production was one Austrian ex-corporal and ex-house painter. He didn't like the show. He didn't like Hindemith. He didn't like the very atmosphere of the fabulous, teeming city. He was determined to wipe it all out one day. And the day was to come soon.

III

IN 1923, THAT DAY was still ten wonderful years and many train rides away from the Viennese Schrammelparadies to Berlin's Kurfürstendamm. I had been watching Hertzka go on trip after trip—leaving from every one of Vienna's many railroad stations and always returning with fabulous tales and a harvest of new composer contracts in his knapsack. Soon I would have to go on such a trip myself or decrumple my law diploma and settle down in Untergrundersheim. The proverbial chance of a life time arrived when Hertzka came down with a cold two days before the first opera of Ernst Krenek, one of his latest discoveries, was to be performed in Berlin. For hours I waited nervously in the wings. But his cold and my luck were holding. A happy understudy, I was on my way.

I arrived in Berlin and met Krenek. It was a revelation, almost a shock: this young, slender man, with an overflow of soft blond hair covering a square head that seemed too big for his smallish body, was just twenty-eight days older than I was. I had met composers before in the awe-inspiring presence of Hertzka and the solemn surroundings of Universal. They were introduced ceremoniously and addressed as Master. "Dear Master Schönberg," Hertzka would say. "My dear Master Bartók." Master Schreker. Master Busoni. Master Reznicek. Master Delius. But Krenek had been born in 1900, as had I. So were Kurt Weill, Aaron Copland, George Antheil. Hindemith was just two years older—and there were so many more. They were my generation.

After a few days in Berlin, I returned to Vienna to report.

My assignment had been to be a silent observer. But I had boldly overstepped my orders. I had talked the head of the Berlin opera, the formidable Baron Max von Schillings (himself composer of a successful opera, *Mona Lisa* and, of course, one of Hertzka's Masters), into signing a contract for a new ballet by Egon Wellesz, not only a Viennese master, but also a neighbor in the Kaasgraben, and had promised the conductor Erich Kleiber the first performance of a new symphony (by a minor Universal master) which wasn't even written. Recklessly I had roamed all over Berlin. Now, riding back on the train, I thought of the Maria Theresa Medal. It was given to an officer in the Austrian army who had successfully disobeyed orders. If he failed, he would be shot at sunrise. If he succeeded, he got the medal.

I entered Hertzka's office the next morning with apprehension. But Hertzka, to his surprise, had enjoyed staying behind. He had nursed his cold, had spent an evening at home, had had a neighbor over for a game of chess. He had loved it. He was delighted with my accomplishments. He sneezed, smiled, and handed me the Maria Theresa Medal: he put me in charge of the opera department of Universal Edition.

And so the trip to Berlin and to the *première* of Krenek's *Zwingburg* was to be only the first of many trips to many new operas. At the beginning, Hertzka would go along—or, rather, I was permitted to go along—but as time passed, I was sometimes sent by myself without the benefit of a Hertzkan cold, till, finally, I became an habitué of almost every opera house of Europe. The hunger and thirst for new works, new faces, new ideas, was not limited to the bubbling activities of Berlin. Almost every central European opera house was eager to get its name in the metropolitan newspapers and national magazines and there was no surer way of getting it there than by trying the untried. A new opera was bound to draw composers, music critics, publishers, reporters, musicians, and professional highbrows from all over Europe, and mayors and other local politicians enjoyed basking in the flattering, if undeserved, reputation of being cultural trail blazers. Town councils and the legislatures of the various German states that had to foot the bills for the yearly operatic deficit found their sacrifices justified when their money-losing wards were mentioned in the metropolitan press as musical citadels and laurel dispensers. Careers of provincial conductors and producers were given a powerful boost by a nod from one of the famous music critics, who would never have gone to Coburg had it not been for an operatic delivery, and many a visiting Intendant from one of the big cities did not take the new opera but took the maestro or stage director from the provincial pond and placed him in his own high-class fishery.

All this was, of course, a delicious set-up for old Mephistopheles and me. It didn't matter why they performed all our new operas—as long as they performed them. Only Vienna remained aloof. When, once in a while, they did try something new there, one could hear, as soon as the orchestra had struck the *first* chord, a loud "What a bore" from the region where the critics sat. Or they would tell you in the coffeehouses after the dress rehearsal of a new opera, the day *before* the *première*, that, considering that this had been the penultimate performance of the new work, the house had been pretty full! When a new opera by one of the local greats, a composing judge, had its world *première*, its *Uraufführung*, in Vienna, they labeled it *Die tote Vorstadt*—the dead suburb—in a deadly pun on Korngold's *Die tote Stadt*, an opera for which they also had a poisonous arsenal of jokes and limericks, based mostly on the fact that the unfortunate Korngold was the son of Vienna's leading music critic. No wonder we took the train, not the streetcar, when we tried out our new acquisitions.

• • •

IN ALL THESE YEARS the gripping tension, the cold sweat, the throbbing excitement of a first night in an opera house has not subsided. During the final rehearsals you have given up all hope. You watch the composer, rushing up to the conductor to suggest a diminuendo here, a rubato there, and, please, could you bring out the second flute just a little more in bar 538? The baritone sang f, not f sharp, four bars after letter T. Could we hold the fermata just a trifle longer? And all the time you sit there and wonder what the hell difference it will make. If it were another *Tosca*, they could have a broken-down zither instead of an orchestra and the second flute could play a tacet solo—it would still be a smash. But you feel in your bones that for all the extended fermatas and no matter what the second flute does in bar 538, you have a lemon on your hands and you already wonder what you are going to say to the composer afterward. Well, you'll think of something.

In the meantime, let him be Richard Wagner for a little while. Look at his face, wrapped in glorious importance as the conductor turns around, calls his name through the dark auditorium, and asks was everything all right? The conductor knows, the singers know, the orchestra and the stagehands up in the wings have known all the time that nothing is all right, that the *première* tomorrow will just be another *dernière*. Only the composer doesn't know. Stageward he rushes, stumbling over the protruding legs of slumbering coaches, score in hand—here, maestro, on page 239, could the chorus come in just a shade louder. So the chorus comes in a shade louder—I didn't hear any difference, but the composer looks *so* happy and sits down, relieved. How pleased he is, how important, how pitifully euphoric in the face of certain death. Let him play Puccini for one more day.

But when the one more day comes, you, too begin to get euphoric. Your bones were wrong before—maybe it was just the dreary emptiness of the auditorium during the rehearsal which smothered it all, maybe they mattered, after all, the rubato, the fermata, the chorus coming in a shade louder. Maybe you were right to send flowers, not a wreath, to the leading lady. The lights dim, and there is the excitement again, the gripping tension, the cold sweat as you sit down in your worn-out tuxedo, faithful companion of all those years, or maybe it is a special occasion and you had to go downtown and rent tails and white tie. It is the moment of truth. Nothing that happened before matters any more. The heavenly croupier removes his hand from the rotating wheel —irrevocably. Maybe the little white ball will yet slide into the right number—your number.

You don't have to wait long. If the first person you spot during intermission rushes over to you and takes your hands and says "Isn't it wonderful," you've won. If the first person you spot asks how is the family and where to do you go for your vacation this year, you can send back your tails to Harris Bros. You've lost.

Once in a while, you win. A few years after *Zwingburg* I again sat next to Ernst Krenek in an opera house. By then, his stock had gone down mercilessly. He had written a couple of additional operas which, like *Zwingburg*, had become mere entries in operatic statistics. When he had tried to get his latest opus produced, it had been rejected by several theaters. Even Hertzka, the perennial, undiscourageable sponsor and sustainer of young composers, had almost given up on poor Ernst. The composer had to peddle his work himself, and when at last the opera house in Leipzig accepted it, they had to copy the music: Hertzka not only refused to print so doubtful a proposition, but didn't even bother to make the trip to Leipzig. I was sent all by myself. Travel expenses to attend a funeral were to be curtailed.

Nobody had played *Jonny*'s number, but as the wheel came to a stop, the little white ball slid right into it. The half dozen producers who had turned down *Jonny spielt auf* were invited to a crow dinner, presided over by a beaming Hertzka, who handed out stacks of hastily printed scores to the diners while not participating in the repast. He was a fanatical vegetarian who had shocked even so devoted and humble an apprentice as me by announcing at the table of one of our composers when a huge platter with golden-brown chickens was handed around: "No, thanks, I don't eat animal corpses." Crow, too, was not on his diet.

After a few weeks we had to call in an artist and had him design a huge map of the world. Wherever *Jonny spielt auf* had been performed or was to be produced, a little Jonny appeared. There were a hundred and fourteen of them, fiddling, blowing a sax, dancing ecstatically, shouting, waving a triumphant hat. One was climbing the Eiffel Tower, one was boarding a ship for New York and Hollywood.

What a wonderful business to be in—waiting, waiting for the right formula to gel, never able to figure it out in advance, because the formula is always different and yesterday's potent witches' brew is today's stale, stale bouillon. The unexpected, the impossible, suddenly gelling, suddenly bubbling over deliciously with guilders and liras, dollars, marks, and rubles swimming in the golden brew, with little zlotys and dinars and kroners as croutons. And when you think you have the sure-fire formula that just can't miss, it draws a deadly zero, when you have all your money on 36, *rouge, pair et passe.*

• • •

For three hours the composer played his opera for us in Hertzka's majestic office on a powerful Bösendorfer, the finest piano made in Austria, so fine that one of the streets bordering the Musikvereinsgebäude was named after it. Every morning I walked through Bösendorferstrasse on my way to work and looked at the Bösendorfer store where an old gentleman presided over many beautifully polished Bösendorfers. He looked like a real Bösendorfer and I was very disappointed when it turned out that his name was Hutterstrasser, which sounded pianomanufactorily enough but still wasn't the real thing.

The Bösendorfer in Hertzka's office had real class, and Mr. Lilien, the composer who had come all the way from Holland to play his opera for us, played it simply hutterstrasserly. He also had a wonderful voice and sang all the parts, and the chorus—the opera was based on a famous play by Maeterlinck and had an awful lot of nuns in it—sounded heavenly, as an awful lot of nuns should sound. Even the second flute sounded alluring when the composer coaxed it tenderly from the Bösendorfer. We were overwhelmed. Leave the music right here, here is a check to cover your travel expenses and a little extra, we'll have it engraved before you get home and printed before you come back, we'll go to work at once, there will be no difficulty with this one, my God, it's a sure-fire hit, believe us, we know, bon voyage. And we all had champagne and our picture taken as Mr. Lilien signed his contract, making a funny face for the photographer, and took his check and left.

A year later, after *Sister Beatrix* had been so sweeping a

fiasco in the city of Hannover that I never showed my face there again, the Bösendorfer was returned to Hutterstrasser and a battered old upright was installed in its place. It was chosen after careful tests as the piano in Vienna that resisted most successfully any attempt to make it sound like anything else but a battered old upright. Nobody would ever coax a second flute from it. Singing composers were barred from the premises. Instead, scores were to be submitted unsingingly to our editors, a bunch of frustrated, underpaid musicians who lived in remote, cluttered, ill-lighted offices, but who were supposed to be able to read a score without the help of singing Dutchmen who could make a Bösendorfer sound like the Vienna Philharmonic Orchestra.

Editors in a music-publishing house are never seen. They live behind closed doors, surrounded by enormous, useless libraries, by Bibles that are only dusted off to look up the spelling of begat, by card systems that convey no information, by giant Websters remaining forever opened on page 203.

For clods like Hertzka and me they show utter contempt—a little less for Hertzka, who, after all, pays their meager salaries, but openly and cruelly for me. All my life they have tried to trap me in a maze of medieval clefs, figured basses, names of sixteenth-century composers and a thing called combinatoriality. There they sit, behind their doors, forever taking vengeance on manuscripts, changing stems from up to down or from down to up in accordance with house rules they have made up—the Universal rule, the Schott rule, the Schirmer rule—unalterable and eternal as the tablets of Moses and the laws of Copernicus, striking terror in the heart of the uninitiated, and then changing the rules again—stems from down to up or from up to down—a new Copernican rule, new tablets of Moses, as soon as the wretched composer tries to comply with the old rules and has finally learned to put his stems up, not down, when, now, they should be down, not up. They love, they worship red pencils, and after they have drowned a helpless score in blood, changing 485 *cres* into 485 crescendos and using one and a half red pencils to make ritenutos out of *rits,* they, even they, smile—or *seem* to smile—before they go home, nobody knows where, to return in the morning, refreshed by dreams filled with red-penciled *cres* and *dims* and *rits* to start all over again.

• • •

NOT LONG AFTER the anti-Bösendorfer action had been taken, the manuscript of a new opera arrived from Czechoslovakia and was, in accordance with the new rules, turned over to the editors at the far end of the corridor, not to have its stems looked after but in order to determine whether it was any good. When it finally emerged from the editorial conclave, the editors scornfully and bitingly recommended that the work be turned down. As they were fine editors, and as neither Hertzka nor I could read a score or had any intention of getting into arguments with people who would only trap us again by proving that we couldn't transpose an E-flat clarinet, the score was returned to the composer with Form Letter C 3 which was neither as polite as it should have been nor as rude as it could have been. Then the telephone rang. Max Brod was on the line, and would I please come to Prague at once—he had just heard a new opera which was bound to become a world success and a man from a big German music-publishing house was already on his way to Prague to hear it. The opera was the rejected score from Czechoslovakia. Max Brod's judgment was not to be taken lightly: he had made the German translation of Janáček's *Jenufa,* one of the biggest winners in the Universal catalogue, and the word "world-success," from his experienced lips, had a heavy, alluring sound. Within an hour I was on the Nordbahn.

The next night, after the opera, we all went to Piscáček's, where we ate the largest knoedels this side of heaven and made a contract on the back of the menu while the publisher from Germany watched dejectedly. As the Czechs liked dejected Germans and had very few occasions to see one, everybody was very happy. The composer, a thin, palish, small man with a balding head that made him look older than his thirty-one years, was Jaromir Weinberger. The opera was, of course, *Švanda Dudák*. During the night, while unforgettably delicious steins of Pilsen beer kept arriving, we made changes in the libretto, turning the very Czech Švanda into an international palatable Schwanda, and as the morning began to dawn, we even asked the dejected German to join us in a final round of Pilsens and all sang—he had a fine, if slightly overbearing baritone—the Polka and even some of the Fugue that would soon be heard around the world. Soon *Schwanda der Dudelsackpfeifer*—what a diabolic joy it had been to make the editors edit the score! —sang his merry tunes in German and Finnish, at the Metropolitan and in Chicago, in French, Danish, Greek, and Dutch, and when I went to Berlin again to hear the work at Erich Kleiber's State Opera Unter den Linden, my friend from the lonely corner at Piscáček's was in the lobby. He came over and congratulated me with visible effort. As I had long since learned to measure our successes by the degree of anguish they caused our competitors, I felt reassured.

Jaromir Weinberger died among the pensioners of a Florida pensionopolis forty years almost to the day after the triumphal *première* of *Švanda Dudák* in Prague. *Švanda* had brought him fame and wealth. It had also brought him forty tragic years of frustration, of loneliness, of trying, and finally of giving up trying to find again the magic formula of success he had once found so unexpectedly. While still in Europe, he tried his luck with three more operas. The enormousness of the *Svanda* success could best be measured by the humiliating fate meted out to its successors.

The composer came to America around the time I had come, in 1938, and for some time we renewed our friendly contacts. I tried to get him performances and placed a few of his works—a few drum solos, some band, some organ music—with various American publishers. We even thought we had discovered, once more, a smile on the deceiving lips of the terrible goddess of luck when Weinberger wrote a set of orchestral variations on an English folk tune for John (not yet Sir) Barbirolli, who played the piece with the New York Philharmonic Orchestra and led it to a sadly brief success. From then on the composer of one of the great international operatic successes of his time remained silent, brooding in lonely retirement in the company only of brave little Hansi from Baden bei Wien, now Mrs. Jane of St. Petersburg, Florida, till, at the age of seventy, he gave up the struggle.

• • •

ALL THE ODDS had been against us, but after the heavenly croupier had called Švanda's number, he had smiled at us and pushed a mountain of gold our way. What had our chances been? In the cold, terrifying casino where the fates of operas are decided, the odds are disastrous, and even of those who win, only a few are permitted to keep their winnings. Of the roughly seven thousand operas which are listed in the most authoritative register as having seen the limelight, if ever so briefly, only—well, perhaps the reader would like to pause for a moment and jot down a list of the real, the permanent, the immortal winners. Did the reader come up with forty, fifty? If we lean over backward and include *Don Pasquale* and *Gianni Schicchi* on one list with such real winners as *La Bohème* and *Aida*, and *Der Freischütz* and *Louise* with *Carmen* and *Meistersinger* and a few lesser Verdis, *Turandot*, *Pelléas* and *Ariadne* with *Rosenkavalier*, *Cavalleria*, and *Figaro*, we might come up with seventy. Seventy out of seven thousand. One to a hundred odds.

And where are the winners of yesteryear? All the little Jonnies have disappeared from the map and, oh, how silent have Schwanda's bagpipes become. Which of the fifteen operas of Adolphe Adam does anyone remember? *Le Postillon de Longjumeau* perhaps—but does anyone *know* it? Auber had thirty-six operas produced. When was *Fra Diavolo* last heard? Boieldieu's *La Dame Blanche* only haunts our childhood memories, and the overtures to the *Caliphe de Bagdad*, to *Zampa*, lie faded and forgotten, among the four-hand music that, untouched, fills our shelves, that once touchingly filled our hearts. How many of Cimarosa's twenty-one operas can anyone name? And when, once in a while, someone tries to dust them off, how dated they are, how labored, how forever lost. What has happened to Paisiello, once so great and mighty a ruler in the realm of opera that he, successfully, challenged Mozart? To Spontini? To *Martha?* To *Tiefland?* To such reigning kings as Halévy and Meyerbeer? *Cosa rara* is immortal because sixty-one bars from the opera are quoted in *Don Giovanni*. But does anyone—editors are not admitted!—know the name of the composer of this, one of the great successes of its time, an opera performed all over Europe, with a libretto by da Ponte?

Who is the composer of *Zaza*, roosting forever with the gnu in the forbidden kingdom of crossword puzzles? Just a few years earlier he had written *Pagliacci*. Ever heard of *Le Maschere?* Its composer was so famous, so successful that the opera was simultaneously premièred by six Italian opera houses. And who wrote *Cendrillon*, *Roma*, *Panurge*, *Cléo-*

pâtre, *Grisélidis*, *Marie-Magdeleine*, *Chérubin*, *Ariane*, *Thérèse*, *Bacchus*, and *Amadis?* I didn't know but I looked it up. Massenet.

There were other gamblers who lost almost tragically. There is the German composer Manfred Gurlitt, who wrote an opera *Wozzeck* and finished it in 1925—but when he stretched his hand out to collect his winnings, another, more powerful voice called out for them. What a fine permanent success Leoncavallo's *Bohème* might have been or Auber's *Gustave III ou le Bal Masqué* or Spohr's *Faust* if the little white ball had not fallen in a slot, predestined for the real winners. . . .

In the early stages of my journeys to the intoxicating Walpurgisnachts of new opera I had met a figure which tragically emerges from the dark, cruel past as these fallen operatic warriors, like so many kings in Macbeth, march by. He was very close to Hertzka, who had been his publisher and friend from the very beginning of his career, one of Hertzka's Masters with whom he kept faith almost beyond the call of duty, and, indeed, to the very bitter end. His name was Franz Schreker—only a name today, just a short entry in the dictionary, but once, not so long ago, a brilliant comet in the operatic sky, bright and sparkling, vanishing, oh, so soon in the night, leaving scarcely a trace among the stars that sparkle forever.

After Franz Schreker's first opera, *Der ferne Klang*, had been performed in Frankfurt in 1912, Hertzka signed him up at once and published the vocal score of the opera, arranged, incidentally, by Alban Berg. The critic of the *Frankfurter Zeitung*, a leading German newspaper, the influential Paul Bekker, pronounced Schreker an operatic genius. The work was an immediate success, performed all over the continent from St. Petersburg and Stockholm to every last little opera house in Germany. After the war there were other Schreker successes—*Die Gezeichneten* in 1918, *Der Schatzgräber* in 1920—unchallenged, just rolling along. Hertzka had the huge orchestral scores beautifully engraved; articles and books on Schreker were published, Paul Bekker proclaimed the advent of a new Wagner, and we had orders in the musical magazine which Universal published called *Anbruch*—Beginning, Rise, Dawn—to have reports on Schreker in *every* issue, twelve times a year! Secretly (very secretly, to be sure, this was dynamite) I hated the stuff, the sweetish, harp-fed music, the blown-up, oversexed corn of the librettos, and the order from the front office to keep Schreker constantly before the eyes of our readers and to like doing it put me and my co-editor, Paul Stefan, to the most severe test of choosing between our artistic consciences and our paychecks. We chose the paychecks, of course, and printed reports on Schreker performances from every city, town and hamlet in every issue. It was disgusting.

Only once a year we could unburden our tormented, humiliated breasts: at carnival time we published a special carnival issue of our magazine, called *Abbruch*—Demolition, Destruction, Dusk—where we were permitted to lambaste everything in modern music that was holy for the rest of the year. Every article, every report was interspersed, every ten lines, with an identical announcement: "Franz Schreker's opera *Der ferne Klang* received a standing ovation and ninety-eight curtain calls at its *première* in Uppergreifswald." And ten lines later: "Franz Schreker's opera *Der ferne Klang* received a standing ovation and ninety-eight curtain calls at its *première* in Untergreifswald." There were forty-seven such interspersions. We felt very good. But when next year's carnival came, it came without *Abbruch*. It was back to Beginning, Rise, Dawn.

After *Schatzgräber* came a thing called *Irrelohe*, and then came *Der singende Teufel* and *Der Schmied von*

Ghent, and by then it had become difficult to find anyone who would say a kind word about Franz Schreker for *Anbruch*. By the time he wrote his last opera, *Christophorus*, Berlin, Frankfurt, and Cologne weren't interested any more, and we had to travel to Freiburg im Breisgau, where I hadn't been since Professor Honiger had given me my diploma nine years before, and Paul Stefan himself had to write a report for *Anbruch* as we couldn't even get the local Freiburg critic to say anything printable about our composer. Schreker died two years later—but he had lived long enough to see his established works decay before his eyes and his new attempts rebuffed and ridiculed. Everybody turned from him—Paul Bekker was no longer a critic, which nicely took him off the hook. He had become an Intendant in Kassel and in Wiesbaden and performed very, very little Schreker. Only Hertzka, magnificently, kept his faith and engraved the scores of *Irrelohe* and *Der singende Teufel* at staggering expense. They ate up all the profits we had made with the earlier Schreker works, which is something everybody in the music-publishing business says you must be sure to avoid and nobody ever does, and drove Universal close to bankruptcy.

• • •

FRANZ SCHREKER was born in Monaco, close to the roulette wheels that spin eternally, grew up in Vienna, where he became a famous conductor, so famous that he conducted the world *première* of Schönberg's *Gurrelieder*, and went on to become the head of the Berlin Academy of Music, an honored teacher and master and a successful composer, rich, applauded, decorated with medals and titles, abandoned, humiliated, forgotten, left to die of a broken heart.

But here comes a very different figure in the procession —a little organist in a provincial town of Moravia which he never left except for an occasional trip into the big world—a lovable, unforgettable, youthful face under snow-white, bushy hair, a slightly martial mustache, brilliant, gentle eyes, a modest, friendly smile. I had occasion to visit Leoš Janáček frequently in his dark studio, overcrowded with music and books—it was only a couple of hours on the Nordbahn from Vienna. I went to hear his Sinfonietta in 1925 with its brilliant, piercing opening fanfare of twelve trumpets. I heard the *Missa Glagolskaja*, the wonderful fairy tale of *The Cunning Little Vixen*, *The Makropoulos Case*, and, of course, *Jenufa*.

There has never been a fate like his, even in this maddening operatic world where eternal glory and oblivion without appeal are so close to each other, neighboring numbers on the wheel with the hundred slots. For more than sixty years of his life, Janáček remained unknown outside of the little town where he was an organist and teacher. *Jenufa*—now regarded as one of the masterpieces of our time—was originally named *Její Pastorkyna* ("*Her Foster Daughter*") after a play by Gabriela Preissova, a lovely, tall, aristocratic-looking lady whom I have seen once or twice and whose noble old face, still kept young by a radiant, indomitable spirit, I will not forget. The opera (Janáček's third—numbers one and two remain unheralded) was first performed in Brno in 1904, when the composer was already fifty years old. It remained a local event, unnoticed by the outside world, soon forgotten and put away. Ten years later, with the advent of the First World War, the waves of Czech nationalism began to rise. Preissova was one of the prominent, politically radical protagonists of Czech independence. Somebody in Prague was looking for a Czech opera to signify the new spirit of a restless nation and somebody in Vienna thought it might be a good idea to let the restless Czech subjects of the Hapsburgs play around with an opera

—it might keep their minds from playing with more dangerous stuff. And so, in 1916, Janáček had his first operatic performance outside of Brno: *Jenufa* was produced at the National Theatre in Prague. Two more years had to pass. Janáček, still unknown beyond the narrow frontiers of his homeland, was now sixty-four years old. By then, the handwriting on the wall of the Imperial Palace in Vienna had become urgent. What could show the Czech brethren more strikingly how close they were to the imperial heart than a performance of a Czech opera in Vienna, in a German translation?

Max Brod, sensitive poet and critic and a composer in his own right, undertook the "impossible" task of translating the work: Janáček's music is so strongly tied to the cadences of the Czech language that it is almost impossible to separate the two. Musical motives spring directly from the rise and fall of the spoken words: the word-melody is transcribed faithfully in musical lines, the rhythm of a word becomes the rhythm of a musical phrase. The orchestra takes up the word-music, the language generates the very fabric of the score.

Brod accomplished the impossible, and has since translated all of Janáček's operas and, of course, *Schwanda,* for which he had summoned me, not entirely unselfishly, as he gladly admits, to Prague. Maria Jeritza was the first German-singing Jenufa, when the opera had its Viennese *première* in 1918—she spoke and sang German with a healthy, quite delicious Czech accent and so all was kept in character. The production didn't save the empire, which outlasted the *première* by only nine short months, but it moved a masterpiece where it belonged. By the time *Jenufa* reached New York, in 1924, it had already been translated into ten languages.

When Janáček died ten years after the performance in Vienna had opened the doors of the world for him, he was famous and wealthy. His smile was still as gentle and modest as it had been before all this belated recognition had burst into the little apartment in Brno. That, too, remained unchanged: crowded, pleasant, wonderfully lived in.

Janáček was born in 1854, in the tiny village of Ukvaldy in Moravia, and nothing can recall more touchingly this wonderful man than a little story he once wrote down, when pressured to write about his life. By then, he was already a famous composer of worldwide reputation. This is what the famous composer chose to say about himself, calling his little story simply

WITHOUT KETTLEDRUMS

Two neighboring villages—one a little higher on a green mountainside. The two teachers of the two villages lived in close friendship. To one of them God had given many children, to the other a little more land. Music and bees were the only friends of the teacher of Ukvaldy. With his music he was invited to come to the church choir in the richer church in the lower village. Thus we children, all together, walked there with our father.

On a beautiful Sunday the teacher of Rychalt returned the visit of his colleague from Ukvaldy. They chatted in a shack in the garden, inspected the swarms of bees. We children had been forgotten. There was the iron work of the local squire: the roof almost touched the road—the step of a child was sufficient and we were sliding down the new roof. It was smooth as ice. Everything else, I have forgotten. I only remember the inspection—after the slide—of my holiday pants: it took place right there on the street. The fact that I seduced the son of the teacher from Rychalt into participating in the sleigh ride on the roof was, however, scarcely the reason for the sudden end of the friendship between the two teachers. Never again did we go down to Rychalt to sing in the church choir. Everything was over. And there, in the choir, were many music stands, a gilded organ and, behind it, the kettledrums!

Easter Sunday was approaching. We sat in school and learned to sing the Mass—just us, the children of Ukvaldy. What good was it to have violins and trumpets and even clarinets? No—without kettledrums it couldn't be a real festive occasion. Towards evening we sneaked down and into the church of Rychalt. And, across the fields, we dragged the kettledrum, uphill to Ukvaldy. I don't remember how we were received there. And I can't recall how the kettledrum got back to its proper place. And our Mass was not festive: no kettledrums. I only remember having felt the timpani sticks dance on my back. Whether our kettledrum raid has brought the two friends together again I don't know. They both sleep (and I am sure, reconciled) near the church door.

And this is the reason why, again and again, I like to toss a little solo to the timpani.

I saw Leoš Janáček for the last time when he showed me the manuscript of his opera *From the House of the Dead*, which he was not to see on the stage. He was composing the music to his own libretto, taking it literally from sentences he had culled from the Russian original of Dostoevski's novel. The music was noted in a strange musical shorthand which he had invented and from which his pupils, who had been taught to decipher it, made the score. On the title page the old man, already in the shadow of approaching death, had written the motto for his last opera, which deals with the poorest, the most desperate, the forgotten and abandoned prisoners in a Siberian penal colony:

"*In every creature a spark of God.*"

IV

THE BELL in my little office sounded shrill, loud and commanding as any bell set in motion by the mighty Hertzka had to sound. Every time it rang—and it rang very often—its call catapulted us out of our seats towards the heavily padded black leather door that led to the inner sanctum. We always opened it—you couldn't knock at the soft, damned leather padding—filled with an apprehension that gripped us as soon as the sudden sound of His Master's Voice, as the bells were called, summoned us to fates unknown. This time there had been no cause for fear. I had been summoned to be introduced to Alban Berg.

At once I felt myself in the presence of a towering personality. Hertzka, smiling, seemed strangely subdued himself. There seemed no one else in the room but the composer. The room was filled with his presence, completely and inescapably, as a light fills every corner and penetrates the dark: bright, warm, reassuring, outshining anything and anybody else.

He was unusually tall but always slightly stooped, as if bowing in grace and elegant humility to the world. His hands were very large, white and sensitive, covered by a fascinating web of blue veins. He had a beautiful face, a smiling, almost mocking mouth, great warming eyes that always looked straight at you. Most of the many photographs that survive do him small justice: they are always a little stiff, a little too beautiful, a little posed, never quite as human as he was—they have neither the twinkle in the eye which we all remember nor the suffering that we also knew so well.

His health was never very strong. He had been battling

with asthma all his life. Tall, elegant, and imposing as he was, he always emanated a feeling of frailty that made us treat him with special care as if, instinctively and worriedly, we were anticipating that this tender, bright flame was not to burn for long. He never became arrogant, never acquired the attitudes of a celebrity after he went up the ladder of success and became revered and recognized all over the world—he did not even become detached, aloof, or different in any respect. He always remained the same: pleasant, friendly, very human. He loved to tell jokes, many of them slightly across the borderline, and after he had told one of his risqué stories he would roar with laughter. There is constant mention of food, good food described tonguesmackingly, bad food taken as a personal insult, in the large volume of love letters to his wife. Of all the famous composers I've known, I cannot recall another in whose presence I felt so much at ease, so little *en garde*, so unafraid to say a wrong word, so much at home.

I visited him often in his apartment in Hietzing, a Viennese suburb, a few blocks from the enormous park of Schönbrunn Palace. He used to go for long walks in the park, talking to friends or alone, thinking, composing, I suppose. Most of these walks—and most of his life—were in the company of his wife, Helene—tall, blond, with her golden tresses wound around her beautiful head and with the gait, the posture, the appearance of a princess. After he was taken in December 1935, she kept the apartment in Trautmannsdorfgasse untouched, unchanged, the way it had been to the very last, even to a flip of cigarette ashes in a tray. She remained always in communication with him. It was never, even many years after the tragedy, "Alban *would* have thought" or "Alban *might* have said"—it was always a direct message, and unequivocal decision coming from the undisturbed studio—approval or disapproval, a yes or a no that had to be obeyed.

During the summer we tried to arrange our vacation trips so that we could visit the two in Waldhaus, their home near an Austrian lake in Carinthia. There, in the midst of meadows and woods, Berg was a peasant among peasants, digging in his garden, going for hefty walks, delightedly driving the American car he had acquired after the first royalties for *Wozzeck* had begun trickling in, a smiling, friendly host to all comers. There, in Waldhaus, he did most of the work of his later years.

Berg quit a government job as a relatively young man and devoted the last twenty-five years of his life to composing. It is difficult to think of another composer of significance who has written so little that means so much, the pages of musical history being so full of the names of composers who have written so much that means so little. Berg's fame, so firmly established and still growing, so it seems, rests on a surprisingly small number of works: two operas, *Wozzeck* and *Lulu*, the latter uncompleted, the Violin Concerto, the second string quartet (*Lyric Suite*), perhaps—but beyond that, if we look at his *oeuvre* unbiased by love and sentimental memories, little has found its way into established recognition.

The Piano Sonata Op. 1, his only work for piano (if one disregards a few unpublished *Jugendsünden*), is rarely heard. A few short pieces for clarinet and piano, dedicated to Arnold Schoenberg and first performed at Schoenberg's private performance club in Vienna in 1919, are better known to the chronicler than to clarinet players or the public. There is only one orchestral work, three pieces composed in 1914 and almost never played. There is the Chamber Concerto for piano, violin, and winds, written for the occasion of Schoenberg's fiftieth birthday in 1924, but belatedly completed on Berg's own fortieth the following year, and were it not for occasional Sunday afternoon concerts for connoisseurs we would not have heard it in many a year. There is a concert aria to a text by Baudelaire (in the German translation of Stefan George), commissioned in 1929 by a Viennese lady of Czech descent whose monetary prowess was sadly superior to her vocal excellence, a fact that always left a thin veil of embarrassment over the piece and a slightly apologetic wink in the eye of the composer when it was mentioned in his presence. There is a handful of songs and the two string quartets—a very early one, written in 1910, and the *Lyric Suite* which Berg wrote for his friend, the violinist Rudolf Kolisch and the Kolisch String Quartet sixteen years later. This is the catalogue of works, the majority of them leading a life of dignified retirement in libraries, books, and respectful memories, which has built up one of the great reputations in contemporary music.

I was, of course, in the audience when the *Lyric Suite*, with its celebrated, stunning *pizzicato misterioso* had its first performance at the—I think—Kleine Musikvereinssaal in the presence of about every musician who lived in Vienna. Oh, how nice it was to go to a concert in Wien! From the office you walked just a block and a half to the Kaffee Kremser on the Ringstrasse, where you remained till concert time. No subway, no traffic lights, no Sorry Garage Filled, no waiting in line for a gulped-down dinner. In the spring and the autumn you sat under the trees, watching the streetcars and the girls go slowly by. In the winter, you sat inside in wonderfully stale air, preserved for generations, at the very marble-topped table where Brahms had breathed the same mixture of chewed cigars, fried eggs, old newspapers, and wet overcoats. All your friends were there when you arrived from the office at four, looking at you with raised eyebrows if you were delayed by an emergency until four thirty. You talked for hours without Juzak or Mukebox, to the pleasant background murmur of billiard balls gently hit by gentle pipe smokers. You had a pair of leisurely *Würstel* and, perhaps, a couple of fluffily scrambled eggs for dinner and you left five minutes before concert time to walk over, slowly, slowly, to the Kleine or the Grosse or the Mittlere. No ticket was needed: you were admitted by what was known as *Gesichtsentré*—admission by face—and you were in your seat, comfortably and very rested, in plenty of time.

I have often thought what this walking-distance, afternoon-siesta, coffee-and-billard conditioning has done for music when watching the haunted, harassed, exhausted music lover of our time emerge from thundering subway trains, drive around choked blocks to find no parking space, wait in line to be permitted to wait in another line to eat, drink, be pushed on an escalator or just to breathe, already looking at his watch and his wife, wondering whether there will be a taxi afterwards that will not wave an off-duty sign at him as the final, crushing chord of the evening. Is he, really and in all seriousness, expected to sit and hear William Steinberg carefully, deliberately, slowly, ceremoniously celebrate eighty minutes of Bruckner's Eighth Symphony in the same mood of receptiveness as did his grosspapa, chattingly ambling in after four hours at the Kaffee Gemütlich?

Most great music has been written by composers and for people who have never heard the words Tow-Away Zone.

The Kolisches, who later played the *Lyric Suite* many times all over the world, were a wonderful bunch of dedicated musical fanatics. The cellist was Benar Heifetz, who ended up at a first desk of the Philadelphia Orchestra. Eugene Lehner (originally Jenö, of course—there is at least one Hungarian in every musical closet) landed a similar job with the Boston Symphony—he was the viola. Felix Kuhner, lately of San Francisco, was the second violinist. Kolisch himself had sustained a crippling injury to his left hand early in life and had to switch the violin to the right hand, holding the bow with the left. He was the most unsmilingly dedicated, the most uncompromising musician down to the last, exasperating detail, when at work and the gentlest, most pleasant, smiling and relaxed friend after he had set down his fiddle. We spent many nights together at the coffee-stained mahjongg tables of the Kaffee Museum, joined by the composer Hanns Eisler and other musicians of similar devotion to atonal music and mahjongg. As the night went on, the mahjongg games became more and more sophisticated and the ladies of the Ringstrasse came in, from time to time, to refresh themselves between chores, wondering at the long-haired (or no-haired) players who had been there when they had set out for the first excursion of the evening and who were still there, bent over the tables, when their last customer had gone and it was time for them—not for us—to go to bed.

The mahjongg players were also, as was Alban Berg (who did not play mahjongg or if he did, played it only secretly), ardent soccer fans and partisans of Rapid or Austria or another of the famous Viennese teams. When there was a game of importance, particularly an international match against the admired Scots, the hated Italians, or the neutral Swiss, the mahjongg players, led by the great Alban, formed a solid intellectual wedge among the Viennese fans, who could hear the giant composer of *Wozzeck* groan in disgust at a missed opportunity by the home team or see him jump up, raising his long, outstretched arms, cheering at a successful *Schuss*, waving his large sombrero.

The four players of the Kolisch Quartet performed their entire repertory from memory. Unforgettable their sitting down on a stage that had only four chairs, liberally arranged, and no music stands. The players tuned their instruments, each of them taking the most comfortable, natural position, pushing their chairs in all directions, sometimes one of them turning his back to the audience and sometimes closing his eyes to look at the music inside—the cellist Benar Heifetz was particularly impressive in reading his part in complete, closed-eye absorption. Kolisch was always very close to the music and the composers of the modern Viennese school—a family trait, because his sister Gertrud soon became better known as Frau Schönberg, a name (or rather an exalted position) she acquired in 1924. We will meet her again, the greatest of all composer's widows, a little later.

• • •

FAME TRAVELS strange, unfathomable roads. In vain one searches in the musical dictionaries, between Zschocher, Joachim, noted German piano pedagogue, and Zsolt, Nándor, Hungarian violinist, for an entry Zschorlich, Paul, Berlin music critic. But Zschorlich should be right there, outzetting Zschocher and Zsolt. On December 14, 1925, Zschorlich wrote a report for his paper, the *Deutsche Zeitung*, which contained the following sentences and ejaculations: "When I left the State Opera last night, I felt that I was not leaving a public place, dedicated to the arts, but a public insane asylum. On stage, in the orchestra, in the audience—only lunatics. The work of a Chinaman from Vienna. My name will be, from tomorrow on, Moses Sewersmell, if this is not a deliberate swindle. Fragments, rags, sobs, belches. Tormented, ugly sounding cackle. A fountain-poisoner of German music. The man who committed the crime of this work relies confidently on the stupidity and baseness of his fellow men and trusts the rest to God and to Universal Edition. He is a musical mountebank, a composer dangerous to the public welfare. And one has to go farther: extraordinary events call for new methods: one has to ask, in all seriousness, whether and to what extent occupation with music can be criminal. This is, in the realm of music, a capital crime."

With these words immortality came on the same day to Paul Zschorlich for his article "Stammering at the State Opera" and to Alban Berg for his opera *Wozzeck*, which had its first performance at the State Opera Unter den Linden. It will always be one of my proudest recollections that I was one of the madmen in the audience that night.

Wozzeck had been almost ten years in the making. The spark that ignited the fire was struck in May 1914 when Berg attended several performances of George Büchner's fragmentary drama *Woyzek* at a Viennese theater and decided to use the play for an opera. A few months later, war broke out. Berg was drafted. Work had to stop, but *Wozzeck* was now forever with him. When one of his pupils visited him in the barracks, he spoke long before the chorus of the sleeping soldiers in *Wozzeck* was written, about his sleepless, tormented nights. "Did you ever hear many people snore at the same time?" he asked. "This polyphonic breathing, rattle, and moaning is the most original chorus I've ever heard. It is like music of primeval sounds emerging from the abyss of the souls."

The whole aspect of the army and the people he encountered—doctors, drum majors, captains, and many poor, downtrodden Wozzecks—drove him closer and closer to identifying himself with the soldier in Büchner's play and his futile struggle against the powers of eternal, universal brass. His delicate health kept him from service at the front, but life in the barracks, the monotony of, to him, senseless training and watch duties, the treatment he received from the noncoms who ordered him around, made army existence a physical and mental torture. What a strange, mysteriously fitting atmosphere for a sensitive artist who had chosen his subject before he had experienced wozzeckian army torments himself.

The opera that was growing in him, however, was much more than a personal reaction to a hated war. Whether he knew it or not, the tale of frustrated love and violent death provided the composer with a libretto whose basic ingredients are the very stuff an opera libretto should be made of, as striking, exciting, basic, and primitive as one of the great librettos of all times, that of *Carmen*. *Wozzeck* is indeed a Nordic *Carmen*, with an identical background of primitive passion, jealousy, infidelity, and murder—a libretto that, like all good librettos, could be sung in Sanskrit or just mimed with scarcely a word uttered and would still strike home. Wozzeck is a German Don José, Marie, the alluring Carmen of a German *Kleinstadt*. The Drum Major—is he not almost a replica of a strutting Escamillo, his splendid Prussian uniform replacing the splendid costume of the toreador, both indestructible, unconcerned survivors of the tragedy they have set in motion? Lillas Pastia's mountain inn has become a dreary *Biergarten:* no sparkling manzanilla makes the blood flow fast—the drunks are heavy with cheap wine and poisonous schnaps. The out-of-tune piano draws the dancers together as do the castanets and guitars of Spain. The passions are the same. The women, doggishly loved by their men, set the same eyes of desire on the heroes, who make their entries and exits at the head of their brass band or their chorus of bullfighters, and they meet the same fate.

The first years in the army left Berg little time for work. Then, in 1916, he was transferred to an office job in Vienna and found enough time and strength to complete the libretto: out of the twenty-seven scenes of Büchner's fragment he selected fifteen—five for each of the three acts of the opera.

In the summer of 1917 he began composing, starting with the second scene of the second act, the street scene involving the Captain, the Doctor, and Wozzeck. It took four years for the music to be completed. In October 1921, he began the orchestration of the finished draft.

All this work, extended through so many years, happened almost in a vacuum. The composer kept his closest friends, among them Anton von Webern, informed on his progress, but there was no encouragement from the officialdom of music. A trip to Germany, where he showed the work to some of the leading opera houses, brought professions of admiration but no results. And no publisher was willing to take the risk of tackling so revolutionary, daring, and, alas, expensive a score: it was too much even for the daring, undaunted Hertzka. Berg decided to publish the vocal score himself—it had been arranged by one of his pupils—and what a job it had been to translate so complicated a score to ten staves and ten fingers. Financial assistance came from Alma Maria Mahler; her part in bringing *Wozzeck* into existence is acknowledged by the dedication of the opera to her. In 1923 Alban Berg announced the publication: "The piano vocal score has 230 large-sized pages and sells for 150.000 kronen. It can be obtained directly from me." Soon he was seen boarding a streetcar with half a dozen of the heavy scores, taking them to the post office for shipment to customers who had sent twenty Swiss francs from Copenhagen, Rome, or Chicago, or delivering one in person to the desk of the Grand Hotel.

At last the first break came. At an accidental meeting in Salzburg, Berg showed a copy of the work to Hermann Scherchen, who suggested that the composer arrange a few scenes for a concert performance. The "Three Fragments from *Wozzeck*" (for soprano solo and orchestra) were the result. In June 1923, Hermann Scherchen conducted the piece at a music festival in Frankfurt, with a local soprano, Beatrice Lauer-Kottlar, singing for the first time in public some of Marie's music. The response was strong. At about the same time, Erich Kleiber, musical director of the Berlin State Opera, accepted the opera for performance.

During the dress rehearsal and the night of the opening there were fist fights, angry challenges shouted across the orchestra seats and from the boxes, deriding laughter, boos, and hostile whistles that threatened for some time to overpower the small but, at last, victorious group of believers.

As the tall, noble figure of the composer appeared before the curtain the riots increased, the bravos and the boos, the waves of enthusiastic excitement and outraged hostility. Berg seemed a little taken aback by it, perhaps a shade paler as usual, but quite unaffected, calm, very sure of his work. We didn't know, of course, what fate had in store for the opera and for us—but we knew, then and there, that we had been present at a historic event.

The violent contrast continued the next morning and for days and weeks to come in the press. We published a booklet "*Alban Berg's* Wozzeck *and the music critics*" which, in a first section, printed the Zschorlich diatribe (in its entirety) and similar comments by Zschorlichites and, in a second section under the heading "Reviews by leading German music critics" (we weren't really very unbiased), the reviews of seventeen critics which, when one reads them now again, were indeed prophetic in their enthusiasm.

But the battle was far from won. The following year *Wozzeck* had its second production, in the Czech language, at the National Theater in Prague. The first performance seemed successful enough. But at the second, violent demonstrations broke out. After the second act, police cleared the theater and stopped the performance. In the excitement, the mayor of Prague suffered a heart attack. With the controversial reception in Berlin and, now, with a theater scandal making headlines all over Europe and a lord mayor the pitiful victim of the new opera, no other theater dared to produce the work. In addition, there were rumors about insurmountable difficulties; the thirty-four orchestral rehearsals that had preceded the Berlin *première* were magnified to prohibitive dimensions.

In 1927 the opera was produced in Leningrad. Now it was a work that didn't only kill lord mayors and outrage German musical decency—it had been embraced by the Bolsheviks! It seemed the end.

Two years later, Johannes Schuler, musical director of a small German theater in Oldenburg, decided to produce the work. The original scoring was too large for his pit. Erwin Stein, court-editor to Schönberg and his Viennese school, made a new score for "normal" orchestra—he had done so before for many seemingly unreducible scores (including the mammoth *Gurrelieder*) with such success that rumors were around that he was at work at a reduction of Bach's Sonata for solo violin.

By the time *Wozzeck* was performed in Oldenburg, only a few years after the Berlin and Prague scandals, everything had changed. Berg himself wrote from the little town stating that what he experienced there was "a miracle." A few years only had been sufficient to accomplish the strange and inescapable chemical process that, generation after generation, changes the ununderstandable into the accepted, the unperformable into music that flows almost effortless from instruments and voices. Unperformable *Tristan* becomes a routine box-office attraction, scandalous *Sacre du Printemps* a repertory piece. A Webern score, laughed off the stage, its performance shamefully interrupted when one of the players walks out protesting that he just couldn't go on with such madness, has to be encored thirty years later and the entire *oeuvre* of the once controversial composer becomes enthusiastically accepted ballet music all over the world. Lines that seemed the stammer of a lunatic are suddenly a charming melody and anyone can whistle Marie's Lullaby more easily, perhaps, than a long spun-out, sophisticated Mozart melody. The nonacceptance of the unfamiliar, generation after generation, changes into the acceptance of the familiar and, unless a work is really strong and enduring, the rejected unfamiliar of yesteryear will soon fall victim to the bored rejection of the too familiar.

"Ovations which we have not witnessed here before," said one local Oldenburg paper. "A success, unequaled in the history of our theater," said the second. "The enthusiasm of the public knew no boundaries," the third. We published a second brochure, including an analysis by the conductor of his rehearsal schedule. "I hope," he wrote, "that these statistics" (and we printed them in great detail) "will once and for all dispel the fairy tale of insurmountable difficulties. If the local success should now be followed by universal acceptance, if the ban that blocked the way for the work will have been lifted—the real purpose of our labors will have been achieved." A year later, almost ten years after the work had been completed, it was a world success.

Hertzka, of course, had long since climbed on the bandwagon: by the time *Wozzeck* was produced in Berlin, the score, once published by Alban Berg himself and offered—with not too many takers—for 150.000 kronen, had the traditional green Universal cover (as, incidentally, had the ill-fated *Wozzeck* by the unfortunate Gurlitt) and only its unorthodox size—publishing composers know nothing about regulation-size racks in music stores and size 317a envelopes—still bore witness to its somehow illegitimate origin. Hertzka had even paid an advance of three million kronen to Alban Berg when he took over the work, which sounds real nice but was only $100 and not too much of an investment if one considers what happened to the property afterward. But Berg had his own sweet revenge. "I won't see much money at first, but I secretly kept thirty copies of the score for myself and will sell them clandestinely," he wrote to his wife after the consummation of the long-sought deal, with a boyish grin that still breaks through the page after so many years.

On the wall of my office in New York I have a memento that I treasure more than anything else that has assembled there. A few years after the Oldenburg event, I wrote to the management there, thanking them for what they had done and expressing the thought that "the Oldenburg opera house has done more for one of the great masterpieces of our time than anybody else." A little later a letter arrived, showing Alban Berg's unmistakable handwriting on the yellow envelope he always used. Inside was the page from the Oldenburg program with my letter. The words connecting the theater with the fate of *Wozzeck* had been circled with red pencil and a red line was extended to my name at the bottom of the page. Before my name he had written two words: *ebenso wie*—just as. It was the most graceful and unforgettable way to thank me for what little I had been privileged to do.

Many years later when *Wozzeck* was shown at the Metropolitan, a headline appeared in the New York *Daily News* which made me miss Alban Berg more than ever before because I knew how much he would have enjoyed seeing it. It read: GERMAN G.I. KNIFES WIFE, CLAIMS INFIDELITY IN BERG'S WOZZECK.

• • •

OF *Lulu* I HEARD only a few symphonic excerpts in Alban Berg's presence when they were played—reluctantly—by the Vienna Philharmonic Orchestra at one of their Sunday-morning concerts. Somehow this attempt to transplant operatic music to the concert hall seemed not to carry the same convincing, inescapable impact that had made the three symphonic fragments from *Wozzeck* an instantaneous hit some ten years earlier. One of my last recollections of Alban Berg is of his serious, searching, carefully listening, only slightly disappointed face when we, frankly, talked about it a few days after the performance. As with every real artist, one could talk to him without restraint about his work.

Berg himself never saw *Lulu* on the stage. I traveled to the world *première* of the unfinished work in Zürich in 1937, two years after his death. It should have been a great artistic event, this posthumous performance of an opera by the composer of *Wozzeck*. But it was much more an occasion wrought with frightening political undertones. The brown curtain had descended over the huge German operatic space, until recently the scene of every daring experiment, more than any other place in the world. Now, the "decadent" music by Alban Berg and the play by Wedekind on which the opera was based were "*untragbar*," unacceptable to the new world of Dr. Goebbels. And so was almost everything else worthwhile creating, experimenting with, believing in.

Zürich, literally, was the last major German-speaking opera house operating without such oppressive censorship and not already touched by the shadow of things to come, as was the whole of Austria. It was an unforgettably ominous atmosphere. Only a few critics had come to a Berg world *première*, and very few producers. There was a party afterward and we all made brave speeches, but we knew that all around us the world was beginning to disintegrate and behind the big words there was little hope or conviction. It would be a long time till *Lulu* would be permitted to take its rightful place among the masterpieces of the century.

Berg did not have enough time to finish the opera. There was one other work, however, which he was permitted to finish but not permitted to hear, the Violin Concerto. And I cannot leave this lovable, beloved figure, so great and deeply true an artist and so thoroughly human a man, without briefly telling the story of the concerto. It is dedicated, as everybody knows, to the "Memory of an Angel"—a Requiem for Marion Gropius, Alma Maria's lovely young daughter; a solemn Bach Chorale is woven into its musical fabric. And, like another celebrated Requiem, this last work was written as a commission and completed, feverishly, against the advancing hands of the clock.

Louis Krasner, a violinist from Boston, had been present when *Wozzeck* had been brought for a single performance to the Metropolitan Opera House in New York by the Philadelphia Grand Opera under Leopold Stokowski. The opera, Krasner told us later, had only been a *succès d'estime* in America. But on him, Krasner, it had made a deep and lasting impression. Early in his life, he had begun playing contemporary music, very much against the advice of his teacher, who had counseled his students, beautifully summing up what was to become the watchword of the American concert trade: "If you want to play modern music, play Grieg."

Ignoring such sound advice, Krasner decided, after the *Wozzeck* experience, to try and get a violin piece from Alban Berg. The occasion presented itself when his concert tours brought him to Vienna, where he made his headquarters for some time. But he tried in vain to hear some music by Alban Berg—there was nothing on the local programs. At last, he was asked to a private home where a group of young people —a brother and three sisters—were to perform Berg's *Lyric Suite*. Krasner listened, entranced both by the music and by the second violinist, whom, soon after, he married and took with him to America, thus ending the brief if brilliant career of the Galimir String Quartet. The music he had heard only strengthened his determination: he now decided to ask the composer of so brilliantly written a string quartet not just for a piece for the violin but for a concerto. Contacts were made through friends and musicians and, at last, we arranged for a meeting between Krasner and Alban Berg.

At first things did not go well. Berg told the visitor that he really didn't think the violin was his dish—or whatever his Viennese words were for a polite refusal. He also felt, so he said, that with two string quartets and the concerto for violin, piano, and wind orchestra, he had done his part for the violin. But the little, very quiet man from Boston (one always felt that he was speaking *con sordino*) had a determined persistence and a fine musical reputation—Berg inquired carefully about his artistic credentials—and perhaps the commission had something to do with it—$1,500 isn't much as today's prices for violin concertos go, but went a long way in Austrian schillings in 1935. So, after a while, I was asked to draw up an agreement between the two. Berg departed for his lake and invited Krasner to visit him in Waldhaus.

The violinist arrived in the morning. They went for a walk and had a hefty Carinthian lunch. Then Berg asked Krasner to play for him. The visitor unpacked his instrument in the spacious music room and asked what he should play. "Just anything," the composer said. "Just do a little *herumpraeludieren*"—a little fiddling around. Krasner began to *herumpraeludier*, playing chord combinations and bits from concertos and sonatas, passages and improvisations that came to his mind and fingers. Later, at the request of the composer, he added harmonics, and then other violinistic tricks and fireworks. Berg was listening all afternoon in absorbed concentration, sometimes busying himself with other matters throughout the house, but always listening and not letting the visitor stop playing when he left the room. When he took Krasner to the train, he pointed to the opposite side of the lake and repeated, several times, seriously and with an obvious sense of responsibility: "There is where Brahms wrote his violin concerto."

Later, when Krasner began studying the work, he found many echoes of his afternoon improvisations in the music room in Waldhaus in the score of the concerto—reflections of some of the chords, of the harmonics and chromatics, even whole types of chord passages that had been absorbed by the composer that afternoon and now made their own, individual appearance in his farewell to the world.

A few months later, in July 1935, the composer wrote to say that he had finished the composition and was now working on the orchestration. "If you may be astonished by this, I am still more," he wrote. "I have never in my life worked with such constant concentration and I have enjoyed the work increasingly. When I have finished the score, I should like to ask you to come to me so that we may go through the violin part together."

Krasner returned to Waldhaus and played the music for Berg. "We discussed several possibilities for changes," he reports, more than thirty years later, still visibly touched by the recollection. "He was always most receptive and willing, but we finally abandoned the agreed changes and decided to let the original stand, except for one place which I felt was uncomfortable for me personally. He rewrote the two measures and as he took his large rubber eraser to rub out the beautiful writing in his original score, I became panicky and begged him to delay making the change in the score until we met again. Of course the orginal text is perfect as it stands and it was never changed."

When Krasner was to play the work for the first time with

orchestra, the composer was dead. The violinist had received a cable in New York asking him whether he could play the concerto the following spring at the ISCM Festival in Barcelona, a year ahead of the originally planned date for the *première*. He arrived in Vienna ten days before the performance date, in April 1936. The "establishment"—the official *Schoenbergianer* and *Bergianer* in Vienna—had decided that no other than Anton von Webern was to conduct the world *première* of the concerto. Krasner spent many hours trying to persuade the reluctant composer-conductor to take on the assignment. At last, he agreed and they left together for Barcelona.

Rehearsals at an international music festival, where every piece is new and difficult, are precious and rare. After rehearsing a whole morning with the orchestra, Webern had completed work on only a few pages of the first movement. In addition to his simply exasperating fussiness, communication between a composer whose rural Austrian (the only language he spoke) was difficult to understand even for a German and an orchestra speaking Catalan drove everybody—mainly, of course, Krasner—to the brink of suicide. After the second rehearsal, Webern locked himself in his hotel room and refused to go on. The festival office asked Krasner to help them draft a release announcing cancellation of the performance.

On the way to the office, Krasner met one of the conductors who had come for the festival. It was Hermann Scherchen, greatest of all pros, enormous gentle-speaking husband of innumerable wives—one of whom (No. 1) he remarried once again, thus giving Artur Schnabel occasion to comment that Scherchen was arranging his married life in rondo form—loving father of countless children, many of them Swiss-speaking Chinese, and unforgettable father-figure of modern music. Scherchen at once declared himself willing to devote half an hour of the rehearsal time allotted to him for other works to the Berg Concerto, the score of which he had never seen before. He was serenely confident that there would be no trouble. Would Krasner come to his hotel in the afternoon to go over the music with him?

The huge German was in bed when the little American arrived. Krasner put his music on the bed—he had carefully pasted the pages of the violin part together so as to avoid page turns. Scherchen, reclining in bed, conducted from the score. After a while he began motioning the violinist to step back—still farther—I can't work on the music when you are so close—and Krasner at last stood in a corner of the room, fiddling away.

The next morning Krasner went to the rehearsal, put his paste-up violin part on a special, large music stand that he had brought along to accommodate so unorthodoxly sized a contraption, and nodded to the conductor to proceed. Scherchen turned around, took the music with one of his majestically sweeping gestures from Krasner's stand and put it on the floor. "But I can't possibly play the concerto by heart, Herr Professor. I never played it without the music—it's a brand new work." "Yesterday you did after I sent you to the corner of my room," said Scherchen, looking at him severely and unsmilingly through his frameless glasses. Then he raised his hands—he never used a baton—and threw himself into the music.

The next night Scherchen swept the orchestra and a musicless Krasner through the first performance of Alban Berg's Violin Concerto. At the end, the audience rose in respect. They had heard the proud and wonderful Requiem of a proud and wonderful man.

THE SUDDEN APPEARANCE of a bright new star—*Hertzka upstartiensis*—in the firmament of music publishing had been a shocking, unexpected, and unbelievable event. There hadn't been a successful intruder into the firmly established hierarchy of international music publishing in many decades. All over the continent, in Paris and London, in Mainz and Berlin, in Leipzing, Moscow, and Milan, even in distant New York, men watched in awe as the new comet began to rise in the East, growing in brightness, intensity and power, with *Jonny* and *Schwanda*, *Jenufa* and *Wozzeck*, the *Three-Penny Opera* and *Das Lied von der Erde*, with everything from Anbruch to Zemlinsky and even the crashing cymbals of the famous march of the Deutschmeister Regiment, which he had bought just for laughs, in its glittering tail.

To try to start a new music-publishing empire as late as 1907 seemed folly. To succeed so brilliantly in so short a time was offensive. Most of the infuriated star-gazers were third- or fourth-generation patriarchs. Their establishments had been founded—Chappells and Booseys of London, for example, Heugel of Paris, Ricordi of Milan, Peters of Leipzig —shortly before or a little after the battle of Waterloo, a time, so it seems, when the world had enough of blood and glory and turned to writing and publishing music. Durands of Paris, who had begun their business with the Valse in E-flat composed by the founding Durand himself and ended up publishing Debussy and Ravel, had been at 4 Place de la Madeleine almost as long as the Madeleine had been there. But they all, not to speak of their much younger colleagues in Moscow or New York, were only nouveaux riches when scrutinized by the wise, old, if already slightly myopic eyes of the real old-timers. In their club, to have been a contemporary of Mozart was not sufficient to qualify. In order to have real class and distinction, one had to go back to 1719, the year in which Mozart *père* was born.

In that year—undistinguished otherwise, no battles, no peace treaties, no kings born or emperors buried, just Leopold Mozart born in Augsburg and Defoe's *Robinson Crusoe* published in London, a peaceful, pleasant year given to the pleasures of the spirit—Bernhard Christoph Breitkopf bought an old printing plant in Leipzig, added a publishing business to it, and thus laid the foundation to the oldest music-publishing house on record, known to this day as Breitkopf & Härtel. He published the first edition of the Schemelli Hymnal, set to music by Johann Sebastian Bach, but his real contribution to the firm was his son, colorfully named Johann Gottlob Immanuel and still reverently talked about as behooves so beautifully named an ancestor and a man who was not only a publisher and printer but also a manufacturer of playing cards, a sinful undertaking that does not seem to tie in very nicely with the publication of a hymnal but must have brought in a lot of thalers. J.G.I. also ran a factory for manufacturing type and invented a special technique to set music in movable type, a process still used today for the publication of hymnals and similar simple musical products. Generations have ruined their eyes singing the praises of the Lord from Johann Gottlob Immanuel's scribbly, spidery, lucrative type.

Johann Gottlob Immanuel Breitkopf also had a son—we are now coming to the third generation of Breitkopfs and still no Härtel—simply called Christoph Gottlob and—no wonder for a man with so undistinguished a name—no chip off the old block. All one knows of him is that he had a friend by the name of—here we are—Gottfried Härtel, who had studied law, had been a majordomo to some count or other and a private tutor to his children, knew French, Latin, Greek, English, and Italian and had—*Gott sei Dank*—only one Christian name. In 1795, Christoph Gottlob Breitkopf took him in as a partner. The two incorporated the firm of Breitkopf & Härtel and took as their trademark the sign of the house in which they had their first office ("Zum Goldenen Bären"), a bear clutching the staff of commerce of the god Hermes while hiding, looking a little embarrassed, behind a shield bearing the head of Pallas Athena, the goddess of wisdom. Breitkopf and Härtel looked at each other across a desk for a little while and then parted. Christoph Gottlob withdrew from the business and vanished forever, and with him any trace of the multi-prenamed Breitkopfs. Nobody knows what happened to him. But he left behind an & that made him immortal. The famous combination of the two names rang down through the ages, the result of a partnership that lasted not quite eleven months.

By that time, Mozart *fils* had been dead for four years and the new owner had landed his first coup: he made a contract with the widow Konstanze to publish the *Oeuvres complets* of the master. Just how complete the complete works were (they were printed in the type invented by the playing-card manufacturer) is difficult to ascertain and rather doubtful, but they established a trend: they were the forerunners of an impressive series of complete editions—the famous *Gesammtausgaben*—which were to become one of the features of the firm—huge tomes, beautifully engraved, printed in an enormous format, accessible only to the large mansions of an uncrowded past and even today forcing libraries all over the world to build extra shelving—huge and steel-enforced—to house and to carry them.

Some of the most important among them were reprinted

during the Second World War in America but, with peace, commerce, and European printing presses restored, they have reverted to Breitkopfs. Throughout a period covering one and a half centuries they have issued, mostly with help from the German or Prussian governments, complete scholarly editions of the works of Palestrina, Orlando di Lasso, Heinrich Schütz, Johann Sebastian Bach, Beethoven, Schubert, Chopin, Mendelssohn, Grétry, Berlioz, Schumann, Liszt, Brahms, Max Reger, Frederick the Great, and Johann Strauss the Greater. The enormousness of these undertakings defies description and the editions have to be lifted to be appreciated. The *Bach Gesammtausgabe*, for example, has sixty-one volumes. Beethoven required thirty-four, Schumann thirty-two, Brahms thirty-six. In addition to hosts of musicologists whose names are familiar only to Nicolas Slonimsky, famous musicians were hired to help prepare the musical texts of the mammoth publications. Brahms participated in the Chopin, Mozart, Schubert, and Schumann editions; Ferruccio Busoni helped with Bach, Béla Bartók with Liszt. My skullcapped sage from the Vienna Musikverein, Eusebius Mandyczewski, worked on Brahms.

In our forays into Europe—like Attila, Hertzka had come from the plains of Hungary—we rode often into Leipzig to be present at performances of such works as *Jonny spielt auf*, Kurt Weill's *Mahagonny* or *Silbersee*, and similar far-out events still farther removed from the Schemelli Hymnal than the ace of hearts. But even upstarts like us were subdued and brushed the dust off our boots when we paid a courtesy call on Breitkopf & Härtel. It was by then an enormous, sprawling beehive where eight hundred people—editors, printers, order fillers, engravers, bookbinders, production managers, designers, executives, travelers, and clerks—were at work. They had huge warehouses to store more than seventy thousand different titles, an engraving shop, one of the largest in the world, serving not only themselves but also many other publishers in Europe and in America, and a printing plant that produced not only music but books in most known languages, among them Arabic, Coptic (I asked them to show me a book in Coptic when they told me about it but they were all out of print, an interesting side light on the rather surprising sales of Coptic books), and Japanese. They also produced the celebrated travel guides of Baedeker in their eye-killing miniprint.

They were the publishers of Haydn and Mozart, of Mendelssohn and Liszt, of *Fidelio*, *Lohengrin*, and *Tristan*, of Busoni and Sibelius, and once even poked a curious if rather conservative finger toward America, my future, little-did-I-know-it-then home, by publishing some of the works of Edward MacDowell, after he had settled in Wiesbaden, their future, little-did-they-know-it-then home. Breitkopfs were also the publishers of the famous authentic scores of every classical symphony, overture, and concerto imaginable. J. S. Bach wrote more than two hundred cantatas, and Breitkopfs had them all in scores and parts with Urtext staring you in the face from every beautiful page. They also published the listing of Mozart's works that has provided the mysterious K or KV numbers identifying every one of Mozart's 626b works compiled by an old bachelor and botanist with a truly Breitkopfian name, Dr. Ludwig Alois Friedrich, Ritter von Köchel.

No wonder that a visitor simply called Emil and his young man were received at Breitkopfs with the condescending courtesy bestowed on a sweaty Roman general by the Egyptian Pharaoh who did not have as many ships and horses but an uninterrupted line of ancestors going back to 1719 B.C. Our host was Dr. Helmuth von Hase, a great-grandson of the first Härtel who, in the slightly Saxon accent that supposedly marked if not distinguished the speech of

Richard Wagner, recalled many a story. They all dealt with the great past and were thus carefully calculated to embarrass and humiliate guys like us who had not been around very long. One of Hase's favorite stories was the one of the composer who had given Breitkopf & Härtel several of his operas, all of which they had published and on all of which they had lost money. Then he came in one day and announced a new project that would put him and Breitkopfs forever in the black: he was offering them the publication rights to a new operatic work that would take four evenings to perform. They told him, please, to go away. He did. It was *Der Ring des Nibelungen.*

There was a similar background of slightly bitter amusement to Dr. von Hase's account of his firm's connection with Eugène d'Albert, a great pianist whose ambitions in life were to be a composer and a husband. Not satisfied with a brilliant career as a concert pianist he married almost as many wives (seven) as he wrote operas (ten). Dr. von Hase recalled the day when M. and Mme d'Albert were expected for dinner at the Hase villa. The father—then the head of Breitkopfs, but really the grandson of Gottfried Härtel and, like him, alas, with only one Christian name—urged everyone to be on guard and not to snicker when the couple arrived: they would see a rather funny-looking couple: Madame towering at least a head over her famous but diminutive husband. When the couple arrived not even the father could retain his composure. Madame d'Albert was a charming petite, scarcely reaching to her husband's famous shoulders: d'Albert had been divorced and remarried between accepting the invitation and coming for dinner.

It was to be his last appearance at the villa. Breitkopfs had published two of d'Albert's operas and in recalling their forgotten names—*Gernot* and *Ghismonda*—one appreciates that even the investment in a dinner for two very small people was difficult to justify to the Board of Directors. As once before in their history, B & H felt that the time had come to part company from one of their operatic writers and when d'Albert offered his next opera, they asked him to take it somewhere else. He took it to Bote & Bock in Berlin (founded as embarrassingly late as 1838), the same people who had sent the polka-and-fugue singing envoy to the *Schwanda première* in Prague. The opera was one of the great operatic jackpots in history: *Tiefland.* Breitkopfs or, rather, Härtels were not the only ones to weep. The author of the libretto, Rudolf Lothar, was so sure that the work would be another d'Albert flop that shortly before the opening night in 1903 he sold his rights to the composer for a few hundred crowns. Another gambler who withdrew his stake a split second before the little white ball was to touch off a beautiful rain of gold pouring down on d'Albert and Bote and Bock.

• • •

NOBODY SHOULD THROW the first stone at the timid gambler, should laugh about the loser, should bow to the winner: they are all gamblers, some just in luck, some in misfortune. The history of our profession is filled with the results—some bad, some good, some simply wonderful—of misjudgments. Very few people are as smart as they portray themselves. Most of our successes are luck, not planning, knowing, judging wisely.

One of the brightest feathers in the cap of any American music publisher, if one is permitted to call it that, is, of course, the musical setting of *The Lord's Prayer* by Albert Hay Malotte. Were the editors of the house so smart as to spot its potential among the hundreds of sacred songs that are submitted to them year after dreary year? Was it a scheming, brilliant executive who searched out the composer and got him to collaborate with Jesus? It was nothing of the kind. It was just another wonderfully rewarding result of misjudgment.

The song had been submitted, unsolicited, but when they looked at the title they said, "Not another one," and decided, sight unseen, to turn it down: a few years earlier they had published a setting of *The Lord's Prayer* by a lady composer and they didn't think it would be nice to publish a competing version, particularly in view of the fact that it was a lady composer. There are so few of them around, and if one of them at last has a song that goes into a second printing and gets published in an arrangement for mixed voices, the least, they thought, they could do was to be nice to her as one should be to any lady even if she is a composer, which isn't always easy, though they all say look at Chaminade, but if one looks there isn't much to see. Anyway, they thought they shouldn't do that to old Josephine Forsyth, and so they marked the new song "Reject." Luckily, a lot of songs and piano pieces and organ solos had come in the same day and all had been marked "Reject," and not out of courtesy to a lady, so the new song was sitting at the bottom of the rejection pile, covered by fifty-nine other rejections that had come in a little earlier, which turned out to be a very fortunate thing indeed. Because when the young lady began working her way down the pile, typing the form letters and how sorry they were and your song just doesn't fit into our present requirements, a music dealer in Pittsburgh called and ordered five hundred copies of Malotte's *The Lord's Prayer:* John Charles Thomas had just sung it over the radio, and could they please get the five hundred copies on the next train because there wasn't any airmail. So they went to the Rejection Slip Department and prayed and searched through the pile, and there it was, there it had been sitting for a couple of days while the young lady was working her rejecting way down the pile, but she hadn't quite got there and so they erased the "Reject" and sent the composer a letter, "We are happy to," and a contract, and they printed the song and have since sold only Our Father in Heaven knows how many millions of copies and have collected simply profane amounts of royalties from records and performances and motion picture uses and everybody admires them and thinks how very smart they are.

• • •

WHEN I SAW Dr. von Hase again, quite a bit later, many things had changed. I wasn't coming from Vienna but from New York. And the old Doc wasn't sitting in his shiny office in Leipzig, surrounded by eight hundred busy helpers, but in a little room in the city of Wiesbaden near the Rhine; the sprawling Breitkopf plant in Leipzig had gone up in smoke during an air raid in December 1943. A few days before, Hase had taken his reluctant family, some of the business records, and the pictures of Bernard Christoph and Johann Gottlob Immanuel to a little town outside of Leipzig. From there, two years later, he, his family, and a few employees in two automobiles, one of them requisitioned from the former chief of the Leipzig police, and a moving van containing a few household goods, some sample copies of Breitkopf publications, and a few statistics, were escorted by the American army on a one-way trek toward the west. After the second day they came to a stop in front of an abandoned community center in Wiesbaden, the American headquarters. The cargo was dumped on the street. The passengers found a few mattresses for the night, chopped down a door to heat a little cooking stove, and, separating them from the pots and pans that had made the trip from the vanishing east, set up their files, their card system, and their sheet music. Then they nailed a little poster to a door that had not been used as firewood: Breitkopf & Härtel, Musikverlag, Wiesbaden.

The next morning they walked around the town, trying to figure out what to do. In the office of the county surveyor they located an old litho press. There was some paper and some printer's ink. They obtained a license from the American authorities. From the little supply of music they had picked almost at random when they had to be on their way within a few hours, they chose two: the Minuet from Grieg's Piano Sonata Op. 7 and an arrangement for piano solo of Schubert's "Unfinished" Symphony. They began reproducing copies on the old litho press, not bothering to put covers on them (and not able to put them on had they bothered). Within a few weeks they had sold every copy. They were back in business.

Today Breitkopf & Härtel have very little time to reminisce. The litho press has long since been restored to the county surveyor's office, and the only recollection of the first postwar editions of Grieg's Minuet and Schubert's "Unfinished" Symphony are neatly framed copies on new shining walls. In Leipzig, too, the new masters of the East have dusted off the rubble and have re-established the Breitkopf & Härtel name, publishing the music, however, with a bear deprived of Hermes' capitalistic staff and of the ancient year of the foundation, neither of which seem to appeal to the philosophy of a *Volksrepublik.* To old Johann Gottlob Immanuel it's probably all the same. He looks with the same satisfied smile on the western *Wirtschaftswunder* and the eastern *Wunderwirtschaft* and as long as they sell two hundred Bach cantatas and tons and tons of Beethoven symphonies, with a little Busoni, MacDowell, and Sibelius thrown in, he couldn't care less.

• • •

FROM WIESBADEN it is only a *Katzensprung,* a cat's leap if one insists on translating what becomes a little earthbound and unbouncy in the process, across the River Rhine to the two-thousand-year-old city of Mainz, snuggled in the junction of the Main and the Rhine, surrounded by villages whose names adorn celebrated wine labels, and the home of another music-publishing colossus with an almost two-hundred-year pre-Hertzka tradition, the house of Schott.

These are the people Richard Wagner took his four-night monstrosity to after Breitkopfs had asked him to go away. By that time they had already lived through three vigorous and prosperous generations before running out of Schotts. They are now owned and ruled by the Strecker family, who appeared on the scene after the last Schott, Franz, had published the *Ring, Meistersinger,* and *Parsifal,* a task requiring the staggering number of thirty thousand plates to be engraved—not to speak of Wagner's personal requirements, which must have been *götterdämmerish.* "Your demands can't be met by a publisher," the desperate Franz wrote to the irrepressible Richard. "You need a prince or a rich banker." Wagner, of course, found his prince and Franz's successors, the Streckers, lived happily ever after on the international copyright which, soon, made the original investment in thirty thousand plates look microscopic.

Schotts have been in the same building, an elegant, beautiful, spacious, patrician home, since Bernhard Schott, the founder, built it, and while it is amazing for anyone in so precarious a business to keep the moving van away for almost two centuries, they have a special reason to stress their immovability: during World War II the center of the city of Mainz was nearly obliterated in an air raid that left almost nothing standing but a little cluster of houses. The little cluster contained the house Weihergarten No. 5, the home of Schotts.

As one enters the grounds through the remains of an old gate, one is touched by history: the wall in the old German city bears the French inscription *Rue de la princesse Stéphanie.* Here, in the faded inscription, is the story of the French revolutionary army, occupying the left bank of the Rhine; here is Napoleon chasing out the Elector who had given Bernhard Schott his first license to be a printer and engraver to his court and whose palace can still be seen down by the river; and then Blücher and, perhaps, the Tsar of Russia sweeping back the tide of history on their way to Waterloo and changing the name of the city from the French Mayence back to the German Mainz, and you wish you knew who the princess Stéphanie was and what happened to her, but nobody can tell you and they'd rather talk about Hans Werner Henze.

Through the remains of the old gate one enters the courtyard with the little pond—the *Weiher*—that gave the garden and the street its name. Here they have serenades from time to time where the members of the Strecker family welcome the better-class citizens of the town with the patrician, condescending friendliness that must, once, have been bestowed on the populace by the Elector or Napoleon or, perhaps, a conquering American general not too long ago. One can listen to the music and catch a cold looking at pretty flowers and well-kept trees and a group of little marble statues playing instruments and one big marble faun who seems to be shrieking back in horror from whatever music they play—an odd pose for a marble faun to take in the courtyard of a publisher who has specialized in contemporary music since they first published Beethoven's Ninth Symphony and *Missa Solemnis* and some of his string quartets.

And then the miraculously preserved house, the elegant, sweeping, comfortable staircase, unmarred by an elevator, and a door marked Wagner Room, leading to a little museum filled with busts and pictures and Gregorian chants written on parchment and illuminated in blue and gold and a letter from Beethoven. There is also a tablet, stating that "in this room, on February 5th, 1862, Richard Wagner as guest of Franz and Betty Schott read to a selected audience for the first time his libretto for 'Die Meistersinger.' Soon after he began composing the work in nearby Biebrich on the Rhine." In an adjoining glass case are the first pages of the *Meistersinger* libretto, written in Wagner's famous neat hand, with inked-in corrections and changes and stage directions, squeezed in as a second thought or crossed out as a third.

Founder Bernhard had two sons who, after their father's death, named the firm, logically, B. Schott Söhne, a name it still carries though there hasn't been a Schott around for several generations. During the French occupation the Söhne became Frères and established branches in the west: in Paris, Rotterdam, London, Brussels. There is still a Schott Frères on the rue Saint-Jean in Brussels, an enormous, cave-like store with a musty publishing department up a dangerously dark wooden stair. Its letterhead, although the firm has been de-Schotted long ago, still carries the inscription *Fondé en 1823.* The London house, too, is still in existence. One can stroll within a few minutes through a publisher's lane, magnificently called Great Marlborough Street, visiting Schotts to the right, Augeners to the left, and Chesters a few steps farther down the street. A little while ago there were also Novellos just a block away, but they, sadly, moved away, and the others, when you come to see them, talk about expensive city quarters and lovely storage space in the country, with a cricket field for lunch-hour recreation and air and sunlight and, oh, so cheap rents and in a little while, I guess, they all will move to Tottenham or Hottentam and I'll never see Great Marlborough Street again.

From its western outposts, Schott's mother house in Mainz received *Wilhelm Tell, Fra Diavolo, The Daughter of the Regiment, Le Postillon du Longjumeau* and many similar products of the Opéra-Comique period and unleashed them on the enormous German-speaking operatic hinterland in translations that still disgrace the Vaterland—they had two hundred or more outlets for their rapidly increasing stock of operatic merchandise in Germany, the Austro-Hungarian empire, and Switzerland. German operas were added—including quite a few by Lortzing, for many decades the sentimental darling of the German stage, and Heinrich Marschner's *Hans Heiling,* first performed in 1833, soon after Weber's *Freischütz* and shortly before Wagner's *Flying Dutchman* and very much akin to the spooky romanticism of both. It was a great hit in its days, though few remember it. I heard it once in my distant youth and still recall Hans Heiling's enormous black beard and very pale face and music that, in memory, still sounds blackbearded and pale.

Wagner, of course, was a meteoric addition to the Schott operatic properties.

There was also a musical adviser and part-time editor on the staff of the firm who, in 1893, wrote an opera based on a fairy tale. Most publishers look with icy disapproval on the creative activities of their employees, resent the fact that they write, compose, or just think, and either fire them if they find out or make them take a vow of future creative and intellectual celibacy. Schotts, in a shocking breach of professional ethics, took neither course: instead, they published the work. They have never fired a composing editor since. The opera was *Hänsel und Gretel.*

Schotts were the only European music publisher that fought off the Hertzka onslaught with haughty contempt. By then, they had become one of the few great international publishers of contemporary music. They were the exclusive publishers of Paul Hindemith and, later, of Carl (*Carmina burana*) Orff, Hans Werner Henze, and many others. They published Stravinsky and Schoenberg's *Moses and Aaron*, Egk and Fortner and Sutermeister, Karl Amadeus Hartmann and Bernd Alois Zimmermann, Luigi Nono from Italy, Jean Françaix from France, Poles, Swiss, and Swedes and a couple of musical magazines, and a house organ in two or three languages.

• • •

How NICE it would be to tell the tales of many more of the fabulous music publishing people who have been and are the mentors, the nursemaids, the bankers, the printers, the disseminators, and the elegant exploiters of composers and writers since time immemorial—how nice it would be and how many enemies I could make, fast and easily. But much of it is known and quite a bit isn't really worth telling and comes out anyhow from time to time when anniversaries—the resounding hundredth, the fanfaring fiftieth, the heavily overorchestrated twenty-fifth—are the subject of brochures or expensive, gold-edged books: stern-faced, bearded ancestors look grim and unsmiling down the centuries, while busy editors fill the rest of the pages with tales of their wonderful deeds, omitting the follies and all the absurdly lucrative accidents—neither foreseen nor planned—that made it possible for them to spend so much money on an anniversary book and to grow all these magnificently groomed beards.

It would be nice, for instance, to talk a little about the Russian publishers—Bessel, Belaiev, and Serge Koussevitzky (yes, *the* Koussevitzky). The Russians were all Ivans-come-lately to the music-publishing trade, beginning operations only in the middle of the nineteenth century when, for example, Vassili Vassilievitsch Bessel started publishing Mussorgsky, Tchaikovsky, Rimsky-Korsakov, and Anton Rubinstein. Twenty years later, in 1888, Mitrofan Petrovich Belaiev inherited a prosperous lumber business and a huge forest of rubles from his father and decided to use his wooden millions to publish and support a whole generation of Russian composers without consideration for profit or loss. He began by publishing Glazunov's Overture on three Greek themes, Op. 3, lavishly engraving score, parts, and an arrangement for piano four-hands and soon added Scriabin, Borodin, Balakirev, César Cui, Glière, Gretchaninov, Liadov, Liapunov, and Nicholas Tcherepnin, not to mention a staggering number of lesser Russian masters who made neither history nor the crossword puzzles.

When Belaiev died in 1903, he left an enormous fortune earmarked for publishing, performing, and giving prizes to Russian music and appointed a board of three Russian composers to rule the business, each of them obligated to appoint another Russian composer as his successor, and so on in perpetuity. It sounded like whatever a Paradise for Composers is called in Russian and prompted Rimsky-Korsakov, another beneficiary of Belaiev's largesse and, as it soon turned out, a better composer than political prophet to announce that Russian composers were now provided for "for all time to come." All time lasted for a little more than ten years, when headquarters, hastily, had to be moved from the Neva to the Seine, where neither Russian composers nor Russian directors were as plentiful as they used to be and where lumber millions in prewar rubles were only sad, uncashable memories.

Serge Koussevitzky, in addition to playing the double-bass and riding up and down the Volga with his orchestra on a steamboat, invested some of the money which his father-in-law had made in the tea business in establishing, in 1909, the Editions Russes de Musique and becoming the publisher of Stravinsky, Prokofiev, and Rachmaninoff.

All these Russian publishers had to have branches in western Europe: Russia had never been a member of the international copyright convention, and works published in Russia were not protected in the rest of the world. So there had to be a Bessel in Paris, a Belaiev in Leipzig, and Editions Russes de Musique became Russischer Musikverlag in Berlin. One day *before* anything was published in Moscow or St. Petersburg, it was issued in the West and became thus fully protected, everywhere that is, with the exception of the United States, which did not play the game by the same rules. Here, the citizenship of the composer was and is the decisive factor, and only people whose country of origin has a mutual treaty with the United States are admitted to copyright protection. As Russia never had a treaty with the United States, no Russian, no matter how white or red, has ever been able to obtain a copyright. From Rimsky-Korsakov to Shostakovich, from Tchaikovsky to Khachaturian, no Russian composer ever made a dime in the land of the free and the home of the brave. However, as no kopeks were coming for *May Fair Lady* or *Porgy and Bess* from Russia to the United States, both sides were equally hurt and injustice was meted out impartially.

It would be even more tempting to tell the story of the great house of Ricordi. But everybody who ever made a musical tour of Milano has seen it at 2 Via Berchet, an easy stone's throw from La Scala, where, in fact, they had once been located, and the story has been told in a movie—*Casa Ricordi*—seen by multitudes at the occasion of the 150th anniversary in 1958 of a house which, to the disappointment of many who had paid their admission with a loftier purpose in mind, turned out to be a music-publishing house, supremely unadorned by a red lantern. Let us therefore just sum up the history of Ricordi by recalling that the founder, Giovanni Ricordi, who had studied the technique of engraving and music printing in Leipzig, undoubtedly with Johann Gottlob or Gottlob Johann, discovered and published Verdi —they never had a contract; it was all based on friendship and complete confidence!—and that his grandson, Giulio, discovered and signed up Puccini.

Verdi lived to be almost eighty-eight. His works were protected by international copyright for fifty years after his death in most parts of the world and a work like *Aida* remained the exclusive property of Ricordi for eighty golden years—from 1871 when the opera was published, to 1951, when the fifty years of posthumous protection were coming to an end.

Ricordi rented out the orchestrations for *Aida* and *Rigoletto*, for *Traviata*, *Trovatore*, and *Ballo in maschera*, for *La Bohème* and *Tosca* and many, many more—scores and parts were never sold but only rented, to be sure the house would retain absolute control, a control which even, during the first few years of the life of an opera, extended to selection and the approval of the principal artists and of the conductor, wherever the new work was performed. In addition, they sold vocal scores, arias, potpourris, arrangements, albums, and libretti. They also—it was a wonderfully lucrative business, they still tell you nostalgically—made and rented out the special instruments that were needed in many of their operas—Japanese Bells for *Madama Butterfly*, the chimes of Rome for the third act of *Tosca*, fourteen different gongs for *Turandot*, the machine that provided the thunder in *Rigoletto* on cue. Ricordi also provided every theater with beautifully designed and strikingly executed designs for each costume and for all the scenery. For every costume there were sketches, painted by hand in vivid, yet simple and easily reproducible colors—for many of the roles four or more costumes changed from act to act. On the back of each sketch was a detailed listing of all requirements: costumes, weapons (with intricate ink drawings of each sword or dagger to make sure they would be in style), shoes, stockings, wigs, hats, plumes, feathers, jewelry, royal or princely crowns (they were different, and must not be confused), diadems, scarfs, slippers, boots, and flowers (if any). The sketches for scenery and costumes were provided for literally hundreds of different operas, not only for those by Puccini and Verdi, who personally approved each sketch, the use of which was obligatory—if a theater did not produce an opera in the official Ricordi setting, it could not obtain the music—but for every opera by Zandonai, Respighi, Boito, and a great many whose names and titles are forgotten.

The present age of the director has done away with such centrally directed and supplied uniformity and all that is left are the pictures of Falstaff, Gilda, and Scarpia or a magnificent painting of a storm-swept first act of a vanished opera, looking down in faded colors from the walls of the palatial mansion maintained by the American representative of Ricordi near New York and guarded by a little dog strangely named Pamina (a figure from a very un-Ricordian, public domain opera that should have no status here) whose only passion in life seems to be to chase after the 5:14 jet from Boston in futile, noisy, never satisfied frustration.

For many wonderful years every opera house in the world, when it performed a Verdi opera, had to rent the music and the sketches and the special instruments from Ricordi and had to pay a royalty for every performance, and when the days of recordings and of the sound film and radio and TV and LP arrived—holy Giuseppe! An now it's all gone—it's all in the public domain, the ugliest word in the vocabulary at No. 2 Via Berchet. Nobody has to pay any more for "*Celeste Aida*" or "*La donna è mobile*"—it's all for free. You can sing it and record it and perform it and when you need the orchestral parts and the scores you don't have to go to Ricordi any more but can rent them for a few bucks from Mapleson on 41st Street in New York.

And when you look at the show windows of Ricordi in Milano, once the proud and haughty display of the greatest monopoly in the world, you find them filled with television sets and guitars and shiny accordions and rock and roll music and you take a disappointed look and go next door to Biffi for a *gelato* of real, monopolistic class. And then you remember that Puccini, too, has just a few years to go before he too will go PD—public domain—and that soon there will be only guitars and accordions left where once the caravans from all over the world arrived to trade gold and spices in exchange for a *gelida manina.*

Oh—there are many more, all with their peculiar speciality. There are the two Marietti brothers, Jean et Philip, Parisians from Corsica, who own and run the publishing house, founded (in 1907—the year Hertzka started in business) by and still named after Max Eschig and situated where it always was, in the rue de Rome in Paris, near the Gare Saint-Lazare—an appalling, unbelievable maze of corridors and chambers and corners and steep staircases filled, loaded, crammed with music, including unclimbable mountains of Viennese operettas of the golden past—*Le Pays du Sourire*, for instance, *La Veuve Joyeuse*, and *Rêve de Valse*, for which one of the Mariettis made also the translations in Corsican French, thus making money as publisher, agent, and author with some special good-will bonuses thrown in just because they are such nice guys. The main office has been kept, chair by chair, shelf by shelf, roll-desk by roll-desk, picture by picture, bust by bust and dust by dust, the way M. Max Eschig left it to the Mariettis a generation or two ago.

The Mariettis are exuding Corsican astuteness in every word they say and in the many words they do not say. When they approach New York (they never fly) mysterious ship-to-shore calls precede their arrival. After one has been dealing with them and the thousand schemes they have up their elegantly tailored sleeves, one gains a much more intimate appreciation of the nature and success of their great compatriot, buried a few Metro stops away at the Invalides.

Not far from Napoleon's tomb, a few blocks from the opera, is the fabulous house of Salabert, where Madame Francis Salabert, Présidente, Directeur Général, the widow of the founder, rules what is undoubtedly the most absolute kingdom left since the decapitation of Louis XVI. Before her husband, a great and brilliant publisher who published both serious and popular music, was killed in an airplane crash on his way to America in 1946, she had never been in the office. When she made her first appearance there soon after, the directors told her just to forget the whole thing: go home and let us worry about your business, we'll send you a check every month. She fired them instantly. Later, most of them were allowed to come back, but they are not permitted to sit in the presence of Madame, unless formally invited by her to do so, and the word "we" is never used. When Madame talks about the business, she says I. When others talk about it, they say You. Her success is as proverbial as her hospitality and it is equally delicious to be driven, in her chauffeured limousine, with poodle and maid, to one of the luxury restaurants near the Elysée where you get a tiny beefsteak with potato chips for the price of a small villa, but can look, for free, at the chestnut trees and the boutiques of the stamp dealers—or to be asked to her apartment on the avenue Iéna for a gargantuan dinner, served in a forest of roses with several Renoirs watching your table manners.

• • •

Breitkopf, Härtel, and Schott; Bote, Simrock, and Bock; Heugel and Durand, Bessel and Belaiev, Ricordi and Sonzogno, Wilhelm Hansen of Copenhagen, where even the girls of the family are named Wilhelm to maintain the tradition, and, I hasten to add, Schirmer—all are names of real people, proudly transformed into a commercial symbol by achievement and age, known throughout the world of music, printed on millions of copies of sheet music, their intitials adorning elegant plaques on palaces all over the world. But who has ever heard the name of Dreyfus? Nobody with the exception of George Gershwin, Cole Porter, Jerome Kern, Vincent Youmans, Richard Rodgers, Oscar Hammerstein, Kurt Weill, Frederick Loewe, Jule Styne, and a dozen or two people of similar stature.

Max and Ludwig Dreyfus had come to America, two young, penniless immigrant boys from Germany, before the turn of the century. They had come from Kuppenheim, in the Grand Duchy of Baden, a very small village in the valley of the river Murg that comes rushing down from the Black Forest filled with trout and carrying logs from the mountains toward the Rhine.

When I saw a photograph of the little house where they and ten brothers and sisters were born I could almost feel the touch of the stone and breathe the smell of country wine and foaming apple cider emanating from the cellar, filling the two-story house, up to the shingled roof, with a penetrating, lively, fermentive sting. I could hear the voices of the peasants and their speech and their dialect as they drove their hay carts past the little house while the single bell of the village church chimed Vesper. I could hear it and feel it because I come from the same part of the world. Looking at the slightly faded picture of the little house where Elias Dreifuss and his wife Emilie, known as Esther, lived and raised their children, and where the old grandmother, still wearing the *Scheitel*, the wig of the orthodox woman, had died one year after her one hundredth birthday, setting a pattern for a family of patriarchs, I remember my own visits to these villages, on a bicycle, during the 1914 war. Food in the city had become scarce, and we were sent out on search for homegrown supplies. As I look at the picture, the invigorating smells of wine and apple cider and of wonderful country bread and of butter come back—the remembrance still makes the mouth water, now that the butterless war of 1914 lives only in movies and old history books, and even the dung heaps that were kept in front of every house in the little village still smell healthy and strong and fertile and, oh, so peaceful.

Elias Dreifuss was a cattle dealer and he walked—walked—around the villages and to the country fairs, buying and selling, and some of the children, among them Ludwig, walked with him, urging the cattle up the mountains and down into the valley. On Friday night, Elias Dreifuss was presiding over the service in the tiny village synagogue.

Some thirty years after they had arrived in America with nothing but a few marks in their pockets and only an uncle somewhere in the South to give them a little assistance and advice, the two brothers sold their business—one of the biggest music-publishing firms in the world—to a motion-picture company, also run by brothers, at a price that still makes those who tell you about it pause in awe.

The spectacular rise of the firm they sold had begun with the discovery of a young Bohemian piano player who had come from Prague as the accompanist of a Czech violinist and with the launching of his Broadway hit *The Firefly* in 1912. Rudolf Friml was a marvelously indestructible, colorful *Musikant*—I remember him from *Rose Marie*, the first large-scale American-French show I had seen at the Théâtre Mogador in Paris very early in my professional life, leaving the theater humming the unforgettable *Kitsch* of the "Indian Love Call"—and I still could marvel at the octogenarian, almost sixty years after *The Firefly*, breezing into my office (we were the publishers of "Donkey Serenade" and of several hundred salon pieces by Friml) with a smilingly admiring new Chinese wife and enormous tapes, the result of his improvisations at the piano, on his way to yet another world tour to conduct orchestras in Munich or Tokyo in medleys of his works, and still after seventy American years, speaking English with the most marvelously spiced, earthy Bohemian accent, every vowel carrying the appetizing image of knoedels, every cadence full of happily unsupressable *joie de vivre.*

Young Friml was followed by young Jerome Kern, whose entire, life-long output, including *Show Boat* and the forever green "Old Man River," the brothers published and controlled. And then Mr. Max met George Gershwin, who had only written a few songs and Max had never heard any of them. But he was so impressed with the personality of the young man that he hired him at thirty-five dollars a week "without any set duties. Just step in every morning and say Hello. The rest will follow." It followed—many hellos, thirty-five dollar payments, and disappointments later—when Al Jolson sang Gershwin's "Swanee" at the Winter Garden. Within a year it sold a million copies and more than two million phonograph records.

Max's health had never been strong. He hadn't been a cattle walker but more of a fiddler and piano player in the old country and had started his American life playing the piano for a publisher and augmenting his income with five-dollar engagements at night clubs while Ludwig was selling picture frames, making most of his deliveries on foot. After they had sold their business, Max bought an estate some sixty miles north of New York where he had once found recovery from his ailments in the woods and the air of Putnam County, and retired. Ludwig, long since Louis, went to London, where he bought Chappell & Co., a music publisher, piano manufacturer, and dealer on New Bond Street, founded in 1810. He was busy, successful, wonderfully rich, the Rothschild of the British music business. He had a grandiose apartment on Grosvenor Square filled with magnificent paintings, within easy walking distance of Hyde Park, where, every morning, his groom and his horse were waiting for him.

Soon he sold more pianos than he knew he had. He published shows and produced them on a lavish scale, frequently running two or three hit shows simultaneously on Piccadilly. He bought Queens Hall, London's most prominent concert hall. When he walked over to Claridge's at lunch time it was a treat just to walk in his enormous shadow and to get in at the tail end of the greetings bestowed on him by the doorman in his high hat and by the one-armed veteran at the checkroom and by the headwaiter and the second headwaiter and the waiter and the wine steward and the first and second piccolo, in a wonderfully tuned mixture of cordiality, ripened through the years, and humble adoration that had never changed and never would.

Then, one day—some fifteen years after Queens Hall had been bombed out during the Blitz—he stood erect, very silent, tapping his cane on the sidewalk, unapproachable and very quiet, as Chappell of London, a landmark and the pride of Louis Dreyfus and of New Bond Street, went up in fire and smoke. Two days later—he had long since passed the age of eighty—he had his first meeting with the architects who were to erect him a new building covering most of an entire London city block.

In the meantime, Max in America had breathed enough of the Putnam County air in Brewster. He was prevented, for some time, from competing as a publisher with the people who had bought his and his brother's business. But he could be an agent. He became agent for Chappell of London. The agent, soon, was the most successful, the most active and the most revered music man in America.

Who will ever forget Mr. Max, frail, slim, small, pale, very soft-spoken, coming into the music room of Chappell in New York for an audition? He sat there, silent, seemingly dreaming, dressed in his celebrated linen jacket, the royal purple of his trade and the symbol of his majestic station. There the great composers and the great writers paraded, not at all great in his presence, ready to accept the verdict of the little man in the linen jacket, and when he leaned a little forward and cupped his hand to his ear and said "I don't hear any music," they hastily scrapped what they had just played for him and turned to the next number, hoping that Mr. Max would just say nothing at all or, perhaps, nod a little or just, quietly, go back to dreaming.

At lunch time he proceeded, on foot for many years and by car as he became frailer and slimmer and still more soft-spoken, to the Astor Hotel on Times Square. Here, for many decades, he maintained an apartment and had his table on the balcony—Mr. Dreyfus's table, the headwaiter would say, unbelieving that anybody would not know which Mr. Dreyfus's table was—where it was the badge of honor to be expected. Mr. Dreyfus presided, sipping a little tomato juice or milk, nibbling on half an egg or a few crackers while his guests gulped down the Astor menu from martinis to peach Melba. As celebrities flocked to the table, lesser lights, from time to time, took their seats among them, trying to squeeze in a little personal business. Between the boeuf bourguignonne and an attempt to get the attention of Flo Ziegfeld, they felt themselves tapped on the shoulder. Behind them stood the host. "Order your dessert and leave, please," he said softly and went back to his seat. They didn't order their dessert and left. Promptly at 1:45 Mr. Max got up. Uneaten peach Melbas remained uneaten as the guests took their prompt, undelayable departure. It was Mr. Max's siesta hour and an iron etiquette swept the eaters out onto Broadway.

After an hour Mr. Max would walk or be driven back to the office, where to the grief of his minions he stayed till very late. He had formed a dozen different companies to accommodate the famous composers and writers who had flocked to his banner. Nowhere did the name Dreyfus ever appear. The walls were plastered with pictures of celebrities, but not a single photograph of the boss was ever permitted to be taken. There were the Williamson Music Company, Stratford Music Corporation, Mutual Music Society, Buxton Hill, G & C–one innocent-sounding company would take care of the business of *My Fair Lady* and *Gigi*, another one of *Sound of Music* and *Oklahoma* and all the other Rodgers and Hammerstein hits. *Show Boat*, *Porgy and Bess*, *Funny Girl*, or the hits of Cole Porter and Kurt Weill, each had its own publishing company and its own name and a certain measure of independence within the Chappell family and a share in the heavenly profits–but they were all ruled in absolute, unrelenting grandeur by Mr. Max to the very end when, at the age of ninety, he had to take his leave. He had not been back in Europe since Hitler had taken over what was left of the little house in Kuppenheim and had smashed even the gravestones of Elias and Esther Dreifuss in the little cemetery. He traveled only from New York to Brewster and from Brewster to New York while Louis came thundering across the ocean, at least twice a year, in airplanes that had a special sleeping compartment and whose pilots and stewards greeted the cattle boy from Kuppenheim with the same mixture of cordiality and veneration that he had left behind at Claridges and that, he knew, would be waiting there for him again upon his thundering return.

VI

THE TRULY SPECTACULAR battles between the big music publishers, mainly between the Schotts of Mainz, led by at least one Strecker, and the Universals of Vienna, guided by Hertzka himself, were fought at the international festivals, the trade fairs of contemporary music. It was ferocious and merciless warfare, marvelous to watch and highly enjoyable to participate in. Year after year they met there in search of new composers, eager at the same time to display their older ones. When they met in hotel lobbies or concert halls they greeted each other with teeth-grinding exuberance and evil smiles. While they shook hands they winked at one of the junior executives who always traveled in their wake—at me, for example—to hurry and buttonhole Stravinsky while the boss was pinning down the competition.

The festivals that had begun to blossom soon after the end of the First World War had done away with national censorship and international separation, had removed the boundaries that had been marked by trenches and graves and released the pent-up musical emotions of a whole generation. Many, many years later I heard Aaron Copland say on an American television program: "I had the good fortune to have been in my twenties in the twenties." We all felt that way.

The earliest, the most unforgettable, and the most pleasant of all the festivals dedicated to new, untried music was founded in 1921 in the tiny town of Donaueschingen, where it flourished, a small-scale delight, for five consecutive years. It was an ideal setting, remote from hustle, untouched by bustle, many train hours away from the next city. The fir-scented air, rushing invigoratingly from the Black Forest into the little town, filled the lungs of the visitors, making them receptive to whatever, musically speaking, was in store for them. Between rehearsals they would stroll through the park, where whirling mountain streams ended their brief, joyous lives in a little pool whose stagnant waters, difficult to believe, sent the Danube on its mighty voyage to Vienna, Budapest, Belgrade, and all the way down to the Black Sea. I was still a law student in nearby Freiburg when, at the age of twenty-one, I attended my first Donaueschingen festival, pushing my bicycle in lovely company up the mountains toward the pass and then racing down the steep incline along one of the mountain brooks that was to feed the majestic stream and into the little town where I was to have my first encounter with the music and the people that were to be my life.

In a spacious castle surrounded by the beautiful park that contained the source of the Danube lived one of the many German princes, who, like many of the little princes, had a little music director to organize the princely music in the town and the church and the castle and who had to make sure that when the Kaiser came as a hunting guest as often he used to, the little town band played "*Heil Dir im Siegerkranz*" with mustache-tickling precision. This music director, however, was a very special music director. His name was Heinrich Burkard. He was a thin, weather-beaten little man, looking like a peasant of the region, and an absolute nut for modern music. He was not content with conducting potpourris on Sunday afternoon, but persuaded his prince—the Kaiser had retired by then and there was not much to do in the little town—to invite a bunch of international composers and performers for three days of world *premières* and so gave himself and the town of Donaueschingen a reputation it has to this day. Musicians and composers were arriving by train, on bicycles, even on foot. Most of them were quartered, for free, in the castle.

The very first Donaueschingen festival (1921) made musical history: it propelled an almost unknown German composer into sudden international fame, the twenty-six-year-old Paul Hindemith, viola player in the orchestra of the Frankfurt Opera. Burkard had selected Hindemith's Second String Quartet, Op. 16, to be performed, but the artists he had engaged to play it refused to get involved with what seemed a forbiddingly extreme work. Burkard was not to be deterred: the work had to be played even if a new string quartet had to be formed for the occasion. It was, and the Amar Quartet, soon to become one of the celebrated chamber-music groups of the era, sprang into existence. Hindemith himself played the viola. The leader was Liko Amar, a Turkish colleague of Hindemith's from the orchestra pit in Frankfurt, where the composer had also found his wife, Gertrud, the daughter of the chief conductor. Heinrich Kaspar played second violin. The cellist was Hindemith's brother, Rudolf.

Rudolf did not stay long with the Quartet. He soon became tired of playing second cello to the oppressive fame of his brother, and when a chance came to exchange the solo desk in the Amar Quartet for a more anonymous fourth desk in the Vienna Philharmonic Orchestra, which also played nightly at the State Opera, he moved himself and the huge St. Bernard that was his steady companion eagerly downstream. He was a most amusing, highly individual bachelor, a quiet drinker and an untiring, acidly cynical raconteur, and as long as one didn't mind his language, richly and colorfully adorned, and stayed away from the subject of *Mathis der Maler* and similar family topics, he was most entertaining if not very inspiring to associate with.

The newly republican Austrian State, at that time, made

room in the vastness of the former Imperial palace for its civil servants, of whom Rudolf Hindemith as a member of the State Orchestra was one. They gave him and his dog two enormously wide and dizzily high rooms facing through high eighteenth-century windows the beautiful inner court of the castle with its cascading lilacs and the statue of Prince Eugene frozen elegantly on a magnificent bronze Lippizan. Hindemith proceeded at once to cover his eight imperial walls and two republican ceilings with murals of an obscenity which would have caused the proprietor of a Pompeian bath to blush deeply. After a year or two, the cellist and the St. Bernard left Vienna. They left behind the beautiful murals, wedded inseparably to the castle walls.

The next tenant was to be Fräulein Saliger, a mature, Walkyrian spinster employed in the administration of the State Opera, where, a Cerberus guarding the innermost sanctum, she had outlasted a succession of directors, among them Felix Weingartner, Franz Schalk, Richard Strauss, and Clemens Krauss. There were no known witnesses to her arrival at and entry into her new abode. But those who, like me, had seen and enjoyed the colorful aphrodisiacs by which the departed artist had turned the rooms where she was to live into a Sistine chapel of debauchery could easily imagine the impact of the event and the screaming dimensions of the scandal.

The Amar Quartet opened the first Donaueschingen festival with a string quartet by Alois Hába, still written in traditional tonal progressions. Two years later, they performed Hába's first venture into the quarter-tone idiom whose fanatical if slightly tiresome protagonist he had become. Hába, who came from eastern Moravia and was one of the many Schreker pupils who began to make themselves heard, spoke, looked and acted like a slightly overdone prototype of a Czech, with his Schweikian wire-brush hair and intense Slavic face, and shoulders that carried so many chips that there was always someone to knock one of them off. Licco Amar himself performed a quarter-tone solo violin sonata, and, later, Hába persuaded a Czech piano manufacturer to build him a quarter-tone piano for which he wrote suites and fantasias, and while few people, if indeed any, ever noticed the difference between a D sharp and a D sharp plus or minus one-quarter, nobody ever admitted it.

The members of the Amar Quartet were wonderful, easy-going people, popular not only with the professionals and, of course, with the composers whose works they played with fanatical dedication, but also with the townspeople, who all knew Rudolf Hindemith's huge dog and showed Heinrich Kaspar where the trout fishing was good. They worshipped little Paul Hindemith with his already slightly balding egg-head, his little pouch, his quiet south-German speech, his vivacious wife, and his wonderful viola tone. He possessed a natural, old-fashioned musicianship that made him and his colleagues improvise hilarious evenings of musical parodies but also gave rise to the rumor—never denied and probably true—that he wrote some of his scores on the train from Frankfurt to Donaueschingen, finishing them a couple of stations before arrival and rehearsing them with his responsive group during the remainder of the trip. When Rudolf Hindemith left the Quartet to become the Michelangelo of the Vienna Hofburg, he was replaced by Maurits Frank, a big, outgoing Dutchman, full of life, of a bouncing vitality, always overflowing with anecdotes. He knew everybody and seemed to like everybody and was known and liked by everybody in return.

It was also here, in Donaueschingen, that I met my first live American composer, George Antheil of Trenton, New Jersey. He was to become my lifelong friend. I soon visited him in Paris where he lived, a professional expatriate, with his wife, Böske. They came to live in Vienna for a few months. He played an opera for me which I thought was simply wonderful—it was called *The People's Choice,* and George explained to me what the words meant—his libretto dealt with an American presidential election—but as we figured out that other Europeans would be likewise puzzled by the title we called it, rather meaninglessly, *Transatlantic.* I persuaded Hertzka to publish it and the Frankfurt Opera house to perform it, but unfortunately George and I were the only people who really liked it, so not too much came of it. Later, I spend wonderful summers with George and Böske and a lot of simply amazing American expatriates in a fabulous house on top of a little mountain in Cagnes-sur-Mer, between Nice and Cannes and, when he was in Hollywood and I in New York, I went often to visit him, till, one day he left us, an unforgettable, colorful, unique figure, another who was in his twenties in the twenties, though, to him, that wasn't always a good fortune.

The Donaueschingen prince, Max Egon, Fürst von Fürstenberg, who paid for most of the proceedings, moved with delight and wonderful manners among the strange people who took over his town and his castle and his park and the inns and the winestuben for three short days. Burkard, later assisted by Paul Hindemith and a few other musicians, chose the music to be performed. They had a brilliant gift for picking many a small composer who, soon, would be important if not great, knowing of course that they could only play it by the law of averages and that, in every generation, there is an abundance of those who will forever remain small and insignificant and will be forgotten after a brief, frustrating day in the light, and a cruel dearth of those who will survive.

When Heinrich Burkard died, the prince felt that perhaps he had done enough for contemporary music and the wonderful little festival came to an end. The odd people who had come, year after year, went elsewhere. When they came again, after another world war, the patron was not an elegant prince any more but a powerful, rich, new, post-World-War-II radio station under the guidance of Heinrich Strobel, an even more absolute nut about modern music than his namesake of yore. Strobel hired a big symphony orchestra for Radio Süd-West and Hans Rosbaud as conductor and made Pierre Boulez from Paris a composer in residence to compose and to conduct avant-garde music which must have lowered the rating of Radio Süd-West something awful but brought Heinrich Strobel several Dr.'s *h.c.* Once a year, Dr. *h.c.* Strobel and Pierre Boulez and the symphony orchestra went back to Donaueschingen for four, then three, then two days of *Musiktage.* The composers and musicians did not come on trains, on bikes, or on foot anymore. They breezed in between jet flights and brought truckloads of vibraphones and electronic equipment to perform their music. It all sounded the same and it was even more difficult to pick the forever-small ones from the maybe-one-day great ones and to know whether there was a single composer among them who would not, forever, remain an entry in a library catalogue, if, indeed, that much.

After they had gotten bored and frustrated listening to each other's music, they held a symposium on "Where do we go from here?"—*Quo vadis?*, so to speak—but nobody had an answer to the question, and so they hurried home again with their tapes and mobiles and electronic devices and their huge scores which it had taken them a long time and a lot of calculus to figure out, although much of it was just empty spaces, with arrows and dots and fuddly curves to be filled in by the players however the spirit moved them and which they could never have written on the train from Frankfurt, even if they had taken it instead of clocking 150 kilometers an hour on the Autobahn.

• • •

TWO YEARS AFTER the first Donaueschingen festival and following a few similar isolated attempts to bring people together for the display and the furtherance of new music, the exchange of ideas, the establishing of contacts, and the creation of a new, postwar musical era, the International Society for Contemporary Music was organized. It gave its first international festival in Salzburg, in 1923, opening it with a performance of Alban Berg's second string quartet, the *Lyric Suite*. It was the first of a long series of yearly events interrupted only by the Second World War (even then, a few makeshift concerts in America tried to maintain at least symbolic continuity).

The new organization for the performance, propagation, and, hopefully, merchandising of new music from all over the world was abbreviated ISCM, its German name, *Internationale Gesellschaft für neue Musik*, IGNM, later on, after the society became a little stale and methodical and almost exclusively dedicated to the cause of international bee-bee music, to be spelled out as *I*ch *G*ehe *N*icht *M*ehr—I don't go any more. The ISCM did not choose its programs by the leisurely Burkard method that had made Donaueschingen so charming, relaxed, and peaceful a place. The new international society had national sections in every music-producing country—dozens of them—and each national section, year after year, formed a national jury that invited its compatriots to submit scores so that it could pick those which were to be sent to an international jury which could pick those to be performed at the next festival. Every one of the many national juries fished as many scores as possible out of the flood unleashed on them by their composing compatriots and sent them to the international jury, and all the composing compatriots whose scores had not been sent were very, very cross and never talked to any member of the national jury again. And after the international jury had announced its decision and had picked what few national scores—if any—could be accommodated on this year's festival, the national jury was very, very cross and never talked to any member of the international jury again. The national section resigned from the ISCM and swore that it would never send another score and the president of the ISCM, Professor Edward Dent, a suave, polished, slightly dour musicologist from England, had to travel to the national section and have national schnaps with them, which he detested, and tell them how important their music was to him and the ISCM and the world at large. When the jury time came again, the year after, they sent in their dues and their scores and had a Duo for Flute and Viola by one of their nationals performed and the national jury and the composer and a lot of fellow nationals came and cheered and liked it, no matter what the world at large thought of it, which was not very much.

The international festivals did not, of course, reflect only the pressures of international politics and jealousies: they also gave birth to a great many important works. A Berg quartet, a Schönberg wood-wind quintet, Bartók's Dance Suite, Kodály's *Psalmus Hungaricus,* the discovery or first exposure of many composers, the participation of famous soloists, symphony orchestras, and sometimes stunning local operatic and ballet ensembles were worth many a flute and viola duo never heard of again.

Most important, however, was the unique atmosphere that united the participants from many parts of the world, bringing about new contacts and stimulating exchanges of ideas, the renewal of old and the founding of new friendships of truly international (and very multilingual) nature, and, last but not least, many practical results: performances, publication contracts, engagements, commissions, jobs. The sustained success of these yearly gatherings would not have been possible without an obvious tendency to shift the festivals from one lovely city to another. The locales, so it seemed, were not picked only for their musical facilities, important as those were, or for the receptiveness of the local populace to contemporary music, which, in most cases, was minute: paramount seemed the realization that it was easier to digest four concentrated days of new music, relieved only by an occasional excursion to a candle-lit rococo concert in a nearby chateau or a serenade on the Grand Canal, in pleasant surroundings and with beautifully situated and marvelously stocked restaurants to gather strength again. The festivals floated attractively from Prague to Venice, from Barcelona to Liège, from the shrimp canapés of Copenhagen to Salzburg's heavenly *Nockerln.* The mammoth platters of Zürich's Kronenhalle or Donaueschingen's Black Forest trout were wonderful to behold after the austerity of a twelve-tone trio. From Siena we went to Warsaw, from Florence to Barcelona, from Amsterdam to Paris.

• • •

AFTER DONAUESCHINGEN'S prince had given up and the sleepy little town in the southern foothills of the Black Forest had closed the doors temporarily to contemporary composers, the elegant, well-manicured spa of Baden-Baden, at the northern end of the mountains, extended an invitation to the *Musiktage* which was eagerly accepted. Baden-Baden was the most unlikely place to be host to a modern music festival. The Romans had come there to cure in its hot springs the rheumatism they must have contracted, hugely, in the dripping, chilly autumns of Germania. Two thousand years later, the nobility of Europe still came to take the baths and to promenade on marvelously kept garden paths along a lazy little brook whose trout, scarcely moving, looked as bored and as old as the promenaders. Among the trout watchers were so many Russian grand dukes that they built themselves their own Russian church, complete with onion-shaped, gold-covered cupola and Greek cross, a strange, eastern watch on the Rhine.

The pretty town kept its nineteenth-century elegance, long after the grand dukes had moved to Paris to drive taxis, leaving only a few grandiosely meaningless Russian names on deserted villas behind. The rest of the nobility had also been lost in war and revolutions, and the waters were taken, in well-appointed establishments, by visitors less noble but just as rheumatic. In the *Trinkhalle* the customers still walked up and down, sipping the dull-tasting water from glasses so hot that they had difficulty holding them, admiring the gaily colored frescos of the sagas and fairy tales of the region, and listening to the strains of the overture to *The Caliph of Bagdad* floating soothingly from the municipal shell. For a few weeks in late summer the town was bursting with crowds, larger, noisier and less elegant from year to year, which came for the famous horse races. Few, if any, of them noticed a plaque on one of the elegant, old villas, attesting to the fact that Brahms had spent eleven consecutive summers in Baden-Baden and had written his Second Symphony and some chamber music here, the only, pitifully insignificant foray of the town so far into musical history. What was a modern music festival doing here?

Maybe fate had picked the town for no other reason than to be nice to me. Baden-Baden was my home town.

Never had I thought, as I left it to follow the family tradition of studying for a degree in solid citizenship, that I would return one day, a Viennese coffeehouse dweller, a promoter of far-out music, a friend of international musical notorieties. Through the narrow streets (they seemed narrower each time I returned) which I had walked so many times as a school boy, I now walked with composers from Paris, performers from Berlin, and music critics from Poland and Prague. In the gymnasium of the school where I had suffered so many humiliating defeats in calisthenics, a discipline not made for me, I saw the heavy, unliftable handbells and the instruments of torture from which my classmates had swung with such powerful, forever unobtainable grace moved into a corner to make room for music stands and props.

And, best of all, I, who had disgraced a family of doctors, lawyers, bankers, and professors by living in sin with (not only, I am afraid) music in Vienna, a Balkan place, far, far to the despised east, I now led a procession of people whose names, if often misspelled, graced the front page of the local newspaper, to a garden party at the house of my parents. One tea-drinking guest—he was not only a militant vegetarian but also a vehement, dangerous teetotaler—was my boss, Hertzka, smiling in a summery, benignant mood and a white linen suit, a splendid backdrop for his majestic dark beard. It was a day of triumph. As I saw my parents mingle with the strange folk they had never seen before and would probably never see again, they seemed to begin to think that, maybe, I wasn't entirely lost, no matter what Onkel Karl had told them.

Among the guests that lovely afternoon in July 1927 was a young composer, exactly my age, his wife, an unknown, ageless actress who had drifted to Berlin from the bitter *Ungemütlichkeit* of a working-class district in the outskirts of Vienna, and a poet, unfamous yet but already conspicuous by his leather jacket, leather tie, vizored cap, and dark, evil-smelling cigar. At night, at performance time, we met them again. The two men were in the audience, the unknown actress was on stage.

The entire evening of the festival had been given over to the performance of new short operas. There was *The Rape of Europa*, one of Darius Milhaud's *opéras minutes*, spoofs on Greek legends, none of them lasting more than ten minutes. It was a bit chichi, but made everybody fairly if not hilariously happy. Then came an opera by Ernst Toch, *The Princess and the Pea*, followed by Paul Hindemith's by now celebrated sketch *Hin und Zurück*, a little opera that, textually, scenically, and formally rolls on to its exact middle and then rolls back, textually, scenically, and musically, to its opening bar. It was sophisticated, very skillfully done, perhaps a little too brainy. Hindemith and his librettist, Marcellus Schiffer (who later wrote the text for *Neues vom Tage*) were applauded amusedly. Then came the last offering of the night, the Kurt Weill–Bertolt Brecht *Mahagonny*, and the spectacular debut of the unknown actress from Penzing, Lotte Lenya.

From the point of view of the music publishers present, it was a pleasant, harmonious night. Hindemith and Toch were under contract with Schott; Milhaud and Kurt Weill belonged to Universal. On the surface, there was a happy fifty-fifty friendliness as the Streckers congratulated Hertzka and Hertzka extended sweet felicitations to the Schotts. But the real laurels of the evening belonged to us. Hindemith and Toch were already established composers, and a little opera, pleasant as it was, did not add much to their book value in the ledgers in Mainz. Ten minutes of Milhaud were just ten more minutes of Milhaud. But *Mahagonny*, the little *Songspiel*, based on five poems from Bert Brecht's *Hauspostille*, set to music which, for the first time and without any advance notice, exposed a stunned audience to the sophisticated, overwhelming, unexpected simplicity of Kurt Weill's new style, was an explosive stick of dynamite, and as it went off that night in Baden-Baden, it generated echoes that were to be heard for a long time, all over the world.

VII

OUR ASSOCIATION with Kurt Weill had begun several years before the Baden-Baden tea party. He and I were both twenty-three years old when Hertzka signed him for Universal.

Who could have anticipated that the small, balding young man, squinting at the world through thick, professorial glasses with eager, burning eyes, quiet in his manner, deliberate and always soft-spoken, dressed more like a candidate for a degree in divinity than a young composer in the flamboyant Berlin of 1923, sucking a conservative pipe with the absent-minded absorption of an instructor in higher mathematics—who could have anticipated that this son of a cantor in a provincial German town would soon shake the staid hotel lobbies of Baden-Baden with the irresistible songs from *Mahagonny* and one day be the uncontested jukebox champion of the world? Maybe, if one looked very closely, the deep-seated mockery on his lips might have hinted at things to come. But even the magnificent sniffer, whose nose reacted so brilliantly to smells no other human nose had yet detected, was sniffing in the wrong direction. There wasn't a whiff of "Mack the Knife" in the air when Hertzka took up the scent.

Weill had been recommended to Hertzka by his teacher, Ferruccio Busoni. The high-minded, serious composer, half rooted in the classical world of Italy, where he was born, half in the soul-searching, Faustian north, where he made his home, was the very prototype of a Hertzkan master and a most influential and convincing recommendor. Great Bach interpreter and transcriber, famous pianist, prophetic thinker and writer, elegant man of the world, a heavy intellectual, Busoni was irresistible to the perennial sucker for Olympians. Inevitably, Hertzka gave Kurt Weill a contract, packed some scores the composer had recently finished in his briefcase, brought them home to Vienna, and instructed us to publish a setting of old German poems for soprano, viola, flute, clarinet, horn, and bassoon, called *Frauentanz*.

It was a fine achievement for a young man still under the tutelage of the aristocratic Busoni, but if there had been a contest for the most unsalable piece of music ever printed, it would have won, bassoons down.

Weill was very happy when he saw his name in print on the title page of *Frauentanz,* and then we published—good God!—a string quartet, a concerto for violin and winds, and a *Quodlibet* for orchestra. But then came Kurt Weill's first opera, *Der Protagonist*. The opera had a libretto by Georg Kaiser, a famous playwright, very much in vogue at the time though sadly forgotten today which only shows that there are Franz Schrekers in every discipline of the arts and at all times—including, I am afraid, the present. It was a great personal triumph for Weill to get permission from Kaiser to use one of his plays as a libretto. He obtained it with few credentials other than his convincing personality.

We published the opera, and it was accepted and performed at the Dresden Opera, birthplace of most of the operas by Richard Strauss. So it was a most distinguished occasion. We ate very well at the Hotel Bellevue and got very good notices (Oscar Bie, one of Germany's most respected critics, wrote, significantly: "All the philosophical theories of teacher Busoni have been swept aside by the reality of Kurt Weill's score"), but only a few additional theaters produced the work, and we were left, soon, with a depressingly high stack of unsold scores gathering dust in the basement of the Musikverein.

It did not worry us too much. We were sure that we had an important composer, and *Der Protagonist*, together with *Frauentanz* and string quartet and *Quodlibet* were classified as "prestige music."

It's a very noble phrase, "prestige music," when it melts on the tongue and you consider, while it is melting, what a great contribution you have made to the higher values of life, how you will be praised in annual surveys, and how posterity will honor and revere you. But it is a phrase not appreciated by accountants at the end of the fiscal year. They do not know, nor do they care, how to spell it and are very unpleasant when they make nasty checkmarks in their ledgers next to *Protagonist* and perhaps a few exclamation marks that really hurt on the page for *Quodlibet*. They chew soggy cigars while they ask how long are you going to throw more of the company's good money after all the bad money you have already lost on this here Curd Wheel, you don't have to tell *me* about the higher values of life, my daughter-in-law plays the trumpet, but what are we going to say to the board of directors when they look at the figures next Thursday? The hell with prestige, it only inflates the inventory.

Such talk is very depressing and it does not help much to try to tell them of all the prestige music—*Tristan*, for example—that was, at some time, sooner or later, much appreciated by a board of directors, because they'll ask you: How do you know this here Wheel will be an R. Wagner, and maybe the old man shouldn't have listened to Busino, who isn't so hot himself, just look at the copies of *Doc Faust* on the shelves at seven dollars a throw—and you have no answer.

Of course, in those epic days the old man's nose was

mightier than the accountants' pencils. He looked at them coldly and asked them to go away and they did and went downstairs to make trouble for Hutterstrasser at Bösendorfer, and Hertzka went right ahead and published Kurt Weill's next opera. It was called *Royal Palace* which, perhaps, wasn't such a good idea in a newly established republic—at any rate, it expired after a few performances at the Berlin Opera House of the Republican Prussian State, and this time we did not classify it as prestige music but wrote it off the inventory before the accountants could get there with their exclamation marks.

Then Kurt Weill wrote us from Berlin that he was about to finish a new opera. This time it was to be a full-length, three-act work. *Protagonist* and *Palace* had merely been one-acters.

Hertzka read Weill's letter several times and I knew what made him do it. A three-act opera, Hertzka thought, costs three times as much money to publish as a one-act opera. The piano score has at least three-hundred, maybe four-hundred, pages and the chorus parts fifty, maybe seventy-five, and all the pages have to be engraved by the engravers' union and printed by the printers' union and bound by the opera-piano-score-and-chorus-parts-binding union. Then there will be an orchestra score, at least five hundred, maybe eight hundred fifty, pages to be copied by hand and the orchestral parts have to be extracted by the score-copying and orchestra-parts-extracting unions: the first flute and the second flute and the third flute and all the other wood winds. Horns and trumpets and tubas, a couple of kettledrums and trombones and a whole battery of percussion instruments, which isn't too bad because the triangle has a lot of inexpensive tacets—and Hertzka smiled a little as he thought of the triangle part. But then he thought of a harp or two and of the strings which play incessantly and have no tacets but a lot of very expensive divisi and of a celesta and a piano part for which the piano-part-extracting union charges a special fee because the pianist uses two hands and two feet but the second flute player only one mouth, and he did not smile any more.

While he was reading Weill's letter once more he thought that, after all this had been done and paid for in cash (because they bring the stuff in in person and wait for their money before they hand it over, even a lousy triangle part)—that then every page and bar and note and rest and slur and dot and all the accidentals that are always wrong or omitted or put on the wrong staff, everything would have to be proofread by the opera-score-and-parts-proofreader union, but maybe I can get around it and make the editors do the proofreading, they get paid by the month so it's much cheaper and it isn't only the money, it is just the sort of thing they hate to do.

This is what Hertzka thought while reading Kurt Weill's letter. At last, he put it down and sent for the accountants. They left Hutterstrasser, to his great relief, and rushed back upstairs and pulled out the ledgers for *Frauentanz* and *Quodlibet* and string quartet and *Protagonist* and *Royal Palace* and spread them out on Hertzka's desk. And Hertzka looked at the ledgers and wept.

• • •

KURT WEILL's contract with us—as were most composers' contracts—was a ten-year, first-refusal deal. It imposed on the composer the strict obligation to submit every manuscript written during these ten years to the publisher before showing it to anybody else and if he did not submit a carefully stipulated minimum of works during his term of servitude, the contract extended itself automatically until he had done so, which might be forever. The publisher, on the other hand, had only one very strictly spelled out obligation: to prepay the postage on any manuscript he rejected and returned, unpublished, to the composer. It could be "any" or it could be "all."

Hertzka, in this case, decided to go a step farther. He invited Kurt Weill to come to Vienna and play the new opera for us.

Soon the little man was sitting at the depressing upright that had been installed in Hertzka's office after the *Sister Beatrix* disaster. As always in Weill's presence, we felt a very strong will and clear determination behind the composer's soft words and ever-present sense of humor. He exuded the unmistakable aura of a professional. Weill played the entire opera, softly singing with a veiled, pleasant, expressive voice, playing the piano in a dry, matter-of-fact, unflourished manner. Hertzka and I followed with the libretto.

We did not like anything about the work. We did not like the libretto, which was by a little-known German playwright and musician who had never written a libretto before, and as we read on we ardently wished he had let it go at that. We loathed the title of the opera which seemed to reflect the worst asphalt cynicism of Berlin: it was called *Na und*—best, if not well, translated as "So What." The music seemed handicapped and weighted down by the story and the lyrics. As the composer played on, one could sense an aura of despair creep into the room.

Many times had we lived through this situation: you are about to be asked to render a judgment which the man who just finished playing and who now turns around and looks at you doesn't want to hear. All he wants to hear is one single word—the word "great." But no matter how hard it is, don't say it unless you really mean it. Don't be polite. Don't be nice. For an operatic composer this might be the very last moment of redemption.

After every operatic fiasco—and who will ever count them—the question is asked: why was it ever permitted to see the light of day? It is asked by horrified onlookers, by students of musical history, by people who have just read the morning paper and tell their spouse with a sigh of relief: Thank God, we don't have to go and see *that* thing. Why wasn't it stopped during rehearsals? Withdrawn by the author, who surely must have seen what was coming? Taken back by the publisher, who should know better? Stopped by the head of the opera house, who must have dropped in at rehearsals, by the experienced man who directed it, by the celebrated conductor who should have walked out of the pit—just by anyone?

It can't be stopped now. The sets have been designed and built. Costumes have been made and paid for. The date of the opening has been announced. Publicity has gone out. Evening dresses have been ordered. The roster has been mailed to the subscribers, and there is the new opera: Thursday this week and Wednesday next. Singers have penciled in the dates a year ago, maestri refuse to conduct *Pagliacci* instead, directors have been hired and are hellbound to direct the undirectable. Nothing can arrest the final sequence of events. The bus is careening down a mountain road, its brakes busted, its passengers huddled, paralyzed, waiting for the final crash, hoping against unhopable hope that maybe—think what happened to *The Barber of Seville:* Rossini went home weeping—they may still land against a soft embankment.

The only time to stop the bus is before it gets under way. Inspect the brakes, discharge the passengers, and send the opera to the junkyard. Don't start the trip.

Even for those who know all this, it's very difficult to tell a man after he has worked for years over five hundred pages of score to throw them away, and few appreciate such advice. Some, to make it more nerve-wracking, invite you to dinner and you accept, an utter fool. After dinner they play the score in the presence of their wife, who has cooked all day and surely expects something in return. You hem and haw and say that the chorus on page 139 is powerful and perhaps the interlude between the fourth and fifth scene in Act 2 should be a few seconds longer, they might not have enough time to remove the drawbridge, but nobody wants to hear this sort of talk after the filets mignons, and the wife gets already awfully tense around the mouth. You hem and haw a little more and ask the man why don't you come to the office tomorrow, it's a more professional atmosphere and it's late and I should be getting along. Nobody offers you a nightcap or at least a little liqueur. You barely make it to the door and you know that as soon as it closes a little abruptly behind you the wife will tell the composer I told you not to ask this character for dinner the filets mignons were three dollars apiece and who the hell is he to. . . .

The next day, at the office, you tell him because you still think he wants to hear the truth about his opera and you surely expect him to appreciate your tact for not saying it in front of the wife, but he gets awfully tense around the mouth and rushes away and never, never talks to you again even after the opera has been performed and ended up in a heap in a ravine something terrible to look at.

Others, who have no wives—and there are such—ask you to come, they have just finished the first act of a new opera and I would like so very much to play it for you and get your frank opinion, you have been in this game such a long time, why, you even knew Alban Berg, I need advice. You come and he plays the first act. You listen carefully because the poor fellow is young and you really want to help him and after he plays for a little while you say to yourself:

this will work out fine, he has only written one act, and if you tell him now you can blame it all on the libretto so he won't be hurt and he will be very grateful because now he doesn't have to write the second and the third and can make some money writing a ballet for Mrs. Harkness.

But after you tell him, he gets very red in the face and slams the piano lid down and you barely make it to the door. The next morning one of his friends calls you: what a terrible thing to do, how can you discourage him at this stage, you have taken all his confidence away, how can he go on, he cried all night, he'll never get over it, we all hate you. He gets over it all right and writes the second and the third act and you are sorry for him, he is young and, after all, *Madama Butterfly* was a flop when it was first performed at La Scala, so you make a trip to Louisville, Kentucky, to hear his opera performed and see the bus plunge into whatever river they have in Louisville, and sink and disappear forever, and it really was no butterfly.

• • •

THE LITTLE MAN at the piano who had just finished playing the score of *Na und* was made of different stuff. There is, and there always will be, a deep-seated, decisive difference between the many who so easily and happily get tipsy from every drop of the stuff they put on paper and the few who laugh off and superbly ignore the effects of such superficial ecstasies and who only get drunk—hugely, grandiosely, magnificently—when they come across the bottle, hidden forever from the sight and the grip of the self-enamored little imbiber and uncork the foaming champagne of creative inspiration.

A happy little imbiber would have finished the audition in wide-eyed, undisturbed expectation, waiting, undoubtingly, for a torrent of applause that was inevitably to come and for an approval, restrained only by a lack of words to adequately express our enthusiasm. Kurt Weill, with the unerring instinct of the real pro, surely had felt for some time the thickening atmosphere of gloom and the creeping fog of embarrassed silence that had begun to settle in the room soon after he had begun playing. When he had finished, there was no need to say much. We explained, briefly, our misgivings. His reaction had none of the aggressive defense or the condescending superiority with which the little imbibers put a publisher—a businessman, a bookkeeper, the eternal petty bourgeois clipping forever Dedalus' wings—in his place. He was no amateur, he was a professional. He listened quietly and with attention.

We expressed our fears that this work would, at this stage of his career, be a setback, perhaps a dangerous setback. Against the background of *Protagonist*, which had established Weill as an important figure in the realm of opera, and of a second work to an original libretto by Georg Kaiser, an opera buffa *The Czar Is Photographed;* which—easier to perform and with an amusing vaudevillian libretto—was just beginning to make its way to many German opera houses, not to speak of the *Mahagonny*-lightning that had struck in Baden-Baden, *Na und* just was not to happen.

Weill closed the score and put it back in his valise. Hertzka left for his suburbian abode and I took Weill across the street to the *Schwemme* of the Imperial Hotel, a smallish bar and restaurant where taxi drivers and mail carriers dropped in for a beer and where one could always find the doorman from the Musikverein, who guarded our offices and whose duties included the putting up of posters, announcing the Philharmonic concerts or similar exalted events. Whenever he left his little loge for a beer at the Imperial *Schwemme*—and he left it for many, many a beer from many a morning to many a night—he locked the door

Fischer von Erlach's
Karlskirche

Eusebius Mandyczewski

Emil Hertzka

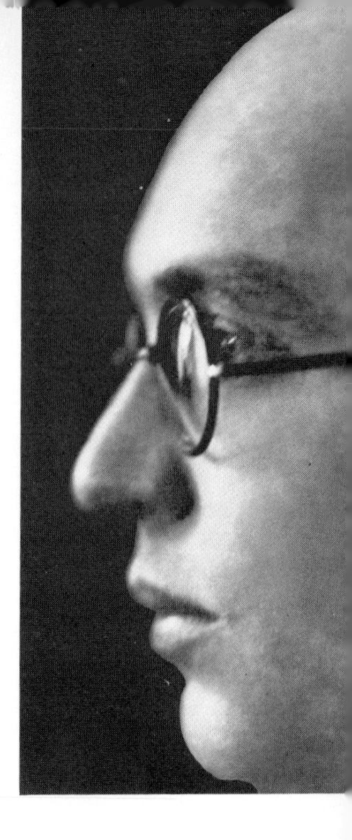

Kurt Weill, Baden-Baden, 1928

Aaron Copland, Paris, 1924

Ernst Krenek,
Palm Springs, 1967

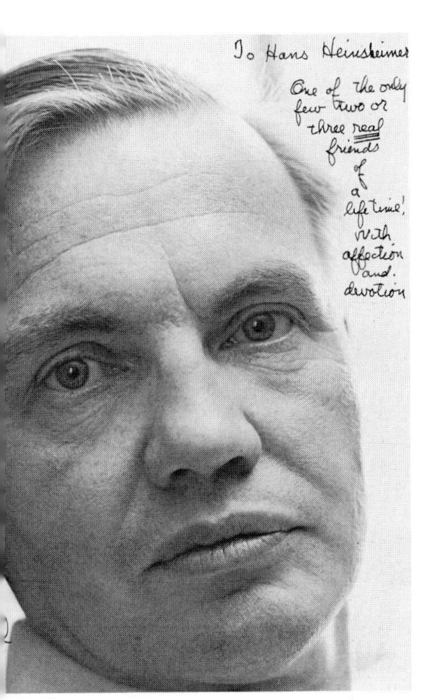

George Antheil,
Hollywood, 1938

Alban Berg, Vienna, 1930,
with self-portrait by Arnold Schönberg and drawing of
Anton Webern by Oskar Kokoschka

Leoš Janáček

Franz Schreker

Jaromir Weinberger

Castle and Spring of the Danube, Donaueschingen

The Donaueschingen Musiktage, 1923:
Joseph Haas, Paul Hindemith, Heinrich Burkard

The Donaueschingen Musiktage, 1963:
Pierre Boulez, Graf Salm, Heinrich Strobel

Music Festival, Venice, 1925:
second from left, the author;
fourth from right, Leoš Janáček

Hermann Scherchen, 1936

Otto Klemperer, 1930

The Kolisch String Quartet, 1927:
Eugene Lehner, Eugene Kuhner, Rudolf Kolisch, and Benar Heifetz

Lotte Lenya, 1928

Alois Hába at the quarter-tone piano, 1938

Arnold Schoenberg and his family, Los Angeles, 1948; left to right: Larry, Arnold, Gertrud, Nuria, and Ronny

Giovanni Ricordi

Johann Gottlob Immanuel Breitkopf

Bernhard Schott

Gustav Schirmer, 1888

Ralph Hawkes

The Dreyfus Homestead, Kuppenheim

Max Winkler

Albert Schweitzer and
Edouard Nies-Berger,
Gunsbach, 1951

Béla Bartók, 1944

Gian Carlo Menotti, Spoleto, 1967

Paul Hindemith and
Willi Strecker at
B. Schott's Söhne,
Mainz, 1951

and put a little cardboard sign on the handle, reading "AM POSTER PASTING." It fooled nobody. Everybody knew, where in an emergency which, happily, never arose, Mr. Vazlacek was to be found. The taxi drivers, mail carriers, Mr. Vazlacek, and the junior executives of Universal and their guests also enjoyed at the *Schwemme* (which means a place where horses are being watered) the juiciest of goulashes, cooked in the fancy kitchen of the Imperial Hotel and served at the wooden tables of the *Schwemme* at prices the guests on the other side of the wall, in the gold-and-purple dining room, would have been embarrassed to leave as a tip on the damask tablecloth.

Weill enjoyed his goulash, told gentle stories during the meal, and spoke of everything but *Na und.* He mentioned it briefly on the way to the station for the night train to Berlin. He would be in touch with us. After a few days he informed us that, for the time being, he had decided to put the opera away.

A few months later I was myself on the way to Berlin where a new work by Kurt Weill was to be performed. We knew little about the new opus. Weill had not submitted any of the music for publication, we had not seen a libretto, we only knew that he had been working on the score until virtually the last moment before the performance. It was to be an unchartered, unpredictable adventure.

Everything had been improvised. A Berlin producer, Ernst Josef Aufricht (he, much later, told the story in a fascinating book of memoirs, called *Erzähl' es, damit Du Dein Recht beweist*, a quotation from the bible which King James doesn't translate quite as strikingly as did Luther and which means "*Tell it to prove you were justified*") had rented an empty theater and had been looking frantically for a suitable play to open it with. He had seen playbrokers and visited about every playwright living in Berlin—and this was 1928, when Berlin was teeming with talent. But nobody had anything that would fit into the smallish Theater am Schiffbauerdamm and satisfy the sophisticated taste of the ambitious Aufricht. The summer progressed. Aufricht announced without impressing anybody too much that he would have to kill himself if he did not find a play to open his theater on August 31, the beginning of the official Berlin theater season. It was also his birthday.

A few months before the gruesome deadline, Aufricht met Bertolt Brecht, who told him that he was about to finish a play—a *Nebenwerk* he called it, something he was doing on the side, so to speak. There was also a composer involved in the project. The harassed Aufricht, impressed with the theatrical possibilities of the work, decided to produce it.

It was to be a happy birthday. The work was the *Dreigroschenoper* (*Three Penny Opera*).

It had been rough. Aufricht, who had never heard any of Kurt Weill's music, had gone to hear the *Czar* at the Leipzig Opera. Weill's music struck him as much too modern to be used in a play—too atonal, as he put it; he probably did not know the word prestige music. He asked his conductor, Theo Mackeben, to make sure to have the original music for the old *Beggar's Opera* of 1738, Brecht's model for the play, ready, just in case the music the atonal composer was to write did not work. One of the leading ladies, Carola Neher, found her part, the part of Polly, too short and quit in a rage. The actor who was to play Macheath, Harald Paulsen, insisted upon adding a sickly, powder-blue bowtie to his costume of an elegant criminal and made it very clear that he would rather give up his part than the blue bow. Shouts, groans, insults, threats, despair, pandemonium. Brecht and Weill decided to introduce the villainous Macheath to the innocent sound of a hurdy-gurdy, in a ballad whose sweet words and detached, unemotional music would be in striking contrast to the ruthless deeds it narrated and would thus go well with Paulsen's out-of-character neckpiece. The "Ballad of Mack the Knife" was born.

The dress rehearsal lasted till six o'clock of the morning that dawned on the day of opening night. It had shown that the play was almost an hour too long. After the actors and stagehands had staggered home, Brecht, Weill, the director Erich Engel, and Aufricht began making cuts. When these were conveyed to the cast, the actor who was to play Peachum announced that he was leaving town on the afternoon train. Aufricht told him with what little voice he had left that he had a wife, several children, and a birthday. The actor stayed. A few minutes later, one of Aufricht's colleagues called to suggest that he should start rehearsals for another play the next morning: *Dreigroschenoper* could not possibly last for more than a few weeks at best.

Night came at last, but disaster was still heavy in the air. The very first music to be heard after the curtain had gone up remained mutely locked in a broken hurdy-gurdy and "Mack the Knife" was introduced to the world by a singing organ grinder without the benefit of accompaniment. The song passed unnoticed and unapplauded. And even after the night had at last ended to thundering applause, a harbinger, as it turned out, for one of the great successes of the musical theater, Aufricht's tribulations were not over. As he went backstage to congratulate and embrace and to be embraced and congratulated, he was faced by an enraged Kurt Weill, who, for the first time in Aufricht's and everyone's experience, raised his voice and screamed. The name of his wife, Lotte Lenya, who had just made history with her rendition of *Seeräuberjenny*—the song of Pirat Jenny and of the ship with eight sails and forty cannon—had been left off the printed program.

THREE DAYS LATER we were on the night train, back home to Vienna. Neither Hertzka, tucked away in the solitary splendor of a first-class compartment, rocking gently by courtesy of the Compagnie des Grand Wagons-Lits, nor I, propped on the wooden bench of a third-class carriage, rattling rudely by courtesy of the Austrian State Railroads, could sleep. Our heads were still spinning. We had witnessed the greatest of nature's miracles: the transformation of the drab larva of a prestige composer into the golden-winged beauty of a commercial butterfly.

As we watched the transformation of Kurt Weill, we, too, found ourselves transformed. Until eight p.m. on that last night of August 1928, the world *première* of *The Three Penny Opera*, we had been the prototype of what Broadway from Berlin to New York calls, if not with contempt so surely with pity, a Standard Publisher. Suddenly, after eleven o'clock, a lot of people who had avoided us through all of our professional lives like a boring plague, tried to find out how we spelled our names and were surprised to discover that we had a telephone. Backstage, minutes after the final curtain, while we were pushed around by hysterical actors, happy musicians, stagehands who couldn't have cared less, falling props, and well-wishers who only a few hours earlier had been prophets of doom, a man who looked like the personification of His Master's Voice and turned out to be just that had clawed his way towards Hertzka and had offered him money if he would let him record a show album of *Dreigroschenoper*.

He did not *ask* for money to record one of our publications—he *offered* it. It was a shattering experience. We had come as close to being a Popular Publisher as anyone who had his place of business in the Musikverein beneath the sensitive Brahmsian slippers of the angelic Eusebius Mandyczewski would ever succeed in coming.

It was a delicious disgrace.

We were, of course, completely unprepared for our new station in life. The only song we had ever plugged was Mahler's *Song of the Earth.* Everything we were now expected to do we had to learn from scratch. The sober rules by and the solemn goals for which the Standard Publisher lives have nothing in common with the flamboyant world of his Popular confrère. Neither of the two knows anything of the other's business. The former thinks of the latter as a contemptible lowbrow—the latter of the former as a contemptible highbrow. Their paths cross only when they take their artfully mingled seats at a director's meeting of ASCAP or GEMA or SACEM or PRS or any of the other performing-rights societies throughout the world who try to gather composers, authors, and publishers into one Peacable Kingdom and whose names all sound like cough medicines. At such meetings three Standards are usually outnumbered by nine Populars, a ratio that clearly reflects their mutual significance.

The Standard Publisher's customers are opera houses, ballet companies, symphony orchestras, a violinist introducing a new sonata at a recital in Baytown, Texas, nuns, happily many of them, who conduct classes in singing, and instrument-playing children whose future role in music will be to produce another generation of singing and instrument-playing children attending classes conducted by music-buying nuns.

The Popular Publisher, too, has a Standard Department, which he calls Educational Department to make it sound less humiliating. It is operated by a soberly dressed egghead at the far end of the corridor who tries to pick up some of the by-products that fall from the rich tables in the front office and arrange them for girls' voices, called SSA, so that the nuns can use them. But when the rest of the staff go out for lunch, nobody asks the egghead to come along and he is lucky to find a couple of nuns to keep him company while he munches a miserable sandwich. To the other members of the establishment, dining at Toots Shor, he is just a tax-deductible joke. Their customers are the TV and radio networks of the world, shiny night clubs and crowded ballrooms that have very little nun trade, juke boxes all over the globe which play only rarely one of the piano pieces of Op. 19 by Arnold Schoenberg and have never heard the name of Milton Babbitt. Recording companies from all four corners of the world are sending them huge checks. If a Standard Publisher gets one of similar size, he knows at once that it was a computer's error. The computer, he knows, printed $749.000 instead of $7.49, which is what the Standard Publisher expects and what he is supposed to get. As he has to split it with the composer, it really is not very profitable by the time he breaks it down, a yellow copy to the Accounting Department and a rose copy to the Royalty Department and a white copy to the composer, and then has to write half a dozen letters because the composer doesn't understand why it isn't more, I bought eleven records myself and if the composer is dead and it's the widow that writes, he will never hear the end of it.

The only time the Standard Publisher gets a check that isn't a computer's error is at the rare and wonderful occasion when one of his Standard Publications gets on the *back* of a Popular record. This one time, he gets $749.000 instead of $7.49, but that isn't so good either because how can he explain to the Standard composer that he is just riding on a

Popular composer's back and that it's going to be $7.49 again as soon as he is on his own, and if it's a widow there will be a lawsuit because we got all this money and what is the matter with them now, they are all crooks and if you don't sue them I'll sue them *and* you.

• • •

BUT NOW *we* were Populars.

The man from His Master's Voice had only been the first of many eager messengers from the enchanted forest of the recording industry that had suddenly become visible to our stunned eyes. Albums rolled off the presses, singles appeared in rapid succession, sound tracks were licensed for radio use. We subscribed to trade magazines whose enormous formats and outlandish, incomprehensible language we were unable to master, as we tried to grasp the meaning of an entirely new vocabulary. Screenings, lead sheets, slick showcase demos, packaging concepts, record exploitation, A&R men, show albums, performance campaigns, disk jockey drives, folios, payola, song books, jingles, bridges, theme songs, teen pops, standards, international tuners, blues, country, western, folks, evergreen, charts, global blockbusters.

We met the most fascinating people, none of whom had ever crossed our doorstep before: movie moguls, network presidents, night club singers, jazz drummers, regiments of lawyers, confidence men with glitteringly suspicious propositions—a whole world of musical commerce. The most penetrating among the visitors were some of the cyclopic giants who inhabit advertising agencies, soulless descendants of commuter trains, who talked to us in muffled voices, blowing stark contempt from their suburban pipes. Their request to use Weill's music for a jingle had to be rejected, not for ethical reasons—we had soon left ethics beyond the point of no return—but because we were about to sign a contract for the motion picture rights of *The Three Penny Opera,* something we had never done or ever hoped for while we still were Standards. The motion-picture people had told us to our surprise—we had absolutely no idea what we were doing and would have signed just about anything in return for a check—that they would not take kindly to the idea that the music played at the wedding of Macheath and Polly should remind the movie audience of bad breath. The Men from the Advertising Agency left us in a state of collapse. We had deprived them of everything they had believed in when we told them that "Mack the Knife" was not available to combat acid indigestion, no matter how much they would pay.

Lotte Lenya had her name printed in the program from the second night on and got star billing, and her song became a great hit. But as she was billed as *Spelunkenjenny, Hure* which, I am afraid, means Divejenny, Whore, we didn't publish an SSA arrangement of her song because we weren't sure the nuns would use it widely, though the girls should have enjoyed singing it. This, however, remained the only silent pipe in the powerful diapason we unleashed on the world and to whose golden chords and silvery voices we listened in rapt disbelief. It was all one, big, great *vox celesta.* When the checks came rolling in, the commas and periods were all at the right spots, and the accountants, furiously chewing their cigars, had to provide for extra columns in their ledgers to accommodate the thousands and the ten thousands where there had only been room and need for miserable tens and for zeros point something or other.

One of the slaves in the arranging department was assigned to make a vocal score of the *Dreigroschenoper.* He was chained to his desk and not permitted to go home and as he had no phone, a *Laufer,* left over from *Rosenkavalier,* was dispatched to notify his family that he would not be back for some time. Mr. Norbert Gingold lost seven pounds during his solitary confinement, but finished the task within four days and nights. The vocal score had only seventy-three pages, which was very little for a Standard Publisher raised on *Parsifal*, and Hertzka fell in love with the engraver's bill, a pretty petite.

• • •

HERTZKA, once before, had a brief brush with the seamier side of music publishing. It was an incident worth recalling, mainly because it proves that the music publishing business is fifty per cent luck, forty-nine per cent nose, and perhaps one per cent sweat. The earlier encounter with Lady Luck, Hure, occurred under circumstances that seem particularly noteworthy if one takes into consideration that Universal happened to be the publisher of *Pierrot Lunaire*. Hertzka—no snob when it came to making a buck—had purchased an old Viennese publishing house, mainly, or probably only because among its large catalog of Viennese songs, dances and similar *Vorstadt* items was one of the most popular marches in the Austrian arsenal: the famous march of the famous Deutschmeister regiment, composed by the conductor of the Deutschmeister band, Wilhelm Jurek. Jurek, a one-march Austrian Sousa, was happily overwhelmed by his success and, after we had acquired his march, paid us many a visit to chat of the old days when he was still leading the band on splendid parades and to enjoy his admission to our exalted premises. He was a large, broad-shouldered, good-looking man, who in his uniform and plumed hat must have looked like the Drum Major in *Wozzeck*, and who undoubtedly, in his time, seduced just as many Maries. His visits were always pleasant diversions from the visitors we were accustomed to. After Bartók, Schönberg, or Webern, Jurek was a composer in whose presence one felt neither pygmeic nor afraid to utter a word that would go down in history as *laesa majestatis*.

A year or two after we had acquired Otto Maass Verlag, an old clerk who had come with the inventory and who had never been permitted to travel from the little shop in Mariahilferstrasse to the shiny halls of the Musikverein, asked for an audience with Hertzka which—the great sniffer even sniffed correctly to whom to grant an audience and to whom not—was granted. Herr Habenzierl brought with him a waltz song, published many years before by Otto Maass, and also a copy of a new drinking song that was just sweeping the German speaking world and had recently been published in Germany. He sat down at the piano and played with one stiff finger first the old waltz song and then the new drinking song. The two songs were identical.

Hertzka left for Germany the same night and came back, four days later, to pour an enormous mountain of money onto the table in his office. He had found out that a singer in a Berlin cabaret had written the identical twin to our little waltz song and had put some rousing words to it that delighted his audiences. It was called "*Trink, Trink, Brüderlein, Trink*," and spread like wildfire. The author, not equipped to cope with the avalanche of his unsuspected success, granted printing rights in half a dozen different versions to different publishers. Hertzka had first called on the singer, who swore that he had never heard or seen our waltz song, but was crushed by the weight of evidence that left no room for innocent violations of copyrights. The publishers took one look at our little waltz song and surrendered. By the time it was all over, the investment in Otto Maass had yielded a wonderful basket of sweet fruit. The man who had labored to discover it was sent back to Mariahilferstrasse and forgotten.

The vocal score of *The Three Penny Opera* sold many

more copies in the first few months of its existence than all other works by Weill combined had sold. When the accountants brought in the ledgers, we realized that God had created Standard Publishers and Popular Publishers in his image but Popular Publishers just a little more so.

Hertzka never hit the big time again. He died a few years later, in 1932, just before the great tide swept away most of his proud accomplishments. He had been mercifully spared the advent of the new order in which there was no room for the old man and for the things and ideas and people he had worked for. He saw the clouds rise on the horizon but he was not there any more when the thunder began to roar and the lightning struck.

THROUGHOUT the few years that Kurt Weill could still stay and work in Germany—he and Lenya left, in the nick of time, early in 1933—our contacts remained close. How fast the sands of time were flowing! Was it really only nineteen months and nine days from the happy, carefree fireworks of the opening of *The Three Penny Opera* in Berlin to the dark, frightening events, surrounding the next Brecht-Weill operatic *première* in Leipzig on April 9, 1930? We had all met again, as we had before in Baden-Baden and in Berlin. It was to be a very different occasion.

The opera, which is what it was called though it had very little similarity to any of the many operas enjoyed by the subscribers of the Leipzig City Opera—the opera was *The Rise and Fall of the City of Mahagonny*, an expanded, full-length version of the Baden-Baden *Songspiel*—serious, aggressive, bitter, nihilistic. It ended in a huge demonstration on stage with the citizens of Mahagonny, an imaginary town in an imaginary America, milling around to rousing, funeral-marchlike music, singing defiance into the audience and carrying signs over their marching cadres: "For the natural order of things." "For the unnatural order of things." "For freedom of the rich." "For freedom of all." "For the unjust distribution of goods on earth." "For the just distribution of goods in Heaven." And, finally, as they carried the corpse of the hero, who had been hanged for the one crime punishable by death in Mahagonny, the crime of not having money to pay a bill, a huge sign, floating over the dead man: "For the continuation of the golden age."

How fast the sands of time! *The Three Penny Opera* had

been the sparkling highlight of the brief, sparkling period that had begun with the end of the First World War and was blotted out by Hitler's rise to power, signaling the beginning of the second. After its explosive initial success, the work led a happy, undisturbed life at the Theater am Schiffbauerdamm and later in a larger house whence it had to be transferred to accommodate the crowds. Within days after its first performance it had been accepted, within weeks it was produced by about every one of the countless theaters which dotted the map of central Europe, a rich, wide *Lebensraum* for the operatic division of Universal, whose enthusiastic, busy, if still juvenile head I had become. We were spoiled. In these exciting days there were five, eight, a dozen new operas every season and we sold our wares successfully throughout the vast territory that seemed to be always begging for more.

The *Dreigroschenoper* topped them all. It was a wonderfully easy joyride. The work did not require operatic singers —it was conceived for singing actors who were everywhere readily available. The score was ingeniously written for an orchestra of eighteen instruments, played by nine players: one played tenor and soprano sax, bassoon and second clarinet, another one alto sax, flute, and first clarinet. One man played banjo, cello, guitar, and bandonion, another one harmonium and celesta, and one trombone and bass fiddle. The conductor doubled as pianist, and only two trumpeters, a timpanist, and a percussion player were not required to play anything else. Little scenery and easily improvised costumes were needed, and every provincial actress with a husband and four kids loved to play a whore.

The play had an enormous audience appeal in those days and months of rising political tension, of black Fridays, jobless Mondays, bloody Sundays, of an ever-increasing tremor in the earth on which we were walking. Brecht's violent, brutal lyrics, served slightly sugar-coated by Weill's music, struck an almost masochistic response in the hearts and minds of the audiences that flocked to hear the play. In the deeper layers of their subconscious they felt a nagging uneasiness that they tried, desperately, to silence. Now some of the frightening realities that rose all around them, threatening their confused and confusing world, were hurled at them from the stage by safely remote seventeenth-century thieves and pimps and a wonderfully invincible hero who proved to them that crime paid. It was all just make-believe, an operetta, a musical comedy, an evening's entertainment.

For the opening at the Theater am Schiffbauerdamm the arriving celebrities of stage, film, and politics had been greeted by celebrity-seeking crowds, illuminated by flashlights, photographed with broad photographers' smiles on elegant lips. Later, there had been champagne for all and fruit juice for Hertzka, the confident waiting for the morning papers, toasts to the first raves, and the sweet hangover of success.

But on our way to the first performance of the new *Mahagonny* in Leipzig, we walked through crowds of Brown Shirts carrying banners and placards protesting the new work in ugly tones. We had felt a new, never-before-sensed, ominous tension during the dress rehearsal the day before. On opening night, it was not long before demonstrations broke out in the auditorium. A little uneasiness first, a signal, perhaps, then noise, shouts, at last screams and roars of protest. Some of the actors stepped out of their parts, rushed to the apron of the stage, shouted back. The performance ended in violence. It was a purely political demonstration, carefully planned as a test of power and, as such, a great success.

The second performance, a few days later, took place before a stony audience, watched over by a large contingent of police in a fully lighted house. Later performances were for specially invited audiences only. The management had got the message. Other theaters that had announced the work and planned to perform it, got the message too and canceled hastily. One of them—the opera house in Frankfurt, headed by Josef Turnau—tried to ignore the signs of the times. There was such a violent, vicious outburst during the dress rehearsal that the authorities let it be known that there would either be no *Mahagonny* or no Josef Turnau the next day. Only Ernst Josef Aufricht, who was running a private theater and did not have to worry about subsidies being voted down by incensed city councilors or a job to be lost by an edict from the mayor, produced the opera in Berlin. He engaged Alexander von Zemlinsky as conductor, which gave the production class, and Lotte Lenya to sing the songs that had aroused all of Baden-Baden, which gave it class and box-office appeal.

Perhaps because the *Lebensraum* given to my operatic department at Universal was shrinking rapidly as the cry for another *Lebensraum* was rising, I had a little more time on my hands and, as the production of contemporary operas in Vienna left a lot to be desired, I got together with a friend who shared my enthusiasm with my lack of funds. We founded the Viennese Opera Production and found the willing ear of one of Vienna's theatrical entrepreneurs whose house was dark between productions and who probably thought that what we would take in would at least pay for the doorman and the heat. Before we knew what we were doing, he announced that the Vienna Opera Production was to have its "first guest appearance" at the Raimund Theater on April 26, 1932, for a limited run of six performances of *Rise and Fall of the City of Mahagonny*, opera in three acts by Bert Brecht, music by Kurt Weill.

We were daring fools, but not without mitigating circumstances: among the cast of willing and unpaid singers, a conductor who was eager to show his mettle and a stage director—me—who had never before stage-directed anything at all, we announced, in a shameless change of the order as it appeared in the score, as our No. 1 artist in bold letters: Jenny—Lotte Lenya (Berlin).

Oh, what a wonderful time we had. Later, one of the critics, the Austrian composer Joseph Marx, summed it up nicely: "Many a theater manager will envy Messrs. Brand and Heinsheimer their improvised ensemble, which never thinks of a raise in salary because they haven't a salary in the first place, rehearses from eight in the morning to four in the afternoon with only a break for a sandwich, without looking at the clock, always enthusiastic about the work, the director, and themselves." The manager of the Raimund Theater had undertaken to pay for the orchestra and had given us free use of the house. The take, whatever it was to be, was to be split among the singers. Lenya had consented to come for nothing.

We rehearsed in the living room of the parents of one of the many who had drifted in and who volunteered as coach or assistant stage manager. Eric Simon, now a clarinetist in New York and the owner of a lovely home in Connecticut, a state which, at the time, he surely wouldn't have known how to spell, played the piano backstage when a piano had to be played backstage and then donned a mustache and a hat to become one of the men of *Mahagonny* on our never sufficiently crowded stage. Another, now a famous Viennese critic, got the singers on stage and saw to it that they had the props they were always leaving behind, ready to carry them on stage himself, if necessary. Hans Weigel had his picture taken by a professional theater photographer and dedicated it to me, "To my"—"from his," posing solemnly and menacingly in an old, frayed jacket he had saved from the destruction it had been assigned to by his spring-clean-ing mother, the proper garment for a man in the mythical city of Mahagonny in an America none of us had ever seen and few of us suspected we would see so soon and for so long.

During intermission—there was only one, we played the three-act opera in two acts—or when they were not busy running with guns and whisky bottles after the forgetful men of Mahagonny, the two volunteers worked on a libretto designed to liberate, at long last, the many famous personages known to every opera lover and never before seen on stage. There was the Marschallin's Feldmarschall, back from the eternal hunt in the Bohemian Forest; there was Scarpia's Count Palmieri before he was executed without benefit of an audience; there was Isolde's mother, preparing her little girl for the voyage to Cornwall with a splendid assortment of poisons and potions. Pamina's father was in love with Donna Anna's mother; Parsifal in *Lohengrin* appeared, wearing his crown; and in the final scene Lillas Pastia, cousin Morold, and the Pope in *Tannhäuser* made a grand entry. Perhaps the most memorable figure, however, was that perennial, decrepit bore, Onkel Greifenklau, from the first act of *Der Rosenkavalier*, who was driven on stage by the never-before-seen coachman Joseph from the second, singing an aria in which he expressed his forever frustrated desire to have lunch alone.

Weill was very impressed with the libretto, which was written in the epic style of a Brecht *Lehrstück*. Unfortunately it has been swept away with many other things by the ensuing events.

As everything was improvised, we let our imagination run as freely as it itched to run. When we at last tranferred from the living room in the Salesianergasse to the stage of the Raimund Theater, I discovered that I did not have the slightest idea how to light a scene. I did not know one knob from another, and when I signaled to the man in the box to give me white he bathed everything in red or plunged us in utter darkness. I was saved from ignominious disaster by a famous German director who happened to be in town and who drifted in at one of our rehearsals—other in-drifters I remember were Alban Berg and Ernst Krenek—and took over, discreetly, tactfully, and successfully.

Lenya and Weill arrived only a few days before the opening. She fitted herself marvelously and gracefully into the excited ensemble of volunteers and rehearsed indefatigably. Weill just smiled—whether because he was pleased or just nice, I didn't dare to ask. To our immense surprise things went so well that we had to extend our season from six to ten days. Even so, we had had it. The Vienna Opera Production went out of this life as quietly and suddenly as it had come in. To me it had been a wonderful experience. I had, for the first and last time, given battle to the stage. It was not a victory, but I had retreated in dignity. I went back to my office, hung one of our posters on the wall, paid Hertzka the royalties for our ten performances on which he had pitilessly insisted, and felt very good.

BRECHT HAD NOT COME to the performance. I saw him in Vienna only once, a few years later, after he had arrived there on the first leg of a long, multilegged exile from Germany. He sniffed the Viennese air, which to all of us still smelled sweet, pleasant, and very safe, shrugged his Marxist shoulders, and said—unforgettably and later often remembered—"This is no place for an exile." He left long before any of us began to detect the first traces of political air pollution in the Vienna Woods and the first streaks of poisonous brown in the Beautiful Blue Danube.

Perhaps he had not attended our performance of *Mahagonny* because, at that time, the artistic partnership between him and Weill had come to a bitter end. (It was revived only once more, briefly, in the all-wounds-temporarily-healing atmosphere of a common Paris exile, where they joined in writing the now celebrated ballet *The Seven Deadly Sins.*) After the *Three Penny* triumph, Brecht and Weill had collaborated on another play with music for Ernst Josef Aufricht, misnamed *Happy End.* Its lone survivor is one of Kurt Weill's most tantalizingly beautiful songs, "Surabaya Jonny." Then, for the 1929 festival in Baden-Baden, Weill made a musical setting of a poem Brecht had written under the impact of the Lindbergh flight. Afterward, of course, the fact that Brecht had written a poem idolizing Charles Lindbergh became a political embarrassment for him, and so the work is almost forgotten today, but I still remember the work and particularly a short scene of great and striking beauty—two fishermen off the west coast of Ireland, one noticing a plane coming from the west and calling out to his companion, and the companion refusing even to lift his eyes to the sky "because it cannot be." The poem and the music were dedicated to "The Unreachable."

In 1930, Brecht and Weill made a short opera for children. *Gebrauchsmusik*—music to be used—had become an important aspect of contemporary musical efforts. It meant music for active participation, not for mere passive listening. The movement was a strong reaction to the ever-increasing difficulties and complications in modern music. Dozens, if not hundreds of rehearsals were needed to perform Schoenberg's *Pierrot lunaire* adequately. Only a few initiated musicians were able to participate in the performance of such a work. *Gebrauchsmusik* was to allow participation in contemporary music to people who sang *Messiah* on Christmas or played in the town band. Krenek had written some rousing marches for brass. Hindemith, among other works for the new medium, had written a charming opera for children —*Let's build a city*— and Brecht and Weill wrote *Der Jasager* (*The Yes-Sayer*), based on a Japanese play, into which Brecht injected his increasingly orthodox Marxist if not Maoist philosophies, whose application to the stage had already caused such a swift and unhappy end to *Happy End*. *Der Jasager* was to be performed by children. A boy, injured during a march over a mountain pass, volunteers to stay behind, willing to perish so that the group may proceed without being delayed by carrying him. He is asked whether he is willing to sacrifice himself and says, of course, Yes—*Der Jasager*. Strangely, the little Maoist, consenting so bravely to perish for the community, could just as well have been *Hitlerjunge* Quex, a legendary self-sacrificer in the rapidly rising Hitler Youth.

Weill made a haunting, subdued dramatical score, beautifully written for children's voices, and when we performed the little work with a group of school children in a Viennese assembly hall, whither I had returned for a brief, but definitely last nibble at the sweet opium of the limelight, we had everyone in unabashed, very unpolitical tears.

It was undoubtedly Brecht's increasing preoccupation with radical, doctrinaire leftist politics that was the ingredient, dissolving slowly but surely the partnership between him and Weill. Those who knew Kurt Weill always had felt that his participation in the Brechtian political treatises for the stage was not the result of common political philosophies or convictions, as they were in the case of Hanns Eisler, who had advanced from the bourgeois mahjongg tables in the Kaffee Museum to official court composer of the Communist party or of Paul Dessau, the post-war musical mouthpiece for Brecht's interpretations of the world. In Weill's case it was much more the irresistible attraction of a great poet and brilliant dramatist for a composer born for the stage who would have sold his soul for a good book and for singable lyrics to hang his music on. There was little common ground between the roughneck from Augsburg who always looked as if he was ready to man the barricades (though he never did) and Weill, who always looked as if he was hoping one day to be a rich man in America, which of course he was soon to be. I have never seen a man enjoy his first automobile—a Graham-Page—more than Kurt Weill, and I will not forget the exuberant, relaxed, boyish pleasure with which he drove the car, with Lenya, me, and a lovely lady of my choice from Vienna over the mountains toward Italy. A short stretch of the pre-Autobahn horrors of the road was in splendid condition, and as he gave the American car all it had, Weill improvised a childishly primitive doggerel, singing with his famous veiled voice:

Ja, so ein Strässchen
Ja, das macht Spässchen. . . .

Aufricht reports that during the rehearsals of *Mahagonny* in Berlin, Brecht was fighting stubbornly for the preponderance of his words—he was never interested in music, only in the political message—whereas Weill wanted the music to be heard and properly interpreted. When a press photographer took a picture of the two together, Brecht hit the camera from his hands and screamed: "I'll throw the fake Richard Strauss in full war paint down the stairs." Nothing could reveal more strikingly the chasm between the two than this comparison of the composer of *Erst kommt das Fressen, dann kommt die Moral* with the rich, contented idol of the German bourgeoisie.

There was, of course, a grain of truth in Brecht's outburst. Weill, in his heart, was an unpolitical man and, when looked at from Brecht's Maoist point of view, undoubtedly "one of the persons in power, who took the capitalist road." He took it vigorously and successfully after he had come to the United States. While other composers mourned their lost paradise, forever bemoaning the fact that there was no publicly subsidized opera house in Amarillo, Weill turned his back upon the vanished East and his face toward the new discovered West, one of the few among the many newcomers to America who knew that those who turned back would—like Lot's wife—be transformed into a pillar of salt, the very symbol of sterility. Instead, he announced: "The Broadway legitimate stage is to the American public what the opera houses and concert halls are to the European. I have always believed that opera should be a part of the living theater of our time. Broadway is today one of the great theater centers of the world. It has all the technical and intellectual equipment for a serious musical theater. It has a wealth of singers, who can act, excellent orchestras and conductors, music-minded directors, choreographers, and designers. Above all, it has audiences as sensitive and receptive as any audiences in the world. These audiences are willing to accept any musical language so long as it is strong and convincing."

• • •

THIS WAS IN 1935. My own American association with Kurt Weill began twelve years later. In the meantime, he had written *Knickerbocker Holiday* and his first American hit song, one of the great Weill perennials, "September Song." While he was working on the music, he wired Walter Huston, who was to play the leading part of Peter Stuyvesant: "What is the range of your voice?" and Huston wired back: "No range. Regards, Walter Huston." As performed by the rangeless actor, the song passed almost unnoticed during the run of the play and became and remained a hit only after Bing Crosby made a recording of it in 1946, eight years after it had first appeared on Broadway. After *Knickerbocker Holiday* came *Lady in the Dark* and the debut of Danny Kaye, came *One Touch of Venus*, came *Street Scene*, and, later, *Lost in the Stars*. There also came a plethora of famous playwrights writing for and with him—Moss Hart, Paul Green, Maxwell Anderson, Elmer Rice, S. J. Perelman, Langston Hughes.

By the time I came to his door, the capitalist road had taken him to a beautiful house and sprawling estate in Rockland County, New York, next to his friend and collaborator Maxwell Anderson, with a private brook (the house was named Brookhouse) and well-kept lawns and a truly capitalistic-looking huge dog.

My mission to the palatial home was not quite in style. I had come to ask the composer of *Lady in the Dark* to go back to the days of his first school opera. I was looking for a *Jasager à l'américain.*

During the summer of 1947 I had given a few lectures on

various aspects of musical life. After one of them, in a small community, a man got up. He explained, that all the big and important things I had been talking about meant little to them. The Metropolitan Opera would never bring its stars to their little town in Tennessee. Was there an opera they could perform themselves, with their own forces, with local singers, a local chorus, a little ballet they had formed, with homemade costumes and self-painted scenery, to be sung in English in a high school auditorium that had no pit, no elaborate lighting, few technical facilities?

Here was again the call for *Gebrauchsmusik!* I remembered *Der Jasager*. I also remembered that, within a short time, I was to start my new job at Schirmer's. What would be more rewarding than to bring them as *Morgengabe*, as a seal on the new marriage contract, a *Gebrauchsoper* that could really be *gebraucht?* A combination of sentimental remembrance, cultural pioneering spirit, and selfish greed had brought me to New City.

After I had told my little story to Kurt Weill, he got up smilingly and took a large-sized score from a desk drawer. Its title page was inscribed "*Down in the Valley*. A folk opera. Libretto by Arnold Sundgaard, Music by Kurt Weill." The score was written in ink in Weill's own clear, clean, unhesitating handwriting.

A little earlier, Weill told me, he had been approached by Olin Downes, music critic of *The New York Times,* whose approaches were not easily ignored by any composer and certainly not by one as public-relations-minded as Kurt Weill, to participate in a project Downes had been asked to organize. A sponsor was interested in a series of half-hour radio programs based on folk music. Would Weill write the music for a pilot production that might induce the sponsor to sponsor? When Weill went to Olin Downes's apartment in the Osborn, on Fifty-seventh Street (it was later to be occupied by Leonard Bernstein), he found there a heavy-set Norwegian from Minnesota with a ruddy, boyish face and wiry hair who had been called in to write the libretto.

Arnold Sundgaard had spent some time at the Barter Theater in Abington, Virginia, where he had plenty of leisure to listen to the radio and go to folk dances. He had become fond of the song "Down in the Valley," and now suggested to Downes and Weill they take it as the basis for the projected work. Both said that they didn't know it. Foreigner Weill was, of course, excused. But it was a rather triumphant moment for Sundgaard when he took a large collection of American folk songs from a shelf in the apartment. The collection had been co-edited by Olin Downes. It contained the song "Down in the Valley."

Weill and Sundgaard finished the work, carefully measured for twenty-six and a half minutes of radio time. They made an audition record for the sponsor and the sponsor said thank you very much, but we'd rather not, and that would probably have been the end of the little work if I had not come innocently knocking at the door. Weill seemed delighted at the prospects of such unexpected resurrection of the spurned pilot project and went to see Mr. Max Dreyfus, who was his publisher and who probably didn't think much of *Gebrauchsoper* and gracefully released the work. It was a little short for what we had in mind, so Arnold Sundgaard was called back to write some more prose and Kurt added a few songs.

Soon Kurt and Arnold came and played, sang and acted the opera for the samovar and the mirrors and the boss and the sales manager at Schirmer's, where I had arrived a little earlier. The sales manager laughed and said what do you want an opera for? Opera is foreign stuff, American kids are doing fine with Gilbert and Sullivan, we sold a thousand copies of *H.M.S. Pinafore* last year and we won't sell ten copies of this thing here, pardon me. But the boss told him to go downstairs and sell more copies of Hanon Exercises and he went downstairs and was not nice about it at all. Later, he sold forty-five thousand vocal scores and eighty-five thousand chorus parts of this thing, and every time he sent a slip asking us to print more copies, he added a little note reading "I told you so."

Before the score was published, one of our editors thought it would be a good idea to have a painting by Grandma Moses on the cover and we went to see Grandma Moses's agent. He said, sure, he had just the painting for us and showed us a picture called *The Spring in Evening*, which was as down-in-the-valleyish as we could have wished it to be and had everything but the jail, which wouldn't have been a nice thing to have on a cover for kids in the first place and would have upset the sales manager some more. The agent asked us to write on a slip of paper what we were willing to pay while he wrote out what he would ask. We exchanged the slips of paper and after we looked at his we said, thank you, we didn't want to buy his art gallery and got up to leave. He was a very refined Viennese gentleman and it grieved him to see us so dejected, so he said, if we could get him an autograph of the opening song from the *Dreigroschenoper* he would let us have the painting at our price, which, we figured, wouldn't benefit Grandma Moses much, but would help everybody else, and anyway, the man told us, she never cashes her checks, but puts them in a large coffeepot in the kitchen, so it was just as well. Kurt Weill was real nice about it and wrote out "Mack the Knife" in his own, unmistakable handwriting and we brought it to the man and Grandma Moses had her painting on forty-five thousand vocal scores and a very small little check in her coffeepot, and when *Down in the Valley* was reprinted in

England the man even gave us a set of brand-new color plates free to show his appreciation.

Kurt Weill's *Down in the Valley*—we called it just that in the published score, not an opera or anything else because we didn't know ourselves just what it was going to be—had some three thousand productions and more than fifteen thousand performances during the first twenty years of its life. It was the beginning of a new performance practice in America and has prompted a whole new literature of similar works for similar performance conditions.

Weill began making plans for a companion piece, soon after the little work had begun its spectacular career. He never got around to it. Less than two years after the *première* performance of *Down in the Valley*, he died, on April 3, 1950, at the age of fifty.

The first of our little group marching with the century had left.

NOBODY HAD PAID any attention to me as I left the ship. I wasn't a composer or conductor. I was no scholar and no baritone.

No brass band waited for me at the pier, no limousine whisked me away, nobody took my picture as I came down the gangplank, and nobody offered me a job. The only person who had come to welcome me was an old friend with whom I had once studied in Freiburg. As I discovered him in the crowd, I happily took my hat off and swung it in a wide arc, as was customary in Europe when you greeted a man.

"Keep your hat on," the old friend said. "We don't do that here. You are not in Vienna any more. You are in America."

I did not mind it. I was excited and happy to be here and I did not mind criticism a bit. I was eager to learn.

This was not just another country, it was another continent. You step ashore and already the first thing you do is wrong. People don't take their hats off when they greet other people in America. I would remember that. I would never take my hat off again.

I turned around and there was Edith, my old friend's wife. "Hello, Edith," I said.

"Take your hat off when you talk to a lady," said my old friend. "You are not in Vienna any more. You are in America."

• • •

THE FIRST WEEK of a newcomer's life in America is an exciting mixture of exalted happiness, wide-eyed amazement, and creeping fear. It is a wonderful week. I arrived in New York late at night, and all I saw on that first drive from the pier to a hotel on the East Side was the sudden blinding flash as we dived into the floodlights of Broadway.

But the next morning I was up early. I stepped out on the street to begin the unforgettable first hike through the ravine of Forty-second Street.

For the first time in my life I saw a drugstore. I went in, climbed on one of the stools, and—for the first time—had breakfast at a counter.

"Toasted English," I heard a man next to me give his order—and "Toasted English," I repeated when it was my turn. I didn't know what toasted English was, but when it arrived I loved the taste and the smell of the muffins, and for weeks to come I would enter the drugstore every morning and order, with the swaggering ease of an old-timer, "Toasted English"—till at last I had guts (and English verbs) enough to ask for a menu and order corn flakes or orange juice and two soft-boiled eggs. While I was waiting for my first breakfast I watched people coming into the store not to eat but to buy hot-water bottles, shirts, and aspirins. It was all new, and so was the punched check the man behind the counter handed me, and his refusal to take my money, and the cashier at the cigar counter who took it.

Back on the street I saw my first skyscraper. I made my first trip in an American elevator, racing to the top floor and down again in dizzy exaltation. I discovered my first Western Union office with sloppily dressed boys lined up on the benches like birds on telephone wires. I ducked—this was 1938—when I heard the first elevated train thundering over my confused head. I saw the marquees of movie theaters rotating their mad ribbons of light at nine o'clock in the morning. I joined the silent watch of the sidewalk superintendents. I saw a row of men propped up high like pashas on their thrones getting sparkling shines from chatting Negro boys while they read tremendous newspapers of a size I had never seen.

The trolley cars were different, the buses, the taxis, the Negroes, the Chinese laundries, the barber poles, the steam shovels, the pushcarts, the fire escapes, the newsstands, the dirt, the speed, the noise, the air, the light, the climate, the smell, the ugliness, and the beauty.

As has everybody, I had brought with me a list of people I was recommended to, and with the trembling anticipation of the explorer starting out on a new and uncharted journey, I began my first expedition through the endless vastness of the Manhattan telephone book. My heart would beat with that extra pang of the lucky discoverer every time I encountered in printed reality one of the names I had brought all the way across the Atlantic in my soiled little notebook.

Anybody you call during your first week of life in America seems overjoyed. Everybody comes right to the phone. Nobody has "just stepped out for a moment," nobody "isn't at his desk right now," nobody "will call you back later."

"You are in New York. Wonderful! You must come and see us. Are you free for dinner tonight?" Of course you are free. You go to dinner tonight and to lunch tomorrow and to cocktails and concerts and shows, and for the weekend you have your choice among Great Neck, Westport, and Mamaroneck.

When you come home at night you find a message to call Butterfield 3–6754. You call and it's a Mrs. Blum. She has heard from her sister in Vienna that you are in America, and my husband and I would so much like to meet you, and won't you come and have cocktails, we're having a few people in on Friday at five.

Friday at five you go to the Blums' and there are thirty people and this is Mr. Heinsheimer—pardon me, *Doctor* Heinsheimer, who just arrived from Vienna, he knows my sister there, isn't that interesting, how do you do? Glad to meet you, Doctor, I didn't get your name, so you just arrived here from Austria, hello, Doc, well, tell us all about Vienna. Pardon me, I want you to meet Mr. Voigt.

By now you have had many cocktails and so has Mr. Voigt, who tells you that he is the president of Associated Music Publishers, Inc., and he gives you his card and asks you to be sure to call him next week, let's say Tuesday at eleven o'clock—he wants to take you out for lunch because you are just the type of man he would like to talk to about a job. You carefully put his card in your wallet, and glad to have met you and don't forget to call me, young fellow, and good-bye, Mrs. Blum, thanks for asking me, yes, I had a wonderful time, good-bye sir, thank you, thank you very much. And you go home and make a note on your calendar call Voigt Tuesday, eleven o'clock.

Yes, this first week in America is a wonderful week. It is your honeymoon with New York. Every day you have free luncheons and dinners and shows and cocktails and all you pay for is your toasted English in the morning and an occasional nickel—this is 1938—for a bus or a subway. But the following Monday you have no invitation and you go and buy yourself a lunch at Jiffi's. You don't look at the dishes, but at the prices, and where it says fifty cents—this is still 1938 —yes, miss, that's what I would like to have.

Tuesday at eleven o'clock you go to a drugstore and call Associated Music Publishers, Inc., and ask for Mr. Voigt, Mr. Ernest R. Voigt.

"Mr. Voigt's office," the lovely sound of a flutelike voice comes over the wire, alluring and reassuring. You tell the voice that Mr. Voigt has asked you to call and will she please put him on?

"What was your name again?" sings the sweet voice, and you repeat your name and will you please spell it for me, and thank you, and will you please hold on while I see whether he is in? So you wait till she comes back and any moment your nickel will drop, but no, there she is, flute-voice is back, and I am awfully sorry he stepped out for a moment.

"He told me to call at eleven."

"I am awfully sorry, but he isn't here right now."

"Well, I will call later."

"No, I don't think that's a good idea, I really don't know when he will be back, why don't you leave your number? I'll have him call you as soon as he comes back, yes, you can be sure I'll give him the message, thank you for calling."

But Ernest R. Voigt never calls back, so after three days you call flute-voice again, but he just stepped out again, yes, of course, I gave him your message but you see Mr. Voigt has been awfully busy these days. This time you don't spell your name and don't leave your telephone number because you begin to understand that Mr. Voigt will always have stepped out for a moment and you take his card from your wallet and tear it up.

Soon you will learn more. You will learn, for instance, to understand what it means when a man tells you:

"We must have lunch one of these days."

You will learn to understand that that man has just given you the supreme kiss of death. You will learn that if a man *really* wants to lunch with you he will take his notebook out and put in: "Lunch Wednesday 1 at the Brass Rail." A man who says he wants to have lunch with you "one of these days" wants *never* to have lunch with you. He just is telling you, in a subtle and refined way, that he doesn't want to see you ever again, that you are thin air to him, and that he will completely forget your very existence before he walks half a block down the street.

You keep on learning a lot of things you didn't think you would ever have to learn, and you learn them all the hard way. But there is one consoling feature: you make wonderful progress with your English. The days are gone when you had to order toasted English because you didn't know any other dishes. You can handle every situation with ease and relaxation. You soon begin to adorn your growing vocabulary with an abundant assortment of "guys" and "buds" and "O.K.s" and "hells" and "you bets" and "swells" and "damns." They are just a little bit too numerous and a little bit too loud, and they stick out of the simple bunting of your language like cheap paper flowers in noisy pink.

People begin to comment on your English. It is ambrosia to your ears and nectar to your heart when they tell you, "It's amazing how you speak English" or when they want to know how many years you spoke English before you came here. At night, before you go to sleep, you read your paper aloud and admire your perfect pronunciation in the solitude of your bedroom. You can't even hear a trace of an accent any more. Your language problems are over; hell, even Felix Frankfurter was born in Vienna and look what happened to him, he ended up on the Supreme Court!

But then one nice afternoon you take a cab. The cabby's name is Emil Wasservogel, and you get in and all you say is, "Twelve West Seventh Street," just four short words, and Wasservogel turns around and says, "*Schönes Wetter heute.*" You could kill him in cold blood. To him you are no Yankee. To him you are just a Riding Dutchman.

You pretend that you didn't hear what he just said. You sit back in the cab and murmur a muffled "Nice day, isn't it?" with all the Yankee accent you think you can muster and Wasservogel turns around and shrugs his shoulders and probably thinks that you are an awful schmock. When you arrive at your destination you hand him a dollar, take your change, give him his tip, and don't say another word. But while you enter the house you hear his cheerful "*Auf Wiedersehen*" echoing all over West Seventh Street.

So it's the accent, you think, and maybe it will take me another year till I get rid of it; Frankfurter, I am sure, had none, or how could he have been a Supreme Court judge?—but otherwise I am getting along fine.

You don't know it, but you still have a long, long way to go.

• • •

SLOWLY your wardrobe, all the nice things you brought with you from Europe, your suits and handkerchiefs and stockings, begin to wear out, and the day arrives when you have to buy yourself a new shirt, your first American shirt. You take it home and take the pins out and look at it. You discover that it's different from the shirt you were used to wearing all your life: you can button it up all the way down. You open all the buttons and put it on. It's the first time that you don't have to slide in a shirt with your arms raised, struggling to get your hands through the sleeves, blindly feeling your way around the room, upsetting the vase with faded roses on the chest, till at last you emerge, your hair, your room, your new shirt messed up. This time you put on a shirt with your eyes open, your head erect, in the proud posture of a free man in a free country.

You get dressed and leave the house. You feel different. That shirt does something to you. You feel that you are one of fifty million American men walking around in an American shirt. You have advanced an important step, a step away from the past, a step nearer to the future. That shirt makes you feel relaxed as you have not been in a long time. You are not quite as much of a stranger any more while you walk through the streets of New York.

You go home and send all your European shirts to the Salvation Army and go out and buy yourself half a dozen shirts at Broadway and Seventh Avenue. And you do it at ten o'clock at night, when there isn't one single store open all over Europe where you could buy a shirt.

The shirt is followed by a suit and shorts and socks and shoes. At long last the tranformation is complete. You feel different, you walk differently, you begin to look different, and slowly, very slowly, you begin to think and to act differently. Your Wasservogels are over.

But there are still many mysteries you can't penetrate. Every day you try to read the sports column, but it's Chinese, just plain Chinese.

"Giants Powder Phillies. Judd faced five men without giving up a run in this second round, as singles by Gordon and Kerr sandwiched a force-out, Trinkle sacrificed, and Rigney walked to load the bases."

Chinese, Chinese, Chinese.

Southpaw, errors, Lombardi refuses to fret at Judd's stalling tactics, the grand-slam homer, a pass, a double play, five trips to the dish, a two-base passed ball, bagging only seven safeties, Kerr came up with a fielding flash in the fourth, roaming behind the third baseman to collar Verban's grounder, and unleashed a long, underhanded, off-balance throw to nip the batter at first.

You know it will always be Chinese to you. You know you will never, never, never, learn what a two-base passed ball is.

But all the time your transformation goes on. When you first arrived in America you had nice cards printed with your name preceded by a "Dr." Being a European, you are a doctor. A doctor of law or of music or of art or of economics or of something or other. Wherever you go, you introduce yourself as doctor till one day you are at a party and please meet Dr. Heinsheimer, hello Doctor, glad to meet you, Doc, how do you do, Doctor. Later you have a drink or two and come to talk with a fellow and he asks you, Doc will you please come in the bathroom with me for a moment? You are amazed, but after all this is a strange country and you better be polite so you go and he puts his hand to his right side and I always have pains here, Doc, I hate to bother you but I thought you might be able to help me Vienna is famous for its good doctors and do you want me to take off my shirt and pants?

From that day on you drop your doctor and are a plain mister and you don't even think any more of poor Professor Honiger, who was so proud and so sad when he gave you your doctor's diploma back in Freiburg on a Friday afternoon, and now it was all in vain. Soon you aren't even a mister any more, but plain Hans.

It didn't sound very *amerikanisch* but I decided to stick to it. I had no trouble and have been living a happy American life as a Hans among so many recent Johns and Jacks. Only my cousin from San Antonio pronounces it Haynes, which, I suppose, sounds more American than an ordinary Hans, particularly to a Texan who was born in Karlsruhe, Germany.

XII

TWENTY-THIRD STREET seemed light-years away from Bösendorferstrasse.

From my desk in Vienna, caressed by the scent of lilacs drifting in from the square below, I had been looking on the baroque columns and the green-golden cupola of Fischer von Erlach's Karlskirche. From my first desk in New York, through a yellowish, unopenable wire-mesh, I faced a rusty water tower on the roof of a factory loft on Twenty-fourth Street. In Vienna, there had been the gentle shuffle of Eusebius Mandyczewsky's slippered feet over my head, tiptoeing among Beethoven autographs and sad, gentle letters by Schubert. Here, there were thirty steam presses, operated by the Peerless Ladies' Dress Company, Inc., groaning, hissing, clattering, shaking the floor above.

The leisurely ambles to and from the golden-brown schnitzels of the Imperial *Schwemme* and the whipped-creamed *Torten* of the Kaffee Kremser had fast become fata morganas from another star. There was, instead, the lunch-hour squeeze in the elevator, bulging already with Peerless shirt-sleeved steam-pressers, and then the rush to and from the lettuce-and-tomato-on-whole-wheat-toast at the corner drugstore, the worst place and the worst repast this side of hell. Had it really been only yesterday that I was walking to work through the morning dew of Prince Eugene's Belvedere gardens and, later, back again past fountains sparkling in the setting sun? Even the memory of flowers and fountains had faded as the Sixth Avenue Elevated, groaning and shrieking past unmade bedrooms and cluttered kitchens, spat me out at the Twenty-third Street station and swallowed me up again at night for the ride home past tired figures, looking motionless from narrow windows on a dewless, flowerless, fountainless, heavenless world.

The enterprise with which I had found my first precarious shelter in the uncharted, frightening vastness of the American publishing industry occupied an entire floor in the middle of a depressing block on Twenty-third Street. Its Hertzka was a tall, very thin, incredibly fast-moving man of tireless, springy energy. Like Hertzka, Max Winkler was a vegetarian (it was he who had suggested that one could actually *eat* lettuce-and-tomato-on-whole-wheat) and a teetotaler, not motivated, however, by lofty Hertzkan principles but by ulcers.

With unwavering precision, only occasionally disturbed by breakdowns on the Long Island Railroad which he took in very bad grace, he would arrive three minutes past eight in the morning and leave, unwaveringly, fourteen minutes past five to catch the 5:34 back to Lynbrook. Between arrival and departure he sold more sheet music than I had ever known existed or could be shipped by anyone anywhere in so short a time. It was a stunning experience. After all those years in the music-publishing business it struck me during my first days on Twenty-third Street that perhaps I knew nothing about it. The whole philosophy of the European publisher was based on the assumption that sales of sheet music were at best a by-product, but were basically for the birds. Money was made through performing fees, mechanical royalties, theatrical productions, motion-picture rights, rental fees. Max Winkler opened up new vistas for me which showed me, on my very first day on Twenty-third Street, that lettuce-and-tomato-on-toast wasn't the only thing I had to acquaint myself with in my new fatherland.

Max Winkler—the story unfolded bit by bit during the daily run to and from lunch—had received his baptism of fire in the epic days of the silent movies. He had started behind the counter of the orchestra department in the Carl Fischer store at Cooper Square, where, arriving from the humblest of beginnings and the lowest of East Sides, he had begun life in the music business at six dollars a week. There he sold and memorized thousands of pieces and titles. Soon, his head was overflowing with the music that the rapidly expanding movie industry needed to illustrate musically what was going on on the screen. It didn't take long for this encyclopedic knowledge to be put to better use than increasing the turnover at Fischer's orchestra counter.

Soon, when he left the store at night, Winkler proceeded to a studio on Seventh Avenue where he was shown a film about to be released. Two hours later, he pressed a button, the lights went on and he emerged with a pad, covered with musical titles. The next day, the list had been printed and rushed to every movie theater in the land—there were about fifteen thousand of them, he would tell us with a mixture of pride in and sorrow for the past.

For some time he faithfully channeled toward Fischer's his cue sheets and the staggering sales they produced. Then he quit and went into business for himself. Soon his Catalogue of Dramatic and Incidental Music had become the bible for thousands of orchestra leaders, innumerable pianists and, so he told us, twenty-five thousand organists playing in the motion-picture theaters. Here they found the Sinisters, Chases, Animals, Sads, Happys, Mysteriouses, Furiouses, and Majestics they were craving for. Winds and storms, rain and Eskimos, gigolos and emperors, streetwalkers and emergencies, vamps and cowboys, colibris and elephants—everything had its proper counterpart in Winkler's musical catalogue. "Open with 'Dramatic Suspense' by Andino," a cue sheet would begin. "At title 'Don't shoot!' shoot with your left hand and switch with the right hand to

Mysterioso Dramatico No. 22 by Borsche. As villain flees play Hurry No. 33 by Minot."

Soon the sales became astronomical, and Winkler put the finishing touch to his efforts by publishing an *Encyclopedia of Music for Pictures*, "*As essential as the picture*," which listed twenty thousand titles. It began with Aeroplanes, Aesop's Fables (see Comedy pictures), African (see Cannibal) and 157 Agitatos and ended, five hundred pages later, with Witches (see also Spooks and Gruesome), Yodl (see also Swiss and Austria), Zanzibar and Zoo (see also Various Animals).

The best of all possible worlds had arrived. Then Winkler attended the showing of the first sound film, *The Jazz Singer*, and heard Al Jolson warble without the benefit of a single music-buying musician in the pit. The best of all possible worlds had come to an end. Within a few months, he told us with masochistic pleasure (see also Funerals and Torture), fifteen thousand theaters in America began installing sound equipment and a hundred thousand musicians had lost their jobs. "In 1926 I sold three hundred thousand dollars' worth of music to the moving-picture theaters," he said, blowing on his tea so that he could hurry back to work. "In one single year we sold four thousand copies of the *Encyclopedia* at ten dollars a copy. In 1927 we sold two copies. And we sold"—by this time we were already racing down Twenty-third Street and I had trouble keeping up with him —"our entire stock of music, seventy tons, to a paper mill for two hundred and ten dollars."

It sounded awful, but as none of us could imagine how much music seventy tons were, the magnitude of the disaster somehow lost its impact by the time we had returned to the sixth floor. Also, he had long since turned adversity into triumph. No sooner had he been deprived of his kingdom of Furiosos and Dawns that he began to look for other frontiers to conquer, and he was now well on his way to become the king of the school bands, the emperor of the xylophone solos, and the unchallenged Führer of piano solos for the very early grades.

• • •

HERTZKA had guided me patiently and, I had thought, not without some success through a world whose uncontested, respected, and humbly-to-be-served center was the composer: a world of music festivals, symphonic conductors, opera houses, orchestras, song cycles, piano sonatas, masters, and maestros. In the world of my new boss there was not a single living composer whose name I had ever heard. Winkler took great pride in the fact that he had never missed the 5:34 back home to Long Island and thus could offer definite proof that he had never seen Carnegie Hall from the outside or, God forbid, from the inside. As for opera, when I once, very early in our acquaintance (I soon learned to guard my tongue) mentioned the Metropolitan Opera and the difficulties they face to make ends meet, he snapped, "If they don't make money, why don't they close the joint?" and hurried away to fill an order for eighty copies of Dapper Donkey (Grade I) by Brunt for B♭ Clarinet.

Order-filling, to Max Winkler, was a sacred, a priestly chore. The whole floor, extending from Twenty-third to Twenty-fourth Street, was a fantastic labyrinth of steel bins packed with music. A pencil between his restless lips, he would pounce on the basket where the orders were stacked up in the morning and which, under an iron rule, had to be empty by the time the trains to Long Island got under way at night. Unhesitatingly, he took the order staring at him from the top of the pile while everybody else, looking over their shoulders to make sure they were unobserved, pushed a bitchy, messy, ink-scrawled order for single copies of seventy different items from Charlotte, North Carolina, down the pile, pulling instead with the instinct and the agile fingers of experience a neatly typed, juicy stockorder from Lyon & Healy, for ten and fifty and hundred lots of easily accessible best sellers that would keep them comfortably busy for the rest of the day.

Winkler hated order-diggers but seemed more hurt than infuriated when he caught one in the act. He would take the despised order from Charlotte, North Carolina, with a silent look of reproach and hurry to bin 37 to get a single copy of First Division Melody Instrument Method, and on to bin 347 for a second euphonium part of "Santa's Holiday" by Piato. Wetting his finger, he tirelessly counted out eleven copies of "Dear Lord and Father of Mankind" by Swift here and two Eck, Quartet Album for Flutes there, marking an occasional item with a hopeful TOP, which meant Temporarily Out of Print, or a crushing POP, which meant Permanently Out of Print, dead, buried and gone, or No. 13—Order is indefinite, give (a) composer, (b) arranger, (c) key of voice, (d) instrumentation, (e) volume number, (f) quantity—which shows the unending frustrations lurking along the path of the order-filler and why there were so many who pushed the order from Charlotte down the pile for the boss to pick up and why thirteen is bad luck.

The boss never seemed to mind. Unerringly he found his way through the Stygian darkness of the bins till he had the order completed, the music stacked in a neat, elegant pile, to be charged and packed and sent on its way down the freight elevator where America's Flying Legions by Lyons, full band, $2.00, were rubbing shoulders with the ladies' dresses descending from the seventh floor. The boss had already rushed back to the basket to snatch the next order from the top and could be seen, reaching high up to bin 68d, Clarinet

Trio by Frangkiser, which everybody else hated to be stuck with because they had to fetch a ladder to get to it.

The narrow passages between the bins were lighted by countless 25-watt bulbs swinging from the ceiling and everytime the boss had finished with bin 68d he pulled a little chain to extinguish the light, pulling another chain at bin 147 to show him, dimly, the way to Octavo 2024, "Bless this House" for three-part mixed.

In the middle of the floor the bins receded to make room for the Holy Ark of the establishment, the mailing room. Eternally and brilliantly illuminated by an assembly of 100-watt bulbs, it housed tens of thousands of stenciled name plates, green for piano teachers, purple for churches, bright red for band masters, pale blue for music directors in high schools, black for sisters, innocent white for libraries. All year round, busy nibelungs presided over by the daughter of the boss punched new names on plates, mercilessly throwing out the dead, demoted, and retired, adding secret little signs and mysterious tabs to indicate whether the addressee was three-part mixed or four-part mixed. Toward the end of the summer, when the windowless solitude of the mail room provided a pleasant, almost alpine atmosphere while in the rest of the place the clarinet trios were coming to a slow boil, mountains of heavy mail bags appeared from nowhere to be filled with envelopes, addressed to the red, the orange, the pale blue, the black. They contained catalogues and announcements, coupons *ask for your free sample copy*, FREE, FREE, FREE! and testimonials to the finest Fife and Drum Corps Builder—an elementary method for "INDIVIDUAL" or "CLASS" or "FULL CORPS INSTRUCTION"—ever introduced in the school system of La Crosse.

Then, the last week before Labor Day, in a ceremony never disturbed or omitted and as inevitable as the advent of the High Holidays which soon followed, the men from Peerless had to walk to lunch and the ladies' dresses had to gather dust on the seventh floor while the elevators, trip after trip, carried mail bags, stuffed to capacity, ready to erupt and to spread the gospel of Harmonized Rest Patterns to the four corners of the land.

Winkler himself was never present at the Ritual of the Mail Bags. Every year, for two months in a row, he went on a sales trip, visiting music dealers, talking to band masters and arrangers, telling and collecting dreadful jokes, selling music in staggering quantities, finding a man who would write him Eighteen Barret & Jancourt Studies or an elementary book for the balalaika. He was blessed with a complete lack of inhibitions which kept him going where others faltered and failed. Once he discovered that a man by the name of John Schaum (the bubbliness of it all seemed to my German mind beautifully mirrored in the name, Hans Foam, but I never said a word about it, having learned my lesson when I once had pointed out that a fawn, cute as it may be, was not the proper image to put on the title page of *Afternoon of a Faun*, easy piano arrangement, advice that was definitely not appreciated)—well, Max discovered that John W. Schaum had sold two different piano arrangements of *The American Patrol* to two different publishers. Both—there was no better recommendation—were very, very easy and both—there was positively no better recommendation—sold very, very well. Winkler—these were his own words—was electrified. He proceeded at once to Milwaukee, where the foamy Schaum resided, and asked him to write a piano course for him. He published, within less than a year, nine books for beginners ("Don't call them that, Marty. Nobody wants to be a beginner. Call them the Red Book, the Blue Book, the Green Book, the purple, orange, violet, brown, amber, gray, and after-gray book") and an Adult Piano Course and a Pop Piano Course and fifteen albums, the ballet, boogie, boys', cowboy, folk song, gay nineties, girls', mountain, opera, parade, polka, ragtime, recital, waltz, and sacred album and fifty Supplementary Books, covering every emergency from Arpeggios in all Keys, Book I via Bach-Schaum, Chopin-Schaum, Haydn-Schaum, Mozart-Schaum, Schumann-Schaum to Theory Lessons, Book III, $1.00 each book. It was such a staggering success that they had to put new steel cables on the Twenty-fourth Street elevator to carry all the Schaum.

• • •

MAX WINKLER was a *unicum* in the world of music publishing. He had accomplished his breathless rush from the ruins of the motion-picture business to a network of family swimming pools and two-car garages by the bold and unbending defiance of every rule whereby other twentieth-century publishing houses conduct their affairs. All he ever cared for or did was to sell printed music. He never attended an ASCAP meeting where his colleagues would gather to watch over the ducats produced by the performances of their copyrights, which had become their bread and—they all had to watch their cholesterol—margarine. He never had to hire bookkeepers to decipher the IBM-contrived royalty statements from RCA Victor or Columbia Records and to distribute their findings among composers, authors, widows, orphans, and the First National Bank of Brewster in trust of. He did not bother with sound film, radio, or television and had lost all interest in Broadway after vaudeville had gone out of fashion and with it the gratis promotion of music that would sell and sell and sell. He didn't know what a rental orchestration for the New York Philharmonic was, he had never drawn up a contract for an operatic production, ballet was a Russian attempt to corrupt the capitalist system, A & R men were not listed in his dictionary, his editors-in-chief were Scissors & Glue, and a composer was a man who could compose an easy bassoon solo.

What was I doing in Binville?

XIII

I WAS SHARPENING pencils that I had nothing to write with, waiting for phone calls that never came, and looking out on the Twenty-fourth Street water tower only because, a little earlier, having absolutely nothing else to do I had taken a stroll up Fifth Avenue. Ernest R. Voigt was still not at his desk right now and I was rapidly running out of my last nickel, trying to reach him. Mr. Carl Engel, the celebrated president of G. Schirmer, to whom I had a letter of recommendation from Hertzka's widow, glanced at it, said "Thank you"—barely—and wished me good luck in America. There hadn't been a dinner invitation from Mamaroneck in a long time. I was in trouble.

A Viennese friend who had arrived here under similar circumstances of duress, a brilliant scholar who spoke fluent Austrian, Italian, French, Latin, and some English, had found employment as an orange-crate lifter in the fruit and vegetable market on Fulton Street and had told me the night before at Horn & Hardart's that there was a job open in the cauliflower department, next to the oranges. It was really very nice, he said, looking at the calluses on his fingers through professorial spectacles: work started at five in the morning and he could easily be at the Public Library, where he was studying Greek, by three in the afternoon. As I couldn't know that, within a few years, he would be the assistant director of the New York City Opera (where he didn't miss a single performance of *The Love for Three Oranges*, smiling sardonically and knowingly through every one of them), as well as secretary-treasurer of the American Dressage Institute, riding his own Lippizan with a family tree going back to Charles the Fifth, I could not appreciate the intellectual and equestrian potential of the Fulton Market and thus passed up the opportunity. Instead, strolling up the Avenue, I was still hoping against dwindling hope, thinking how I could manage to stay in my profession.

Near the Fifty-third Street entrance to the subway bound for Fulton Street, a hatless, very well dressed, ruddy man with sparkling, restless eyes and a little black mustache called my name and asked me what I was doing in America. After I had told him the truth—it didn't take long—he offered me twenty-five dollars a week if I would work for him. I accepted in front of Cartier's, which, in retrospect seems an elegant way to begin a twenty-five dollars a week association. He vigorously hailed a cab and took me downtown.

The man was Ralph Hawkes of London, whither he was to sail back at midnight the very same day. No more providential needle was ever found in a larger haystack against greater odds. During the ride downtown, Hawkes told me where we were heading for and why.

During what Max Winkler (we were, of course, heading for his beehive on Twenty-third Street) liked to call, more with corn than with nostalgia, the "golden days of the cinema," he had become the American agent for the catalogue of Hawkes & Son, music publishers in London. The present Hawkes was the grandson of the founder, who had begun his musical career as a State Trumpeter to Queen Victoria before opening a publishing business in 1865. Grandfather, father, and son had published large quantities of music for military band, instrumental solos, and instruction books for various instruments, in the tradition of the band of the Scots Fusilier Guards, in which the State Trumpeter had served. They also had been lucky in their choice of orchestral music. Such titles as "The Glow Worm," "Venus on Earth," "Valse Septembre," "In the Shadow," and "Nights of Gladness" meant as little to me as did the names of their composers—Lincke, Finck, Godin, and Ancliffe. But they had been welcome fodder for the bottomless pits of the silent movie theaters and had been entered in gold in Max Winkler's *Encyclopedia*. "In the Shadow" alone had sold more than a million copies. Thus the marriage between Hawkes & Grandson and its American agent, Max Winkler, had been a very happy one.

By the time the Holocaust of the Sound Film reduced all this to ashes, Hawkes had amalgamated his catalogue with the firm of Boosey & Co., music publishers in London since 1816 and the copyright owners of such famous ballads as "The Holy City," "Macushla," "Danny Boy," "Bless This House," and similar best sellers, generally known more by their titles than by their composers, whose names were meaningful mostly to the banks where they deposited their royalty checks and to descendants who never had to go to work.

Hawkes band music, so easily adapted to the American school band, and Boosey ballads, so easily converted into choral arrangements, some of which would be printed in thirty thousand and fifty thousand lots at a time—it all was made to order for the exploding school and church business of Max Winkler. Again, under his imaginative, uninhibited exploitation, the best of all possible worlds seemed to have arrived for all concerned.

There was, however, an unsuppressible highbrow streak in the soul of Ralph Hawkes which could never be satisfied by the sales of "Colonel Bogey," no matter how many ships were needed to fill the orders from America, and it didn't find a proper response on Twenty-third Street. It was because of this nagging, ever-present streak that I found myself so unexpectedly in a taxi cab turning west on Twenty-third Street. I was to look after the serious music of Boosey & Hawkes.

We arrived unannounced. Max Winkler climbed off a ladder, took the pencil from his mouth, handed an uncompleted order to a resentful clerk, and put on his jacket. Hawkes explained my presence.

Winkler made no response. He just shrugged his shoulders and led us rapidly through bin forest to a little partition at the far end of the floor. A porter, busily unpacking crates of band music just arrived from England, interrupted his handiwork, dusted off a saggy little desk, tried to open its drawers, failed, gave up, and went in search of a chair. The immaculate Hawkes carefully groped his way back through packages and bins, entered the front elevator, keeping himself haughtily aloof from the steam-pressers who fell into embarrassed silence in his presence, and departed for Pier 87. I was alone with the scores of Prelude to *Irmelin* by Delius, *Cotillon* by Arthur Benjamin, and *Pomp and Circumstance* Nos. 2, 3, 4, and 5. *Pomp and Circumstance* No. 1 was not under my jurisdiction. As *Land of Hope and Glory* it occupied bins 57 to 61 in eighteen different arrangements. Of Nos. 2 to 5 there were one score each and a set of parts, all thickly covered with dust. They had never been used. They were for me.

I wrote my first letter to Hope Cunningham, administrator of the WPA orchestra in Chicago. It was not a success. I had addressed her—how should I know? There was no Hope in Europe—as Dear Mr. Cunningham. She resented it very much and Prelude to *Irmelin* was never performed in Chicago. Then a letter arrived from London.

Ralph Hawkes wrote that he had made an exclusive publishing contract with an American composer who had a work performed in London. The composer was soon to return to

America and I was to present myself to him upon his return. The score of the new work was presently to be published in London. I would receive a liberal supply of copies to promote it. The work was *El Salón Mexico;* the composer Aaron Copland.

Before I could offer the respects I had been instructed to pay at the Hotel Empire on Sixty-third Street, where Copland lived, a tall, gangling, bespectacled, broadly smiling man arrived on Twenty-third Street and asked for me. I offered him my chair, but Copland preferred to park himself legèrely on a corner of my little desk. He had brought with him a package: it contained an ink copy of *Music for the Theatre*, one of his early works, which had had its *première* performance in 1925 under Serge Koussevitzky. This was an arrangement of the work for two pianos. A German title, *Tragödie im Süden*, was written across the English original and a ballet scenario, in German, was penciled over the music. Slowly it all came back to me. It was my own scenario! I had met Aaron Copland many years earlier at a music festival in Germany whither I had gone—sans Hertzka—to represent Universal. I had told him that I'd like to try to get his score performed in Germany and suggested, it might be easier to launch it as a ballet. He had eagerly agreed.

Nothing came of it. *Tragedy in the South* was never performed and the score later had found its way back to the composer. I had almost forgotten the incident, but Copland had not. A bridge suddenly opened up to the past and, perhaps, to the future. The dust on Elgar's *Cockaigne* Overture had lost some of its hopeless gloom.

I was back in my world.

• • •

As LUCK would have it, *El Salón Mexico*, the first work by Aaron Copland to be published under the new contract with Hawkes, was to be Copland's first popular breakthrough. An esoteric, experimental American composer whose music had appealed mainly to the League of Composers crowd and to a few determined specialists such as Koussevitzky and Stokowski had written a piece of music that had the public appeal of the *Grand Canyon Suite* but the quality, design and sophistication of a first-rate composition by a composer of recognized stature. In 1925, when Walter Damrosch had performed Copland's Organ Symphony, he had publicly declared that anyone writing anything like this was sure to commit murder within five years. Instead, thirteen years later, Copland wrote a work that conductors could program without blushing in embarrassment or trembling with fear. The public ate it up and highbrows were bravely hiding their disappointment, hoping that one day the prodigal son would return to the anemic, the brainy, the unpopular.

What a break! *El Salón Mexico*, an American *Bolero* with its hypnotizing rhythm and melodic sophistication, suddenly moved my dusty cubbyhole right into the center of American music making. Beautifully engraved large scores arrived from London and went out to a mailing list of potential performers which I had improvised: there was no color reserved in Nibelheim for symphony orchestras, conductors, or similar nonsense. I culled the names from the huge booking issue of *Musical America*, enjoying myself hugely on this exciting trip, this first discovery of musical America. I wrote to Washington for a list of WPA orchestras. I revived connections with conductors I had known in Europe and whom I rediscovered in encouraging numbers here in my new life in America.

Soon the work was played all over the land. I typed labels to send out the music, I counted and checked the parts from Piccolo to Double Bass and made sure that if they ordered 8, 7, 6, 5, 4 they got eight first violins, seven seconds, six violas, five celli, and four basses. I found out which orchestra manager wrote irate letters when the rental fee for the material was too high and which one didn't care, and adjusted my policy accordingly. I typed invoices with relish, I unpacked the music when it came back from one orchestra, counted to make sure that they had returned 8, 7, 6, 5, 4, and all seven percussion parts and sent it off again on its way to another performance, another invoice, another postcard to the composer "We are pleased to tell you that," another victory bulletin to headquarters in London. My silent telephone sprang to life as recording companies joined the general acceptance. I learned and learned and learned. When Bernard Herrmann played the piece over a national hook-up on CBS which produced an ASCAP revenue paying for my salary for several months, even Max Winkler lost the worried look he had unfalteringly reserved for me and asked me to lunch. "Order anything you want," he said, and I knew that I had arrived. I remained prudent in victory, however. I ordered lettuce-and-tomato-on-rye and he seemed gratefully relieved. We remained friends forever.

Over coffee and apple pie (he insisted on *à la mode* for the occasion) he even suggested we publish a piano arrangement of the Copland score, but for God's sake tell him to make it easy, you guys are living in the clouds. I reported to Copland verbatim. Copland, always practical and cooperative, was delighted. He suggested a young musician who had recently come to town and who, so he said, should be able to make a piano version of *El Salón Mexico* that would please both, Winkler and Copland, a combination that seemed almost impossible to achieve.The young man was also badly in need of money and would therefore do the job for a really miserable fee. This, of course, clinched the deal. We asked Copland to go ahead and order it and after a few days a young Adonis delivered the arrangement, played it brilliantly and convincingly on what was alleged to be a piano in Winkler's office and left, happily, with his little check. His name is still on the piano version of *El Salón Mexico*. The young man was Leonard Bernstein.

Against the background of all these exhilarating events it seemed utterly incomprehensible to me that Aaron Copland, who was thirty-eight years old when all this happened—it was easy for me to know: he was yet another member of our little vintage-1900 group—was in a position to sign a long-term, exclusive publication contract during a visit to London. A Krenek, a Weill, a Milhaud, a Hindemith—just about any composer I had known in Europe had been signed up by a publisher practically in their teens. Here was a well-known, if not already famous American composer, several times a Guggenheim fellow, a founder-member of the League of Composers, a respected man of letters, winner of a Victor Talking Machine competition, a man rapidly approaching retirement age who had not and never had had a publisher in America. And as I looked around, it was easy to see that he wasn't the only one. His case was the rule, not the exception. I was puzzled.

We talked about all this and why it had been and had to be like this many years later. By then, Copland had become so successful, famous, and rich that he had attained the great status symbols of American accomplishments: an unlisted telephone number and no name on the mailbox—just watch for the driveway after a big yellow sign on the road that says Hidden Driveway, and turn in. At the end of the long, winding driveway was a sprawling, beautifully proportioned house with a large studio filled with books, records, paintings, an enormous picture window overlooking acres of woods and meadows, trees, shrubs, and flowers, all part of the estate. Refreshments were served by a Belgian couple and everything, the Belgians, the library, the paintings, the Steinways, the Highest Fi, the Mercedes-Benz, the view of the Hudson and the mountains—all had the mark of a very well-off country squire and reflected the affluence that had come, during these thirty years, within the reach of a serious composer in America. But he had not forgotten how it had been. Standing before a wall-to-wall shelf housing the publications and recordings of his own works, he still reflected in voice and manner the joy he had felt when, back in Frankfurt in 1927, I had expressed interest in his *Music for the Theatre* and had taken the score back to Vienna with me. "I was simply overwhelmed by the thought that a publisher, any publisher, would pay any attention to me," he said. The Belgians silently refilled the glasses and retired to their caretaker's villa and we sat there, watching a cardinal splashing in a bird bath fitted elegantly in the landscape, and talked about the struggles of the past and the achievements of the present.

• • •

AFTER COPLAND had returned to New York in 1924 from three years of studying in Paris, he rented a studio on West Seventy-fourth Street and sent out little cards soliciting pupils —he outlined the shape and the littleness of the cards plastically and convincingly with his large hands—but there was not a single reply. Around that time, however, Walter Damrosch made his frightening prediction, which made good newspaper copy, and Koussevitzky performed a work of Copland's. "I got a little publicity, a little attention." But he needed more. "These were the mid-twenties. Money was freely available. I was looking around for someone to help me." He didn't look in vain: Mrs. Alma Wertheim provided a yearly retainer of a thousand dollars toward the composer's sustenance. It was soon supplemented by a Guggenheim, Copland getting into the very first pilot project launched by the Guggenheim foundation. "They had to find fifteen guys," he explained. "Thomas Whitney Surette, a successful and influential music educator from Concord, Massachusetts, was the music adviser for the Guggenheim committee. He knew Nadia Boulanger, and she suggested me, and so I was the only musician among fourteen writers, painters, sculptors, and scholars." The prize was twenty-five hundred dollars. He could live, he had performances, he lectured, he organized concerts, he slowly approached his status as Dean of American composers—but he still had no publisher.

It was suggested to Mrs. Wertheim that an additional step was imperative. Subsidies, performances, praise in magazines and newspapers, prizes and publicity were of little avail if the music was not available. The commercial publishers were not interested. It was easy for their colleagues in Europe, whose outlets were state-subsidized opera houses dotting the map, symphony orchestras that did not have to worry about a deficit, radio orchestras that flourished under the noncommercial European system and that had become a wonderfully rewarding market for the publishers, as they paid the same fees for a midnight performance of a modern symphony as they did for a prime-time performance of variations on "*Ach du lieber Augustin.*" Nothing of this existed in America. What existed was the depression. The music publishers of the establishment just didn't want to get involved in organ symphonies, esoteric piano concertos, or a piano trio called *Vitebsk*.

It had not always been like that. An earlier generation of American composers had been widely and expensively published in America—G. W. Chadwick, Horatio Parker, Edward MacDowell, Henry Hadley, Charles Martin Loeffler, and others were all born within less than twenty years of each other—between 1854 and 1871. It had been a generation of academicians writing in a post-romantic European tradition, and even if they gave their music American names, *New England Sketches*, or *Indian Fantasy*, the music wasn't any more American in sound and spirit than the "New World" Symphony. They were respected members of the establishment, they had social status, they had studied in Frankfurt, Stuttgart, Leipzig, Vienna, or Berlin and remained strangely rooted there. MacDowell, of course, had become a classic, and when *To a Wild Rose* fell into public domain it bloomed in every American catalogue, tamed, domesticated, deprived of whatever wild glory it once had. *The White Peacock* by Charles Griffes still displays its impressionistic tail. But most of the rest is forgotten. Henry Hadley had met with the most frightful fate any composer can possibly meet: a society for the performance and perpetuation of his works had been founded, equal to a public declaration that nobody else ever performed his music. Scores and scores of faded little publication cards marked with a mournful "Discontinued" is all that survives in the files of American publishers of most of the overtures and symphonies, the songs and sonatas, the oratorios and operas and tone poems that had once been so expensively engraved and so beautifully printed on paper so heavy and rich that it savagely if unsuccessfully fought destruction. But they all once had their place in the sun, they all had been published.

For the new generation, there was no place to go. So Mrs. Wertheim was prevailed upon to start a private and very much nonprofit music press specializing in the new American music. She owned a place in Cos Cob, a little settlement in Connecticut, and the new enterprise was named, as mysteriously as appealingly, Cos Cob Press. Cos Cob published most of Copland's existing output, his Piano Concerto, the Organ Symphony, *Music for the Theatre*, the trio *Vitebsk*, and other works, and it published scores by an impressive number of composers who later became famous and recognized, and by amazingly few who did not. Emerson Whithorne, perhaps, did not fulfill every hope. But a catalogue which, within the few short years of its operation, published Walter Piston, Roy Harris, Louis Gruenberg (including his opera *The Emperor Jones*), Randall Thompson, and Roger Sessions in addition to Copland speaks brilliantly for the taste and judgment of Mrs. Wertheim's musical advisers, a committee headed, of course, by Aaron Copland.

The music was prepared for publication and administered by Mr. Edwin Kalmus, a Viennese nephew of Hertzka and brother of the young man who, so obligingly, had made room for me by calling it quits just when I had asked Hertzka for a job. Kalmus had come here as a very young man to become the uncontested reprint king of America. Tirelessly he searched the copyright records in Washington for a flaw here, an expiration date there, coming up, again and again, with wonderful public-domain discoveries which he added to his catalogue to the dismay of their rudely awakened owners who did not know the peculiarities of the American copyright law. Kalmus, at that time, had his reprintery and a little music store from which to sell the fruits of his learned labors on Fifty-seventh Street, and he began, from there, to administer the Cos Cob publications. The music was engraved in his native (and, oh, so much cheaper) Vienna and printed and stored in the basement of his store. When asked, later, what interest there was in America in the music Cos Cob brought out, Kalmus answered unhesitatingly: "None whatever." The scores, he then explained, came usually back unopened from conductors and performers and as for sales—Kalmus just shrugged his shoulders in long pent-up disgust. Charles Ives's *Concord*

Sonata, he added with an unsuccessful attempt of a smile, turned out to be our best seller. It sold three hundred copies.

Unfortunately, this happy situation came to a sad and sudden end when Mrs. Wertheim divorced her husband, who had maintained an attitude of friendly neutrality toward her investments in contemporary American music, and married a man who took a position of unbending belligerency toward such foolishness.

Aaron Copland participated in all these ups and downs with enormous zest. By the time Mrs. Wertheim sacrificed Cos Cob Press on the altar of love, he had become, in addition to all his other accomplishments, honors, assignments, and headaches, the moving and leading spirit of a group of composers—many years later Lehman Engel still called Copland "the father of us all." They organized concerts, exchanged views and scores and discussed in endless sessions the fate of unpublished American music. Marc Blitzstein was one of the group, as were Lehman Engel (who really didn't care much—he wrote well-paid theater music and put his symphonies unresentfully on the shelf) and Virgil Thomson, just returned from a long stay in Paris. After very lengthy discussions (Thomson was always convinced that the evil world would take advantage of them and added endless protective clauses to the proposed contract, more to the amusement than the grateful approval of his friends), they decided to form a cooperative publishing venture and to take up where things had been before Mrs. Wertheim's fatal decision.

Every one of the group knew someone who would advance a little money to get the venture started. Laws and bylaws were drafted and a music-minded lawyer volunteered many hours of his working time to satisfy the suspicious Thomson. The basic idea was, to recover expenses and then to pay ninety per cent of all income to the composer! It was well intended but, as Lehman Engel evaluated it later "perhaps a little short-sighted. It meant that the press never had any money." The only silver lining was a declaration by Charles Ives, who, when approached by Engel, enthusiastically offered any of his works they'd care to publish and declared himself willing not only to pay the expense for their publication but also to assign any income earned by them to the press so that other composers may be published at his expense. The sales of Ives, alas, had not much improved since the gloomy days of Cos Cob's *Concord* Sonata, and so the gesture, deeply appreciated and gratifying as it was, gave more moral than material succor to the group.

This was the background against which the famous Arrow Press entered life. Soon it published—a committee of four composers made the selections—the most representative works of many serious composers of the thirties. The winged, silvery name seemed always to indicate to me the swift flight of something elegant and fanciful, new music soaring aloft, piercing the heart of its enemies. It grieved me when Lehman Engel told me—in a garden restaurant on Fifty-fourth Street shortly past noon—that the group, having been unable to agree on a name, assembled in an automat on Twenty-third Street (because it was near the hotel where Virgil Thomson lived and lives) and spotted, through the window, a little place called Arrow Lunchroom. "It doesn't mean a thing," somebody said. "Let's call it Arrow Press."

Again, as in the days of Cos Cob, they used their own judgment on what to publish. Kalmus took care of whatever business there was and added the abandoned Cos Cob publications to the Arrow list.

It is a very impressive catalogue, more, perhaps, today when we know what happened to the music and the composers they published under such awkward and difficult circumstances than it was in those days when nobody knew where all this was heading for. Within a short time the position of the serious composer in America was to change radically. Performing-right societies such as ASCAP and BMI made new, liberal assessments of the value of serious music. Their basic philosophy "A song is a song," which used to apply equally to "Yes We Have No Bananas" and a violin concerto, has been heavily changed in favor of the latter. Music departments in hundreds of universities specialize in contemporary music and many of them have composers in residence. Commissions had become the rule, not the exception. The Koussevitzky Foundation alone commissioned close to a hundred new American scores and helped in their publication and recording. A provincial orchestra, such as the one in Louisville, obtained huge amounts to commission, perform, and record contemporary music. Larger orchestras got into the habit of celebrating anniversaries by commissioning and performing new American scores.

For the young there was the Prix de Rome and the Prix de Fromm. For the more advanced, Ford and Rockefeller money was waiting in the wings. For the arrived there was Pulitzer and the National Academy of Arts and Letters. Radio and TV deflected some of their largess in the direction of new music. The chronicle of long-playing records was heavily interlaced with the type of music that had been gathering dust in the Kalmus basement, and contemporary composers were chosen to be musical ambassadors, heads of conservatories, and presidents of music centers. There was a definite trend toward unmarked mailboxes and cardinals with private baths.

Copland's new association with Hawkes, his entry into the catalogue of a "commercial" publisher signified the end of a period. One by one, others joined him. Within a few years, an entirely new, different composer-publisher relationship, based on the new realities under which serious music began to expand, developed in America.

Again, as once before in the heroic days of yore, I was permitted to participate.

XIV

RALPH HAWKES WAS made for our profession.

He had limitless drive, unsuppressible ambition, reckless courage, enormous luck, a sure sense of timing, and the all-important trait that cannot be learned, acquired, or bought: an instinctive reaction to the slightest jerk of the inborn divining rod, the only reliable guide in the arid desert of music publishing, where so many, equipped with compass, maps, and a doctorate in music from the University of Oregon lose their way and are never again heard of. He also had the most important prerequisite of a music publisher: he was not a musician. He was not led astray by personal taste, misguided by prejudice, cockily opinionated, burdened by tradition, blinded by jealousy, allergic to open fifths, fatally influenced in his judgment by an oboe passage on page 57 that doesn't really *lie* for the oboe, so let's turn the piece down, and it turns out to be *Sacre du printemps.* He had never heard of parallel octaves nor did he know what Josquin des Prés had done for this world, if indeed he had ever heard of him or it or her.

He was a born music publisher.

It was therefore inevitable and only a question of a short time before my cubbyhole on twenty-third Street would become a Department and before trader Max and dreamer Ralph would have to go their separate ways. *El Salón Mexico* had been bad enough. But when the first score by Hawkes's latest acquisition, Benjamin Britten, arrived from England it wasn't only for string orchestra and high voice, who is going to buy *that?* It was also called *Les Illuminations,* what the hell does it mean, do you people want me to send a dictionary with every copy, I told you guys you are living in the clouds, what do you think this is, Paris, France?

So, soon Ralph Hawkes crossed the submarine-infested Atlantic with the stiffest of all upper lips, hired a binless office next to a French restaurant on upper Fifth Avenue, and returned on a plane that left him stranded for three weeks in Lisbon where, speaking several languages, he had a great time mixing with the international spy set and recovering all his expenses plus some extra at the gaming tables of Estoril before finding precarious transportation back home to London.

Soon he cabled momentous news: he had acquired the copyrights in most of the operas by Richard Strauss. The original German publisher, a London refugee in need of money, had approached Hawkes to find out whether he would like to buy his catalogue. I could easily imagine, even at a distance of three thousand miles, what must have gone on in the mind of the state trumpeter's grandson when, suddenly, he was within reach of being the publisher of *Der Rosenkavalier*, *Elektra*, and *Salome*. And Richard Strauss, although currently an enemy alien, was still alive. His works would be under international copyright protection for fifty years after the composer's death, which meant, as it turned out a little later, comfortably into the next millennium. It was not only a glittering, irresistible treasure, it was also the supreme mark of nobility within the music publishing fraternity. Hawkes, I knew, would have given his right arm for it.

The London firm, in addition to its publishing division, had a large plant in which they manufactured instruments. It had grown and flourished, equipping the bands of the farflung empire, among them the unfathomable multitudes of beautifully uniformed (Hawkes also manufactured the uniforms) musicians employed by every maharajah in India. Now, during the war, the plant had been converted from making clarinets, basset horns, and bandoleers to the manufacturing of elevators that lifted bombs unto planes. It was a very profitable business. And so the elevators that lifted the bombs on the planes that dropped them on the German opera houses so that they couldn't perform any operas by Richard Strauss any more, paid for their acquisition by the enemy. It was an elegant twist of fate, appreciated on both sides of the Atlantic.

The Strauss deal had not been the first time that Hawkes had profited from Hitler's follies. In 1938, after Austria had been occupied by the latter, the former went to Vienna, where the new bosses of Universal—the previous crop was walking Fifth Avenue, Regent Street, or the Champs-Elysées in search of a job—were glad to sell him such embarrassing properties as Gustav Mahler's symphonies and other works by composers who, otherwise, would have had to be burned publicly. There was also one composer who wanted no part of the new order, although he would have been acceptable, had he chosen to remain. Instead, he made a long-term contract with Boosey & Hawkes to have his works published in England and America. He left Europe under the most harassing circumstances and arrived, with his wife, almost penniless in New York.

• • •

I HAD MET Béla Bartók many years before in Vienna. He frequently came to visit us on his way to or from Budapest, and every time his short, businesslike calls were very special occurrences in the routine of Universal. He was already an important composer, famous in a restricted, not easily defined way, but not at all successful if success is measured by the usual yardstick of public acclaim, large printings, performances, and money. Yet, these visits—never improvised, always announced in a formal note which stated not only the day but the exact hour of his appearance, arrangements he would keep unfailingly—caused nervous apprehension and uneasiness. The deep respect, extended to him by everybody from the shriveled old lady at the door to Hertzka himself, for whom, after all, visits by celebrities were daily after-breakfast exercises, was a special brand, of an intensity and seriousness rarely rendered any other of the many famous composers who walked through our doors. Even the great Arnold Schoenberg, so terrible in his wrath, so offensively biting in his criticism, so easily hurt by a wrong word, a wrong gesture, a seeming lack of submission, could sometimes quite easily be pacified by a well-placed joke or induced to tell one himself, and if he could get in a pun, he came right down from his pedestal, grinning, pleased with himself and becoming almost human. Bartók lived in an unsmiling, hushed world where there was little room for our human frailties and no pardon for our sins.

When he arrived with his young wife in America in the winter of 1940 on what was to be his last and final trip, our connection became much closer. He had already completed his by now celebrated collection of piano pieces, *Mikrokosmos*, for his new British publisher, while living in Europe. Some of his most important works, among them the Concerto for Orchestra, were written or prepared for publication during his American period, most of them during the war. What a job it was. Ships were torpedoed, the London plant of Boosey & Hawkes was blitzed, mail, manuscripts, and proofs were agonizingly slow in transit, but if there was the slightest deviation from his very personal and carefully thought-out notation—a bar number placed above a bar line instead of in the middle of a measure, a "dead line," as he called one bearing only rests, or, his pet obsession, a possible inconsistency in punctuation, abbreviation, or musical notation—a third, a fourth, a fifth proof had to be sent across. The war was not permitted to interfere with the proper appearance of a semiquaver. It was very, very trying, once in a while, to work for a man with such sidereal principles.

The intense and complicated administration of his musical output kept us in almost daily communication. I visited Bartók often during the summer in Vermont and in a primitive little summerhouse in Saranac Lake, where he had gone for health reasons. There, again and again, our conversations were interrupted by the composer putting his finger to his lips so that we might not disturb the chipmunks, which he loved and which seemed to love him as he deserved to be loved.

Our contacts were intensified by the fact that Boosey & Hawkes, in order to assist Bartók and his wife, the pianist Ditta Pásztory, in their attempts to get engagements, had started a little concert bureau of their own. Thus I worked for him in a double capacity, as publisher and as manager, almost to the last day of his life.

In his own time, and even more today, after the radiation of his work has extended beyond anything he himself had ever experienced, Béla Bartók has been referred to as "the great Hungarian composer." He was Hungarian, of course, in the technical sense of the word, and he loved his country. His music had its roots deep in his native soil. Before he died he was visibly moved by his nomination to the new Hungarian Parliament shortly after the country had been liberated from German occupation.

Yet one could never think of him as a Hungarian or, for that matter, as belonging to any nation, group, or race. He was a human being, pure, strict, of an almost abstract, sidereal quality, governed only by the laws of decency, integrity, and faith, which he applied uncompromisingly to his own conduct and whose breach by others he never forgave.

His angelic righteousness made him unfit for a world where everything had become a give-and-take, where every hand washed every other hand, and where there was an angle to everything. He neither knew of nor tolerated angles. In his music as well as in his life the very thought that he would ever compromise, accommodate himself to the demands of the day, to practical considerations, to any detour from what he felt to be right, was unthinkable. He would never take the easy way, always the hard one.

He had penetrating, clear, oh so serious eyes, demanding, quiet, uncompromising, a beautiful, wise face, calm, stern, seldom ruffled by a short rapidly subsiding wave of bitter, puckish laughter.

He was shy, very quiet-spoken, constantly on the alert, suspicious of everyone and everything. Never did I hear him raise his voice. When others would shout, he would clam up, retire silently, his face even more drawn, into an icy sphere of disapproval that was much more difficult to take and to dispel again than any temperamental outburst would have been. He was small, almost tiny, terribly frail. His thin body, the sharply pointed nose, the noble forehead with the soft, silken hair, the transparent, childlike hands, the slow, swinging walk (as if he walked on clouds)—his was the appearance of an ascetic, a thinker, a brooder, a ponderer, never at ease, relentlessly driven by an inner flame that eventually consumed him in the literal sense of the word.

The first impression that struck me when I saw him again here in America was how little he had changed. His hair had become white, but his face, his eyes, his body seemed never to change in all the years I knew him. He seemed quite ageless—he had never looked really young, and even through the years of his sickness he changed little outwardly.

He had come to America as a refugee under the most trying, difficult, and forbidding circumstances. Again, in taking upon himself a fate that he shared with thousands, he was quite alone. If ever anyone chose freedom for no other reason than because he could not live without it, it was Béla Bartók.

Neither he nor his wife was Jewish, and no racial uneasiness prompted him to choose emigration as a way to safety. Nor did any political associations make it advisable to leave. A single *Heil!* would have been sufficient to make him safe and comfortable. He had a secure income as a professor at the Conservatory of Music in Budapest, a house, a pension for his latter days, his books, his garden, his vast collection of folk music from many countries—Hungary, Romania, North Africa, Turkey—which he had noted down and recorded in decades of scientific work. He had his own language, his lifelong friends, the beloved surroundings of home. Nothing compelled him to leave it all and to seek the precarious shelter of a foreign shore: nothing but his unbending heart, his complete and absolute inability to compromise, to make peace—even with lip service—with the forces of evil. Compromise was unthinkable. It would have destroyed his very soul.

In leaving, he risked much more than many a famous man would have risked who stayed on, took the devil's blood money, and counted—quite correctly—on the forgetfulness and forgiveness of the world. Bartók's was not a glamorous name sure to be accepted by the Western world and to be safely installed in a new existence of honor and wealth. When he set out with his wife and his son on the perilous journey—weeks of traveling through Europe, their baggage lost somewhere in Spain, barely reaching Lisbon for the freighter that brought them across—he faced an uncertain future: poverty, a violent climate, disruption of his scientific work, a city whose noises and nervous vibrations pounded day and night at his emaciated body and supersensitive mind. He also was to face an artistic hierarchy too busy with the advancement of its own glory to pay much attention to the quiet, small man who could be hurt by one unguarded word and repudiated forever with the shrug of a shoulder.

But there was never, in the years of his exile, either doubt or regret. His determination, as always, was absolute. After he had put the ocean between himself and the enemies of everything he had been living for, he even refused to speak or to write German. He spoke, instead, a very selective, highly cultivated English, slightly stilted, choosing his words slowly, striving perceptibly always to find the right expression. His speech retained a quite undefinable foreign flavor. It was highly civilized, rich, and often amazing in its variety of vocabulary and the elegance of its grammar. Even when we were alone and the conversation might have been easier and much less of a strain on both of us if conducted in German, he would never use the language of the enemy.

His letters, too, after he came to America, were always written in English, composed by the hand of a master and just as dense in their texture as they had been in the old days. Only once in a while he would question with a (?) his own proper use of a word or a phrase, sensing infallibly the slightest error or foreignism in a language he had spoken for only a short time.

Bartók's letters were always written by hand, in a small, clear script that looked as if every word had been put down slowly and deliberately. Every thought, it seemed, had been completed in his mind before it was put on paper, just as if the words were musical notes, the result of an intense process of formulation. There were no unnecessary phrases in these letters, and wherever possible, he used postcards, filling them to the edge. Little time or space was ever wasted on courtesies, on how-do-you-dos, on anything personal that had no connection with the subject of his message. When, after his death, we went through his letters to help provide "human interest" material for a man who wanted to write Bartók's biography, we found almost nothing that would shed light on his character or his life.

The letters covered the paper from top to bottom. Even the margin was usually used for a postscript or two. If the letter did not fill the page, he would tear off what wasn't used, mailing only a closely covered scrap of paper. His room was always overflowing with little paper strips and torn-off pieces of printed matter, every one of them covered with notes, figures, symbols, and a special musical shorthand understandable only to him. All these notes, clippings, letters, books, and pieces of manuscript paper and music, were scattered throughout the room, overflowing from the piano to the floor, covering chairs and tables—an appalling accumulation. Seeming aimlessly scattered throughout the room, they were in reality exciting witness to a mind that never rested and was occupied simultaneously with many problems and ideas. Every one of them was always present and ready to be consulted whenever he might need them.

• • •

NEW YORK was the powerful, unconquerable enemy. Traffic frightened him deeply. He would never walk against a light, and even when he crossed with a green light he was tense and disturbed, hurrying across the street in short, hasty steps, like an animal that has left its protecting woods, and which faces, wide-eyed, the roaring uncertainties of the metropolis. The climate, New York heat and New York cold alike, was a constant source of preoccupation. Noise, and particularly any emanation of music penetrating his privacy, caused him physical suffering. The vicinity of a radio meant painful disruption of his creative work.

Sometimes he seemed to delight, in a strange and almost self-destructive way, in the difficulties and setbacks he experienced; he used to relate them in great detail, an ironical "I told you so" in his voice. At the same time, he would discard any good news we had for him with a deep-rooted disbelief that his fortunes would ever take a decisive and permanent turn for the better. The difficulties of finding an apartment where he and his wife would be allowed to practice were at first insurmountable. When, finally, friends located a place in Forest Hills in which practicing pianists were not regarded as breachers of the peace, he only shrugged his shoulders—there would be other difficulties, he asserted. And he was right. After the Bartóks had moved in and the two pianos had been delivered by an obliging manufacturer, it was discovered that they could not be placed in one room. Triumphantly Bartók reported that they had to practice in two different rooms, separated by a corridor, unable to see each other, with coordination established only by ear.

During the first year or two after his arrival, Bartók appeared as soloist with a few symphony orchestras, but dates were few and scattered. The joint recitals he gave with his wife were not very successful. The programs he chose reflected, again, his uncompromising mind. Not many organizations were prepared to forego the commercial appeal of other two-piano teams for the unbending austerity of the Bartóks. The fact that they never performed from memory proved an added handicap. Their appearance on the stage in the company of two page-turners seemed old-fashioned and was easily misinterpreted as a lack of preparation or courtesy by audiences that were accustomed to flashier displays of virtuosity.

And Béla Bartók's bows were certainly a concert manager's nightmare; stern, professorial, unsmiling to the extent of chilliness—of a great, very moving dignity, but bare of everything the public had been trained to expect from a performer. Nothing, of course, that anyone would dare to suggest to him would change his attitude toward his programs and their presentation, and his hopes to earn a livelihood on the concert stage were sadly disappointed. Later, as his illness progressed, even the few concert appearances and lecture recitals we had been able to book for him had to be canceled.

Life was grim. Offers to accept a position as a teacher of composition—they had come from several educational institutions—he turned down unwaveringly. He was determined not to teach composition, the one thing everybody wanted him to teach. He seemed to feel he had nothing to teach, nothing to give to others in the one field where he was great, an undisputed master! He was willing to teach piano, but only a few private pupils studied with him for short periods. He accepted, though, a few scientific assignments. One of them, offered by Columbia University, kept him busy for two years, and provided him with a slim academic salary.

He had, during that time, a little studio in one of the brownstone houses owned by the university on 117th Street. There he spent several hours each day, transcribing on paper a great number of recordings which had been made in various European countries: folk songs, dances, and melodies, played and sung by the shepherds and peasants of eastern and southeastern Europe, all very difficult in rhythm and intonation, decipherable only by a highly trained and incredibly patient mind and a sensitive ear. These notations, a unique mixture of scholarly exactness and creative genius, were just as close to his heart as his own music. With infinite, tireless care he listened to hundreds of recordings, wrote down the tunes in all their inflections and variations, using his own method of musical notation to put them faithfully on paper. Detailed footnotes and carefully worded explanations, minute in every detail, accompanied most of them.

And this was the same spirit that dreamed up the powerful pages of his own music, freely soaring through fantastic space, trying the impossible, speaking with Prometheus' fiery tongues—only to return again to the painstakingly accurate realm of science.

• • •

THE COLUMBIA ASSIGNMENT, limited as it was in scope, had been a great help. It had provided the composer with a minimum of security; and regularity of income was, to Bartók's methodical mind, the only possible way to make a livelihood. Many of the composers it has been my good fortune to be associated with conducted their lives under the assumption that everybody—publishers, agents, opera directors, symphony orchestras, juke boxes, and heirs—would make mountains of money from their works as soon as they died. They decided—not, it appears, without some justification—that they might as well cash in on all this while they themselves were still around. They saw no reason to balance their books. They felt fully justified in borrowing on posthumous glory.

To Bartók, such imaginary bookkeeping was unthinkable, though he, more then any other contemporary composer, would have been lavishly entitled to it. Twenty years after his death, the Concerto for Orchestra, whose *première* he had only survived by a few months, was available in fourteen different recordings. The Schwann catalogue listed 173 different recordings of some fifty different Bartók works. When I asked an ASCAP official what Bartók's earnings now, after twenty years of posthumous fame, might be, he smiled cryptically but not at all correctively when I estimated a figure in six dollar digits. But, while he was alive he drove everybody to despair in his unbreachable refusal to mortgage his or anybody else's future. His trip to the United States had been paid for by wealthy admirers in Switzerland who considered such action a privilege and an honor. To their horror he returned the full amount, as soon as he had made a little money in America. His young son had joined the American Navy soon after the family's arrival in this country. He was glad to know that his pay was regularly sent to the father; the boy didn't need it and was happy to help. But when he came home the father handed him a bankbook. There he found every penny he had been paid throughout the war years. "It wasn't mine," the father told him. "It's yours."

We ourselves had received instructions from the London head office to do everything to assist him and to advance him any money he might need. But when we had at last persuaded him to accept an advance on his royalties, he insisted that the full amount be deducted from whatever he had earned at the end of the year. Hawkes tried to fool him by sending a hunk of money to ASCAP, asking them to add it to Bartók's next check. He insisted upon getting a detailed account as to how the money had been earned, by what performances, when, where, and by whom! ASCAP stammered in well-intentioned embarrassment and the composer returned the money. Bartók's views about finances were never those of an artist. They were those of a puritan, and they were sometimes quite exasperating.

But something just had to be done. During a previous

visit to the United States he had made a few recordings of his piano works for one of the smaller companies in New York. The owner of the business, an American of Hungarian descent, was a great admirer of Bartók. He called us one day; he wanted to come up and see us. It was rather important, he said.

He knew that it was quite impossible to offer Bartók any money he didn't think he had earned. So he had devised a scheme whereby he would falsify the royalty statements he was about to send to the composer. Instead of accounting for the few hundred records he had actually sold, he would show a sale of 10,897—it had to be a very definite figure, not a hazy ten thousand. It seemed to sound more sincere. The royalty statement, as was usual, was to be sent to the composer through us, his publishers: even the slightest deviation would have aroused Bartók's suspicion. Our bookkeeper became part of the plot; entries were made to substantiate the crime, and statement and check went out to the composer.

When I saw Bartók a few days later, he asked me at once whether I had seen the statement. He was very pleased, happily excited. I felt miserable. Even if this was a conspiracy I would always be proud of, such deceit seemed almost criminal in his presence.

A few days later he called me on the phone. "I want you to take steps against Columbia Records," he said. In a sudden foreboding of what had happened, I felt my swivel chair turn into molasses.

He explained that he had just received another statement for gramophone records sold, this one from Columbia. They accounted for 349 copies.

"It's quite impossible," Bartók said, quietly but in stern determination. "Here is a little company selling 10,897 records, and at the same time a big outfit like Columbia accounts for a few hundred. I want you to investigate."

Somehow, with the help of the man who had pushed me into this web of benevolent fakery, I got out of it; but it took a lot of nervous explaining, and once in a while I was sure that Bartók suspected me of being in conspiracy not with the real culprit but with the accounting department of Columbia. At last the incident was pushed aside—I wouldn't say forgotten, for Bartók never forgot anything—as a more important event took the stage: the strange circumstances surrounding the creation of Bartók's last big work, the Concerto for Orchestra.

• • •

IN THE SPRING of 1943 the sickness that had gripped Bartók for some time had worsened noticeably. He was running a temperature regularly at certain hours of the day. He followed the symptoms with visible apprehension. He became weaker, more irritable, more difficult to approach. He had to cancel lectures and instructed us not to book him for recitals any more—he was sure he would be unable to appear in public again. He turned down a scientific assignment offered him, in spite of the fact that the university which made the offer explained that he was welcome to the honorarium and could begin work at any time, no matter how indefinite, in the future. But so deeply was he filled with his sense of responsibility that he was unwilling to accept as long as he was not absolutely sure that he would be able to deliver his part of the bargain. Sometimes it was very difficult to have to deal with so stubborn a display of angelic principles.

At last he could not stay any longer in the dingy apartment at Fifty-seventh Street and Eighth Avenue in which he had been living. He was brought to a hospital on the East River. For some time, ASCAP, the American Society of Composers, Authors and Publishers, had provided him, at their expense, with the best medical specialists. To their eternal honor—Bartók was not even in a technical sense a member, as he belonged to the British Performing Rights Society in London—they now made themselves responsible for the costs of the hospital as well.

Serious as his physical condition already was, it seemed to be aggravated by the growing feeling of solitude and bitterness which had taken hold of him. He saw himself as a neglected stranger, away from the main flow of musical activity in America. Once in a while he remembered with bitter nostalgia the days of his European past. The artists and conductors who played his music in America were, to a large extent, old acquaintances, many of them former Hungarians. Only a few of the great stars showed interest in his music, and when Yehudi Menuhin played his Violin Concerto, Bartók was so deeply moved by the unexpected attention of a great artist that he wrote a new sonata for Menuhin.

But now all this was forgotten as the composer was brooding, sick, poor, in the enforced inactivity of a hospital room. We had little to cheer him up. Small things did not matter. There were no big ones to report.

It was then, in the summer of 1943, that something happened in the room in Doctors Hospital in New York that strangely and mysteriously resembles an event in another sickroom 152 years earlier: the sudden appearance of the "mysterious stranger," who had come to commission the dying Mozart to write the Requiem. This time, in streamlined New York, the messenger was no mystery man. He was a well-clad, elegant gentleman of very aristocratic bearing. His name was Serge Koussevitzky.

The visit came as an unexpected surprise to the sick composer. Koussevitzky was one of the conductors who had never played any of Bartók's important scores. I don't think that the two men had ever met before. Koussevitzky most certainly was the last man Bartók, bitter, sick, thinking himself rejected by the public and the leading men of music in America, could imagine crossing his door.

The conductor was alone. He took a chair, moved it close to the bed, and began to explain his mission. He had come to offer Béla Bartók a commission from the Koussevitzky Foundation—a commission carrying a stipend of one thousand dollars and the assurance of a first performance by the Boston Symphony Orchestra. The composer was free to choose any form of music he cared to write. There was just one condition: the score was to be dedicated to the memory of Mrs. Natalie Koussevitzky, the conductor's wife, who had died a few years earlier and in whose memory the foundation had been established. It was to be a Requiem, after all!

Koussevitzky himself later told me the details of the conversation, and as he recalled it he seemed genuinely moved. Bartók, touched without doubt by the personal appearance of the conductor, who could have sent a letter or had the message delivered by one of his disciples, declined. He could not accept money for a work he might never be able to write.

The conductor had been prepared for just this situation. Before the foundation had decided to give the commission to Bartók, friends of the composer (Fritz Reiner and Joseph Szigeti among others) had approached Koussevitzky and the members of his board of trustees, urging that Bartók be chosen. They had stressed his precarious circumstances and the difficulty of helping the proud man with anything he might consider charity. It had to be a real commission, even if, because of Bartók's delicate health, nothing whatever came of it.

Koussevitzky explained to the reluctant composer that he was bound by the trustees' decision. A commission, once decided upon, could not be taken back. The money was given to him no matter whether he was willing or able to deliver the piece. These were the terms of the covenant. He had, in fact, under the rules of the foundation, already brought with him a check for five hundred dollars—which he was obliged to leave with Bartók, together with an official letter stating the terms of the commission.

Bartók made no reply. He suddenly began talking of other matters. He asked the conductor, almost urgently, to stay on. The two men had a long talk. Bartók did most of the talking, unburdening his troubled mind. He covered many subjects and became flushed with a new and very touching confidence in life. It was almost an hour later that the nurse came in and the conductor took his leave.

Undoubtedly the learned specialists who attended Béla Bartók in the sickness which two years later consumed what was left of him will have more logical explanations for the incredible recovery that set in almost immediately after Koussevitzky's visit. All we know is that soon they found him to be so much better that they released him from the hospital. He left New York for Asheville, North Carolina. He found a quiet room in the outskirts, where neither traffic lights nor radios interfered with the absolute concentration that he craved. At last he smelled fresh air again, saw the sky, felt the soil. The Hearst Building, the Fisk Building, the entrance to the Independent subway station, the newsstand, the assortment of sweat and dirt he had viewed from his window on Fifty-seventh Street were replaced by flowers and trees. And the constantly tormenting screams of auto horns and police sirens were drowned in memory by the concert of birds. Their cries and calls can be heard in the second movement of Bartók's Third Piano Concerto, which he sketched in Asheville and completed, with the exception of seventeen bars, in a grim race with death in the summer of 1945. He had returned to the sources of nature. In the last pages he ever wrote, the Hungarian, the European, the great citizen of the world set a small, lovely monument to the birds of North Carolina. . . .

He was happy again. "Don't send me special-delivery letters or telegrams," he wrote us a few days after he had arrived in Asheville. "I get all my mail only once a day. Everything is delivered at the same time—mail, papers, special deliveries, wires. Here, time makes no difference." He had no piano. Once in a while his room was very cold. He went for walks, always alone. There was nobody to talk to, only one family where he occasionally took a meal and where he would practice the piano from time to time. He asked us to send them a selection of his music as a token of his gratitude.

His letters, deviating strangely from the austerity we had come to expect, sounded almost elated. He included short health bulletins, giving us a graph of his morning and night temperatures with slightly ironic but not at all pessimistic comments. Most important of all, he asked for music paper —lots of it. Then, suddenly, he wrote that he had completed a major part of a new work he was writing for Serge Koussevitzky. He was sending us the score to be copied. Soon a second and a final third batch arrived. It was the Concerto for Orchestra.

He did not return from Asheville in time to be present at its tumultuous *première* in Boston in December 1944. But he observed its immediate success, its acceptance as one of the great masterpieces of our generation. He knew that this time he had touched the hearts of his audiences, and he was present to hear it and take many of his gentle, very touching, terribly serious bows when the work was played in New York.

• • •

When I saw him a few months later, he rested at last. The little funeral parlor on Lexington Avenue in Manhattan was filled with a hushed, deeply stirred crowd. There were no representatives of organizations, no honorary pallbearers, nobody who had come because he wanted to be sure that his name would be in the register. I don't believe that there was a register. No reporters were there, no pictures were taken as the mourners, stunned, filed out.

But there were many people who had not known him and who had suddenly felt that they must come to pay their respects. Suddenly, this very day, he had become great. As I took a last look before they closed the coffin, I felt again, more strongly than ever before, that this tiny face, so beautiful, so great in the peace of death, drawn even now by suffering and still reflecting an unending struggle, was not only the unforgettable face of a great musician. It was also the face of a great man, a shining example of bravery, faith, and an indomitable spirit that will live on long after the frame that carried them has been taken back, forever, by the dust.

SLOWLY, as the first half of the century began to pass, its musical giants were passing with it.

What a marvelously creative, spectacularly variegated epoch it had been. It had seen the emergence and the passing of Puccini, Ravel, Prokofiev, Hindemith, Villa-Lobos, Respighi, Manuel de Falla, Arthur Honegger, Béla Bartók, Karol Szymanowski, Kurt Weill. It had seen the full blossoming of Gustav Mahler, Richard Strauss, Jan Sibelius, Arnold Schoenberg, and Igor Stravinsky. It had witnessed the brief, brilliant career of George Gershwin and, for the first time, the arrival on the musical scene of a whole generation of significant American composers.

The first half of my century had also seen the advent of the most radical musical innovation since Western music had taken its first steps: the formulation, practical application and widespread acceptance of an entirely new principle of musical construction, the composition with twelve interrelated tones, as its creator, Arnold Schoenberg, had named it. Schoenberg himself had been the most famous of the revolutionary Viennese school, Alban Berg the most successful, Anton von Webern the most influential. Webern's entire oeuvre fills only four long-playing records and, during his lifetime, his recognition did not go beyond a small circle of admirers. But posthumously, his style deeply influenced the thinking and the technique of young composers everywhere, more than did the music and the style of his teacher, Arnold Schoenberg. It was a strange, rare musical phenomenon, a belated assertion of power surely never expected by the thin, tormented, ascetic introvert who fell victim, before the half century was over, to a shot fired by an American soldier as the composer stepped into the curfew to light a cigar.

Never in musical history had there been such a Babel of different musical languages, spoken at the same time. The epoch had produced *Madama Butterfly* and *Wozzeck*, separated by scarcely twenty years. Ravel's *Daphnis et Chloë* had been offered to an increasingly confused world during the same year that had heard the first performance of Schoenberg's *Pierrot lunaire*. John Cage was a contemporary of Gian Carlo Menotti, almost to the year of their birth. The epoch, now coming to its end, had prepared the ground for aleatory flights into psychedelic musical happenings, for the electronic fantasies and spectacular tone combinations of Karlheinz Stockhausen and Milton Babbitt, for the third-stream fusion of jazz, traditional sounds, strict twelve-tone technique and free improvisation by Gunther Schuller, for the brilliantly nervous, imaginative projections of past, present, and future sounds by Hans Werner Henze, for the searching, never satisfied restlessness of Pierre Boulez. Soon composers were questioning not only the principles of traditional music but also the adaptability of traditional concert halls, theaters, orchestras, and performers to their flight into new dimensions.

Many of the traditionalists among composers began to be tormented by doubts of their own musical *raison d'être*. Some—one of them the aged survivor among the earlier twentieth-century masters, Igor Stravinsky—began to adopt or to experiment with some of the new ideas and devices. A few remained defiantly aloof. Others began to falter, to brood, to retreat into inactivity or into busying themselves with extraneous chores, the re-dressing of old masterpieces or the re-formulation of some of their own earlier works, written before they were faced by the inescapable confrontation with the new post-Hiroshima world of musical expression. To many it became increasingly difficult to silence a growing uneasiness and to carry on as if nothing had happened. Their material seemed to disintegrate as they were groping, handicapped if not paralyzed, searching for a message, a meaning in a messageless, meaningless world.

They weren't ready or able, or perhaps were too set in their ways, to mirror the loneliness, the despair, and the rebellion of the times in words and music as John Lennon and Paul McCartney did in the sadly disturbing songs of *Sgt. Pepper's Lonely Hearts Club Band*, which swept the world and, strangely and confusingly, propelled a few despised crooners from Liverpool onto a level where serious composers—not, one supposes, without envy and, perhaps, rather onesidedly—proclaimed them colleagues and compared some of their songs with the best that Schubert had written. "Lucy in the Sky with Diamonds" taking the place of *Die Schöne Müllerin. We read the news today, Oh boy . . .* Are we to believe it? Where are we heading? Where are we to turn?

It was a difficult time of change, transition, disorientation, reorientation for the composer, a time of confusion and mounting frustration for the performer and for the listener. But what was the music publisher to do? Where was he to turn? What was to be his guideline in the midst of the spreading erosion of accepted values and time-honored standards?

It wasn't very long since an American publisher published fifty songs during a single year—not hit songs, but standard songs, lieder. Today, the same house publishes five —and if they really dared to face reality, they would not even publish these. For generations, these songs had been one of the mainsprings of the publishing profession. The great ballads—"Bless This House," "The Holy City," "On the Road to Mandalay," "By the Bend of the River," dozens, hundreds of them—and the great art songs, from Schubert's *Winterreise* to Barber's "Sure on This Shining Night," from Handel to Reynaldo Hahn, seemed to flourish forever. What has happened to the popular ballad and the great art song? Still there arrive in each morning mail feeble, pale reflections of what used to be true ballad sentimentality, true expression of love, true faith in God and, in the words of the Psalmist, true joy. But when we look at the manuscripts, hopefully and very much wanting to like at least a few of them, we have to close them again after looking at a bar or two and send them back to the well-meaning people from whom they have come. They, even they, in their little faraway RFD towns, unwittingly have been deadly infected by the erosion. Not even they can sing any more about the dreamy, beautiful moon, now that it is covered by antiseptic lunars and sterilized luniks. There comes no serenity, no tranquillity any more from the Sea of Serenity and the Sea of Tranquillity when they see its bleak cragginess on their TV screens. Who can write a ballad "In Praise of the 37-mile wide Sinus Medii?"

Could "*Feldeinsamkeit*" still inspire Brahms now that its solitude is punctured by transistor radios, penetrating every remaining *Einsamkeit* with the drumbeat of damnation and the guitar strums of desperate togetherness? Samuel Barber has probably written more successful art songs than any one else today. He has been silent as a writer of lieder for a long time. There is no music any more in a Shining Night, lighted by the fires of violence, pierced by rockets, darkened by fear and hopelessness. And when one of the fearless yet ventured into the forbidden garden, he called one of his most heartfelt songs "*Dorme Pegaso.*" Pegasus has gone to sleep.

Where is one to turn?

Everywhere Pegasus has gone to sleep, waiting to be awakened again. During the first half of the incredible century, the Viennese operetta all but governed the international world of lighter music. Has there ever been so complete an extinction with such lightning speed? From the turn of the century on there had scarcely been a year without a new world-success by Johann Strauss, Franz Lehár, Leo Fall, Emerich Kálmán, Oscar Straus, and a seemingly forever inexhaustible supply of minor, Danube-based masters bringing joy to the world and money to producers around the globe. There is no trace of them now. Suddenly everything they had sung about was gone, the countesses and the butlers, the hussars and the merry, merry widows, princes and waltz dreams, the land of smiles, populated by gentle, funny, pigtailed Chinamen who had never heard the sound of Mao.

Sometimes, after the war that had done away with everything they had lived by, we would see Franz Lehár, waving sadly from a balcony at the Hotel Baur au Lac in Zürich, where he spent his days in nostalgic retirement or see Emerich Kalman ambling idly, though still elegant and very well groomed, but tired and spent, through the lobby of the Plaza in New York. It seemed difficult to believe that they were still there in the flesh, so thoroughly had their world been extinguished.

The thriving publishing house that once had published and administered on a world-wide basis most of the succession of hits they had produced and which had been located on an upper floor in the very heart of operetta land, the Theater an der Wien in Vienna—it, too, had disappeared. Its owner once had operated both the publishing house and the theater and his beautiful daughter had married, in true operetta style, the handsomest leading tenor of Vienna. But when the war was over they all had disappeared and they performed Alban Berg's violent, murderous *Lulu* on the stage that once had accommodated Richard Tauber singing

"*Dein ist mein ganzes Herz*" a thousand and one nights.

It all had vanished. The chocolate soldiers had gone to war and never come back.

Seldom had there been a period of greater variety, of greater productivity, of a richer heritage than this half of the century. Now the giants, one by one, were taking their leave.

• • •

ON AN AFTERNOON late in 1951, a few months after Arnold Schoenberg had died at the age of seventy-six in Los Angeles, his widow, Gertrud, was sitting on a yellow leather sofa in my office, looking mercilessly, in an erect, very unsofaish posture, at the President of G. Schirmer, Inc. Mr. Schirmer was slumped uncomfortably in a chair next to my desk, trying to avoid the determined stare of the thin, powerful woman facing him. She was dressed with defiant carelessness, her graying hair in slight disarray, her face, drawn, agitated, pale, showing no signs of make-up, her glasses dangling threateningly on a black ribbon.

The widow had come to New York (and was from there to proceed to Europe on her mission) for a series of lightning raids on music publishers, performing-rights societies, recording companies, and others involved in the administration of Schoenberg's work. In everything she did, planned, thought, or said she was guided by a few basic, simple, one-track-minded premises: Arnold Schoenberg was the greatest composer of the twentieth century. His music and his writings, every note and every word, were to be revered in undoubting devotion. His works, in terms of cold unintellectual cash, were the most valuable musical property in existence: whoever had them had obtained them too cheap; whoever wanted them was a potential cheat, robber, or thief and had to be dealt with accordingly. In spite or, perhaps, because of its paramount importance, she was deeply and unalterably convinced that Schoenberg's work was disgracefully neglected, if not deliberately sabotaged, by the musical business community and by most artists, conductors, and entrepreneurs. It was her mission to expose the conspiracy, to do battle with a hostile world, to rectify the wrong, to see that justice was done. Her world, like the world of her husband, was populated by an awful lot of bad guys and by very few good guys. It was very difficult not to be considered one of the former and, hard as I tried throughout the years, I never quite made the latter.

Everything she did from the day Schoenberg closed his eyes to the day, fifteen fighting years later, when she was to close hers, was predicated upon these simple, unshakable truths. She would never permit even the thought, so suggestive after all these bitter years, that Schoenberg, one of the most famous figures in twentieth century music, remained strangely removed from musical reality. His works were published and available, but they were not heard very often. Toward the very end of his life he wrote to a musician who had participated in the recording of his String Quartets and had doubts about the quality of the recording and wanted Schoenberg's advice about whether he should have the record released: "My music is almost entirely unknown in America and present-day Europe. Thus it has to be my main concern to make use of every opportunity to let people hear it. Even if the record would be as bad as you say, I have to be very glad if anyone, even a small recording company, sees to it that as many people as possible come to know at least some of my work. I am sure you will put the interest of a composer of my age and my misfortune before yours."

To the public which so readily accepted the music of other giants of the age, Schoenberg remained a name more to be feared or respected in a detached, unemotional way than beloved in happy abandon or accepted in joyful surrender. His impact as a pioneer and a former of new musical thoughts and techniques was not belittled or denied. His acceptance as a composer remained hazy, his place in the repertory astonishingly small when compared with that occupied by other contemporary masters or even by contemporary composers not quite in the master category. Some of his works seemed more a grammar of a new musical language than words, sentences, feelings expressed by it. "I am asked to conduct concerts with my works in Los Angeles and San Francisco," he writes during his first year in America. "But the conductors of these orchestras, have, during thirty years, not played any one of my works and I find it nearly impossible to encounter a public which knows only what they have been told about my music. Have I now to appear only as the composer of *Verklärte Nacht*, which 'has been surpassed' by many younger composers or as the 'devil in person,' the 'atonalist,' the 'constructor,' the 'musical mathematician,' etc.? I hate this way to consider a composer only from the view-point of history instead of enjoying (or not) what he says."

Schoenberg was to be the first of the composers of his century to be honored with a complete edition of his works, twenty-nine huge volumes, beautifully engraved and printed, with critical comments prepared by an international staff of experts, published with a subsidy of the Volkswagen Foundation of Germany, strange as this association between the beetle of the Autobahn with the most esoteric musical Rolls-Royce may sound. But in spite of such posthumous recognition, Schoenberg's music, among the younger generation of his posthumous world, remained respected in a cool, slightly condescending manner and was neither ardently loved nor unreservedly accepted.

Nothing of this existed for Gertrud Schoenberg. As she

waged her relentless battle, she did not even mind being called the *lästige Witwe*, a German pun changing the *lustige*, the merry, into a burdensome, a pain-in-the-neck widow. Quite to the contrary: she carried the designation, known and repeated all over the German-speaking musical world, defiantly as a badge of honor. "I know you call me the *lästige Witwe*," she wrote me not very long before her death. "But *schimpfen*—bawling out—seems the only way I can get results. I am very tired of it and would so much prefer to praise instead and to take your joke as a joke and laugh about it, but, so far, unfortunately, it cannot be done."

It never could. As the copyrights in Schoenberg's earlier works—the *Kammersymphonie*, for instance, *Pierrot lunaire*, the early songs and piano pieces—came up for renewal (under American copyright law the rights revert to the composer or his heirs after twenty-eight years), she refused (what is customary and usually done without fuss) to reassign them to the original publishers for the second term of copyright. I could easily commiserate with some of those who had thought for twenty-eight years that they were good guys when they suddenly discovered that, like most of the rest of the world, they weren't, because most of these works had first been published by my old homestead, Universal of Vienna. Instead, Gertrud Schoenberg kept the copyrights for a new publishing house, Belmont, of course, which she operated in the basement of her house in Brentwood Park in Los Angeles with the help of her sons and another faithful helper or two. There she filled orders (or filed them unfilled if they came from a bad guy), attended to copious correspondence if she felt like it and didn't if she didn't, made packages herself and administered everything in accord with her own moral and human standards. The poor and deserving were rewarded, the rich and suspicious were punished, and many were refused outright or ignored.

What little respect she had had for the music-publishing profession (and it had always been very little indeed) was shattered when the German radio in Hamburg approached her with a request to let them produce the first performance of Schoenberg's unfinished opera *Moses and Aaron.* She asked, nay, commanded the German publisher of the work to quote them so staggering a fee that the publisher, an old experienced house, refused to convey so outrageous and, so they told her, unrealistic and unobtainable a demand to one of their best customers. The widow didn't budge a pfennig, and the Hamburg radio, after having batted a few futile eyelashes, paid the full astronomical amount she had originally asked for. Obviously, after that she never trusted anyone but herself, and publishers could choose between being considered (and plainly called) knaves, fools or—more often than not—people who were corruptly and immorally in cahoots with their customers whose good will meant more to them than their most valuable and important composer, but you are not going to do it to *me*.

A few years after the Hamburg performance, *Moses and Aaron* was to have its first stage presentation at the opera house in Zürich, at the occasion of an International Music Festival. She demanded a fee that made the Alps tremble. As the manager of the theater threw up his thrifty Swiss hands in unbelieving despair, she told him, calmly, to go to the Zürich City Council and ask for a special appropriation of city funds. "Just tell them it is a work by Arnold Schoenberg you want to perform and see what will happen," she told him, smiling confidently. The man did as he had been told to do, the city council voted as she had said they would, and *Moses and Aaron* began its international career in Zürich in 1957. She was present at almost every performance in Hamburg and Zürich, and then in Berlin, Paris, and London, and invited those who had said that the opera would be "unperformable" to join her to see the unperformable performed. "I will be happy to welcome you in Canossa," she added, charmingly and triumphant. Sadly, she had to miss the first American performance of the work in Boston in 1966. She was already too ill to leave the house in Los Angeles which the Schoenbergs had bought thirty years earlier and in which two of their three children were born.

• • •

HER VISIT on that afternoon, late in 1951, was her first visit as a widow to the publishers of her husband's Violin and Piano Concertos, the *Ode to Napoleon* (on Lord Byron's poem), the Fourth String Quartet, the Second Chamber Symphony, and other important works of Schoenberg's American period. She had given us very short notice. She had simply telephoned me in the morning to say she would be in the office at three o'clock. Even the boss, Gustave Schirmer, who hated meetings bound to be difficult, personal, and probably unpleasant, and who would much rather sell musical toys down in the store than talk to twelve-tone widows, had not dared to try to escape.

Gertrud at once went to the attack. One of her friends (she had spies all over the world) had asked for a copy of a Schoenberg score at the Los Angeles Schirmer store, and all the salesman had to offer was a shrug of his uninformed shoulders. A performance of the Violin Concerto in Helsinki had almost been canceled because the music arrived late from America, and when it arrived, the score was falling apart and had to be fixed by a Finnish bookbinder. "He did a marvelous job," she added, acidly. "You should hire him." As she had entered the building she had looked at the store windows. They were filled with music for *The King and I* (which had just opened on Broadway) and "similar wastepaper of tomorrow," but there was no Schoenberg score in the window. And the two-piano version of the Second Chamber Symphony was still not published, and when she had had someone write for it, she had received a miserable yellow postcard marked by "some ignoramus in your organization 'Not our publication.'" She took a postcard that looked indeed very miserable and embarrassingly yellow from her pocketbook and thrust it at us.

The boss looked at it in brooding resignation. He knew, of course, who had sent it and who always would send little yellow postcards to the wrong people so that he had to sit here and have composers' widows pull them out of their pocketbooks and thrust them at him, accusingly demanding an explanation. He also knew that there was nothing he or anyone else could do about it because the man who sent out the little yellow postcard would only yell at him and say how the hell should I know who that dame is. The boss had been in the music-publishing business for a very long time. He was wise, old, seasoned, and a little tired of it all, and he knew that the men with the little yellow postcards live in a little yellow postcard world of their own to which he had no access and he also knew that we would never publish a two-piano version of the Second Chamber Symphony, but he couldn't explain any of this to the widow so he just sat there in motionless, resigned silence for a moment. Then he said, rather gently, looking into an empty corner of the room: "Madame, we have done a great deal for your husband and are still heavily in the red."

It was a statement, fully borne out by the Schirmer ledgers, but perhaps not exactly the thing to say when addressing a tigress. With a rapidity and alertness singular even among composers' widows, who are always ready with a harsh riposte, Gertrud straightened herself into an even more rigid position, pointed an inescapable finger at the boss, and, without a moment's hesitation and in her flavorsome Austrian accent that added steel to her words, began to speak.

"Mr. Schirmer," she said, carefully pronouncing every word but never pausing as she proceeded, "Mr. Schirmer, one day you will be dead. You will go up to heaven and knock at the gate. And Petrus" (her German Petrus seemed much more formidable than a gentle American Peter, and I saw the boss cringe) "will come out and ask who you are and what you want. 'I am the great Mr. Schirmer,'" she continued, the greatness and self-assurance of a surly corporation president arriving at the Pearly Gates in her mimicking voice. "'I have a big publishing house and many music stores and a huge printing plant and I made a lot of money.' And Petrus will look at you and will say: 'Down to hell you go!'" The word "hell" reverberated through the office as she pointed mercilessly toward the netherworld. But at once her scornful face dissolved into a smiling, pleasant expression of happy, quite unexpected redemption. "And then you will say, 'But I also published Schoenberg and lost money on him,' and Petrus will step aside and say, 'Come right in.'" And with a sweeping elegant gesture she admitted poor old Gus to Paradise.

• • •

GERTRUD SCHOENBERG's messianic dedication to and belief in a future that was to fulfill what the past had failed to offer was, of course, the result of her sharing a life that had, most of the time, been a lonely, uncompromising battle and that had become almost unbearably difficult after Schoenberg had come to America in October 1933. Once he had predicted that "the second half of this century will ruin through overestimation what the first half has left of me by underestimation." But as he found himself at the very doorstep of that second half of the century, overestimation seemed still very remote. A letter he addressed to those who had congratulated him on his seventy-fifth birthday, in 1949, sent out as a facsimile of his own clear, unmistakable handwriting, was headed in bold, defiant script by a much more sober and saddened credo: "*Erst nach dem Tode anerkannt zu werden . . . !*" To be recognized only after death! And whatever recognition had come to him in Europe as a composer, teacher, writer, and innovator had found only faint echos in America. His music, his ideas, long since reflected in the work of many European composers, had little impact on American musical thinking and style. His famous book on modern harmony had not yet been translated into English. His twelve-tone technique had found few followers in America.

He arrived almost unnoticed. Lehman Engel was the only musician at the pier—he had come as a reporter for an insignificant musical magazine. But so overwhelmed was he by the strange man from Europe that when he spoke about the event after more than thirty years, his face still was flushed with excitement and, searching for words, he repeated, over and over again, "He was a lion—a lion—there is no other way I can describe him—a lion." Mrs. Claire Reis, perennial guardian angel of composers in America, had prepared a special Schoenberg concert of the League of Composers at Town Hall. Schoenberg was pleased, surprised, and probably sadly deceived by the large turnout but slightly amazed when, after the pianist, to his horror, accompanied a singer through half of one of his songs in the wrong clef, the audience, obviously convinced that these were the famous Schoenberg dissonances, forced him by frenetic applause to rise and take a bow.

The champagne, served after the League of Composers' concert, soon evaporated. Schoenberg, his wife (then still signing her name as a much less majestic Trudy), and little baby Nuria (now Signora Luigi Nono of Venice, with bambini of her own) went to Boston, where the composer was to teach at a small private conservatory. Not a single student registered for his course. Soon, the family returned to New York and to the Marienbadian corridors and enormous rooms of the Ansonia Hotel on Broadway.

From the beginning of his life in America, Schoenberg's main contact had been Carl Engel, who, just at that time, had moved from the Library of Congress, where he had been heading the music division, to the presidency of Schirmer's. The brilliant musicologist, composer, writer, editor, linguist, wit, cook, widower, and poodle fancier (he had also once hired himself out as a butler to get away from it all, but was ignominiously unmasked when his patrons came home early from a party and found the butler playing the "*Appassionata*" with undeniably unbutlery perfection) was to become Schoenberg's lifelong friend, admirer, supporter, and publisher. Following the Boston fiasco, Engel drew up a list of forty-seven universities and schools of music which, he felt, could be expected to engage Schoenberg as a lecturer. After consulting Schoenberg, who had just accepted a lecture date at a music club in Baltimore at a fee of $100, travel expenses included, Engel, before drafting his letter of solicitation, reduced the fee for a single lecture from $200 to $150 and for a series of three from $500 to $400. And when Schoenberg suggested that he would like to have his wife travel with him, Engel had to caution: "I quite realize what a comfort it would be to you to have Mrs. Schoenberg accompany you on your lecture trips. But if this should become an absolute necessity, I greatly fear that the prospects for engagements, not too rosy at best, would still be dimmed." Schoenberg had prepared a list of five lectures: "My Method of Composing with Twelve Interrelated Tones"; "Problems of Harmony"; "Tonal or Atonal Music?";

"Analysis of My Variations for Orchestra"; "Analysis of My Orchestral Songs, op. 22."

Of the forty-seven colleges and universities approached by, after all, not an agent, but one of the most distinguished men of musical letters in America who addressed most of the recipients of his letter by their Christian names, only twenty-two replied, not a single one with a definite acceptance of so incredible a bargain. "Ten can't make up their minds," Engel reported. "Ten said politely no. Two seem a possibility or at least 'hope-awakening.' " (The letter, like many of Engel's letters to Schoenberg, was written in a most elegant, immaculate, almost classical, and brilliantly witty German, interspersed with Latin quotations and numerous puns and plays with words. They, like Schoenberg's very idiomatic answers, are very difficult to translate into English.)

One large Eastern college wrote, rather indignantly: "I must say that the college never pays more than $75 for a lecturer and that Mr. Schoenberg's fee of $150 would not pass the committee." And this was the composer of *Gurrelieder*, the former head of the master class at the Berlin Academy, the originator of the twelve-tone technique of composition, the teacher of Alban Berg and Anton von Webern, the author of celebrated books on harmony and counterpoint.

Soon Engel wrote to Mrs. Reis: "As was expected, Arnold Schoenberg is finding it rather difficult here to make a living. His fees for performing rights are not many. His teaching is now, during the summer, quite negligible. Moreover, he needs time and quiet to finish some new compositions and to write a textbook that he had been planning for several years. This textbook, I believe, might prove salable and Schirmer's would not be disinclined to consider publication." (The textbook was *Models for Beginners in Composition*, published by Schirmer after almost unsurmountable technical difficulties had been surmounted, in 1942, translated and published in many languages and, indeed, very salable.) "What can we do for him? I am turning to you for counsel because you need not be told what a black eye it would give us if we, as a country, had to see Schoenberg off again without having been able to afford him the chance of finding a livelihood among us. Do you know anyone with a country place that has an empty gardener's lodge or some small building that Schoenberg might be allowed to use this summer?" (Engel had previously written in a similar vein to John Erskine, president of the Juilliard School, after Erskine had refused to consider Schoenberg as a lecturer: "Schoenberg is nothing to me," Engel wrote. "I am just fool enough to think that if we let the man and his wife and baby go again, a red blush should cover the map of the U.S.A.")

Claire Reis soon reported that she had approached an impressive list of people who could be expected to have an empty gardener's lodge, but that nobody had anything to offer. One very wealthy patron, however "regrets that he does not know of any flat where Schoenberg can live but he gladly sends the enclosed check of $100 to help see him over the summer. I made further inquiries at Mrs. M. but she, too, knows of no vacant place–I wish I had further suggestions–can Mrs. Coolidge not 'tuck him away' on a Berkshire mountain?" Apparently Mrs. Coolidge couldn't, but as she later commissioned Schoenberg's Fourth String Quartet, she is untuckingly exonerated. Carl Engel felt that "I cannot just offer the check to him as alms," and so wrote to Schoenberg (who was in the meantime tucked away in Chautauqua) that someone would be willing to give $100 for a page of manuscript. Schoenberg was grateful and delighted. He sent a *Riesenpaket* containing a single, large sheet of music covered on both sides with sketches of *Moses and Aaron* and signed on both sides. "Should you find it better," he writes to Engel, "I could send one from my large supply of canons but I thought that these canons, being 'tonal' are not as typical for me as a composition is. However, as I said: if necessary I'll exchange it." Engel dispatched the unexchanged page to the benefactor. "I am sending you this page in the hope that it will not be unwelcome," he wrote him. "If you do not care to keep it yourself I am certain the Music Division of the New York Public Library would greatly value this sample of Schoenberg's handwriting—the Library of Congress has one of his string quartets in autograph."

There is a letter of acknowledgment on the expensive stationery of the benefactor's downtown firm, signed by the secretary to the benefactor and addressed to Mr. Carl Siegel, President, G. Schirmer, Inc.

• • •

In September 1934, the Schoenbergs traveled to California, which was to be their permanent and final home. Schoenberg taught at the university, had private pupils, conducted occasionally. He never returned to Europe. Before he left, he had discussed a publication contract with Engel. Among the projects discussed was *Moses and Aaron*—"As you know, my opera is almost completed," he wrote, still from Chautauqua, in August 1934, and, a little later: "Only fifty more pages to do—a matter of a few months." He never was able to finish it.

When the Schoenbergs arrived in California, a wire announcing acceptance of the Cello Concerto (after Monn) and of the String Quartet Concerto (after Handel) was waiting at Schoenberg's first California address, General Delivery, Pasadena. Two days later, Engel in New York received a telegram from the Universal Credit Guide of Los Angeles: "Please wire collect advise source of income credit moral responsibility how long known Arnold Schoenberg German composer." His proud reply was wired, collect, the same day: "Arnold Schoenberg internationally known for last thirty years among world's most prominent musicians. Ignorant of present source of income except for fifteen hundred dollars due from us as advance royalties payable in five monthly installments. Moral reputation of the highest."

For the next ten years the relationship between Schoenberg and Carl Engel, surviving a continuation of ups and downs, remained warm, almost glowing, based on the most sincere mutual respect and admiration. Schoenberg's letters are interspersed with reports on impending additions to the family and proud announcements of their arrivals, bulletins on his health, particularly on the deterioration of his eyes and his asthma, and on the health of his family, reports on his and, later, his children's tennis feats, jokes, advice, suggestions for gadgets which he adored and constantly invented, curses, and praise.

There was a sustained, touching attempt on the side of the publisher to help the difficult-to-please and even more-difficult-to-sell composer. There was an equally touching attempt by the composer for ever trying "to find out whether there is a publisher who believes in my future, although he doubts in my presence," to adjust his own, ever-present material needs to the situation of the publisher, who, particularly during the war, again and again pleadingly, sometimes desperately, rarely only showing any signs of irritation, tried patiently to explain that he had gone far beyond the call of friendship, that he was not the owner of the business and had to go to his board, again and again, to obtain additional appropriations for a present that looked bleak and a future that remained evasive and uncertain. Schoenberg used to address his letters to Mr. Carl Engel, President, and then proceeded to prefix them with Dear Mr. Engel, lieber

Freund. Finally, Engel wrote him: "Please drop henceforth the pompous and odious title 'President' when addressing me. I am a very plain 'Mister' and not a Geheimer Oberverlagsrat Excellenz." Then, in 1942, Schoenberg offered Engel the *Du* of *Brüderschaft.* "You know," he writes after Engel gratefully and rather humbly accepts this deformalization of their relationship, "that I would not become servile in order to catch an advantage, but that at least for fifteen or twenty years I have not offered such friendship. Even with my dear and devoted friends Josef Polnauer and Erwin Stein I am still *per Sie.*" And again, even here, he inserts a little glimpse on eternity to reassure his friend: "I can understand that Schirmer's are disappointed about the failure with my works which they published. But I do not understand that they put the blame on me. I am sure that, in the long run—and I write for the long run—you will not lose money on my works but will make great profits."

For Engel's sixtieth birthday, in 1943—it was to be his last—a group of friends and admirers tried to surprise him with a collection of articles and other contributions, a so-called *Festschrift,* all written for the occasion. Schoenberg contributed some birthday canons which delighted the recipient. He called them "a veritable masterwork of contrapuntal art, spiced with your own and unimitable humor. You have bestowed 'immortality' on me, as Beethoven did in '*Auf einen welcher Hoffmann geheissen*' and '*Auf einen welcher Schwenke geheissen.*' Their names have survived only because of the canons Beethoven wrote for them. And if posterity will ever disentangle the mix-up among the angelic host, I shall be remembered by a canon, compared with which Beethoven's are *Waisenkinder* [orphans], written '*Auf einen welcher Engel geheissen.*' " Schoenberg fully rose to the occasion. "I must confess," he replied, "that you might be right. These canons might bring both of us into the history of music."

Engel kept his faith to the end. On April 27, 1944, he sent Schoenberg a long telegram, urging him to accept a Koussevitzky commission. Ten days later he was dead.

As a final gesture for his friend, Schoenberg offered to make an orchestral version of Carl Engel's Tryptich, originally composed for violin and piano. Nothing came of it. Nothing came of the Koussevitzky commission. The string had been cut.

Never again would the composer get letters from a publisher who knew that Beethoven had written canons for one *welcher Hoffmann geheissen* and one *welcher Schwenke geheissen* and who, in one of his last letters, had written: "It doesn't happen often in my old days that a new piece of music puts me in ecstatic confusion. Your piano concerto has done just that."

And never again would the composer be able to write to a publisher: "And don't let me forget to say that your friendship and your support of my work has removed one big worry: it has made it possible for me to pay for my house, so that my wife and my children will have a roof over their heads when I am gone."

There would be many "Faithfully yours" and "Dear Sir" letters between publisher and composer. But the warmth and the joy and the fun and the understanding of two friends had come to an end. Soon Trudy Schoenberg would become the avenging angel Gertrud and she would be addressed as Madame and told that we were still heavily in the red. And after that, there would only be the *Gesammtausgabe*, twenty-nine volumes of Arnold Schoenberg's works, rolling off the presses on cold, clickety-clack Volkswagen money, waiting for the judgment of history.

SCHIRMER's had been waiting for the call for thirty-nine years. When it came, out of a blue July sky, in 1949, the caller was M. Edouard Nies-Berger, organist of the New York Philharmonic Orchestra and, for the moment, guide, secretary, interpreter, and amanuensis to Dr. Albert Schweitzer. Dr. Schweitzer (he had never before been in America and was never to come back) was in New York on his way home from Aspen where he had delivered a speech at the occasion of the two-hundredth anniversary of Johann Wolfgang Goethe. Nies-Berger, whose father had been one of the great *docteur's* earliest friends and to whom the old man had transferred the friendship and affection of these days, had phoned to say that Dr. Schweitzer would have two hours—no more, no less—to talk to us about his edition of the complete organ works of Johann Sebastian Bach. It was electrifying news: before World War I, Schirmer's had published five of the eight volumes that were to comprise the complete edition. Ever since, they had been waiting for the missing three. It had been a very long wait.

Half an hour before the appointed hour, we assembled in the board room, a little group of editors, editorial assistants, executives, I, mainly because I spoke German and French and Nies-Berger had forewarned us that Dr. Schweitzer spoke no English, and the boss. A scout had been dispatched downstairs to send word as soon as the visitors entered through the revolving doors. A second patrol had been placed at the upstairs elevator to receive and guide the arrivals to the board room. Everybody in the little group had thought that, after dealing with famous people all their lives, they were celebrity-proof. But this time everybody was looking nervously at the ancestral portraits and the samovar, waiting for the signal from below. It came, with kingly punctuality, and we all got up and stood around the table like schoolboys waiting for the principal. The secretary of the company, a distinguished lady who had grayed ushering musical stars into the presence of a succession of bosses and had never been seen paying a flicker of attention to any of them beyond a painted, frozen, official smile, had a copy of *Time* magazine with Dr. Schweitzer's picture on the cover in one hand and a pen in the other. It was obvious to all that she was going to ask the doctor for his autograph, something she had never done in the memory of the samovar, and her precedent-breaking intentions and the brash paraphernalia that betrayed them heightened the general tension.

Then there was a slight commotion outside. Everybody turned toward the door which was pushed open by a flustered guard and Dr. Albert Schweitzer, looking exactly as everybody had expected him to look, came in and began shaking friendly hands in German and French. M. Edouard, a thin, tense, very intelligent-looking man of medium height and indeterminable age, murmured translations for those who needed a little assistance. The doctor autographed slowly and carefully the copy of *Time* magazine, took his seat, as did everybody else, and the two-hour—no more, no less—session, hoped for with forever dwindling hope for more than thirty years, began.

• • •

THE SCHIRMER contract files are a gray maze of drab steel cabinets. Every night they are locked, every one of them, by one of their vestal keepers and the master key is carefully hidden in a desk drawer where any competitive spy, sneaking in at night to find out whether we paid ten or fifteen dollars for an arrangement of "America the Beautiful" for Brass Choir would look for it at once. The files are crammed with tens of thousands of contracts, bills of sales, assignments of copyrights, settled lawsuits, permissions to make an Australian edition of the Adagio for Strings, and memorandums advising future generations that, as per Mr. Schirmer's instructions, the search for heirs has been abandoned after seven registered letters (see attached exhibits one to seven) have been returned, undeliverable, from the post office in Ithaca. In one of the files is a dirty brown cardboard folder, covered with a sticky white powder that an insurance company, several generations past, is rumored to have insisted on as a fire-preventing device and that still, long after its original purpose has been forgotten, messes up the hands and garments of those looking for enlightenment —here is a folder marked "Schweitzer, Albert," and in it a contract, dated "*le 6 juillet 1910*," in a pale blue cover and tied with a ribbon that has not lost its red brilliance in all these years. In very faded typescript it begins:

> *Le Présent Contrat entre G. Schirmer (Inc.) de New York, Etats Unis, d'une part et les Messieurs Charles M. Widor du Conservatoire de Paris et le Docteur A. Schweitzer de l'Université de Strasbourg, de l'autre part, sera executé comme suit . . .*

The document then stipulates that *les messieurs Widor et Schweitzer* are to deliver to Schirmer an edition of the Bach Organ Works in eight volumes, *revue, corrigée et critiquée*, that M. Widor is to receive a considerable honorarium in French francs and le docteur Schweitzer a less considerable one in German money, that the musical and literary texts are to be prepared by the writers according to previous specifications and that the text is to be translated into English by the publisher who will also issue the edition in the original French and German texts.

The difficult and complicated work of translating, editing, and printing must have commenced at once. In 1912 and 1913, five beautifully engraved and impressively ornamented volumes were published, containing the Preludes and Fugues in four volumes and the Organ Concertos and Organ Sonatas in the fifth. Each volume stated that this was a "Critico-practical Edition, provided with a Preface containing General Observations on the Manner of performing and Suggestions for the Interpretation on the Compositions by Charles-Marie Widor, Professor in the Conservatoire at Paris and Organist at the Church of St. Sulpice and Dr. Albert Schweitzer, Privatdozent at Strassburg University and Organist of the Société J. S. Bach of Paris."

A detailed publication plan for the entire edition of eight volumes was included in the foreword. It also explained the basic idea. "The edition is based on the text of the great Bach edition, which it presents without additions of any kind. The player has the piece, in its traditional form, before his eyes. It is not meant that he should receive it laden with the details of an interpretation which, by being incorporated with the musical text itself, advances the claim to be authentic. Editions for practical use, having the musical text overladen with fingering and pedaling, marks for dynamics and phrasing, etc., do not promote art in a desirable way." This was the important basic idea, proclaimed at a time which cherished overedited, romanticized editions of the masters. "The Editors advocate the 'simple' interpretation and in this edition urge its claims for acceptance. They have left the musical text untouched, so as not to violate the principles of a true critico-practical edition, and have recorded their conception in prefatory general disquisitions on tempo, phrasing, registration and alternation of manuals."

The Chorale Preludes were to be published in the concluding volumes 6, 7, and 8. The manuscript of these three volumes had been prepared and copied and needed only final revisions. Schweitzer and Widor (who was Schweitzer's senior by eleven years, had been his organ teacher in Paris, was a famous organist and composer, and like Schweitzer, lived for more than four score and ten years, dying in 1937 at the age of ninety-three) had agreed on every detail before in 1914 Schweitzer left for French Equatorial Africa, where he had planned to put the finishing touches to the manuscript before sending it to New York for publication.

But his next communication is dated December 1919. It comes, significantly, from Strasbourg: a world war had come and gone and the little change in spelling from the German Strassburg to the French Strasbourg tells some of its history. The letter, a long, handwritten communication, is written in German. Headed *Brief über die Ausgabe der Orgelchoräle an die H. H. Verleger Schirmer, New York*, it addresses itself to Dr. Theodore Baker, Schirmer's editor for many years.

> Lieber Herr Baker—so we both are still alive. To write to each again makes us seven years younger. I wrote you several times during the war from Africa, about the Bach Chorales and also to hear from you personally. There was never a reply. Did you receive my letters?
>
> In the summer of 1914 the three volumes of the Organ Chorales were ready. I had only to wait for some material on the origin of some of the chorale melodies which were to come from experts in the field and for the opinions of some organ professors who had read my notes. At the end of the summer you were to receive everything. And in the spring of 1915, again on holiday in Europe, I would have read the proofs. But the war came. I could not dare to send the manuscript on account of the submarines—and the war would have made publication impossible. When, in 1917, I was transferred against my will to Europe

> [Schweitzer had been interned and then deported back to Europe as an enemy alien by the French], I left the ledgers with the manuscript in Africa—first because of the submarine danger (I did not want you to have to lament my death in the ocean together with the loss of the manuscript!) and secondly, because I was an internee whom any sergeant could have deprived of anything written. After I had left, everything was seized. The manuscripts were in a large box, tin-lined to protect them to some measure from the termites.
>
> After the war I petitioned from Alsace (it is now more than a year) for the release of my seized properties to get hold of the manuscript as soon as possible and to deliver it to you. M. Widor, too, tried his best. Result: promises—and nothing else. One of my friends who arrived from Africa recently and had planned to bring the manuscript with him arrived empty-handed.

Schweitzer continued his letter by proposing to take three months off his teaching, recitals and work on "a philosophical book which was to be ready for the Christmas trade next year," so that he might have the time to reconstruct the manuscript from sketches and notes recovered in Europe.

> I promised the dear master Widor to begin and I will keep my word. On the first of January you will receive the music for the first volume of the chorales, soon after the remaining sections. On February 1 the introductory notes for the first volume will be completed, and by March the rest. I hope my strength will hold. Afterwards, I'll sleep for three weeks!

By the time the letter arrived in New York, an important event had occurred at Schirmer's. Rudolph E. Schirmer, the progressive, far-looking, and imaginative head of the firm (one of the two sons of its founder) who had initiated the negotiations with Widor and Schweitzer during one of his regular trips to Europe and had signed the contract with the two in 1910, had died a few weeks earlier. Thus, in January 1920, a "Dear Sir" reply was sent by Schirmer's to Strasbourg (which was spelled Strasburg—as if the return of the city to France was only partly recognized by the management of a firm whose founder had immigrated from Thuringia).

"Dr. Baker referred your long and interesting letter with reference to Bach's organ works to me since his functions are editorial and not executive," it began, icily, putting everyone in his right place. It then proceeded to explain that the music publishing industry in America was classed as one of the non-essential industries during the war, and that, as a result, the music business had suffered a substantial setback and, in addition, was disturbed by labor troubles "which still further made things very uncomfortable for us."

Having thus prepared the ground, the letter stated that "the sale of the editions of the five published volumes has been most disappointing," and then continued:

> I regret to have to inform you that the publication of the three volumes will have to be deferred and delayed until business conditions have become normal again. Hence, there is absolutely nothing to be gained by you by sacrificing your other projected work to a continuation and completion of the three volumes still outstanding. We prefer to bide our time and wait until your material has reached you from Africa. For all parties concerned, this has been a rather disastrous experience.

While this seems strong language, particularly when addressed to a saint, it is always easy to criticize in retrospect. In 1920, Schweitzer and Widor's ringing proclamation on the spirit of their *Urtext* edition, while looking boldly and prophetically into the future, had little support in the present. Of the five volumes published before the war, only a few hundred copies had been sold.

There was a short acknowledgment from Dr. Schweitzer (now, on his part, using "Dear Sir" as an opening), and here the curtain descends. "Dr. Schweitzer evidently is peeved and that makes the situation very embarrassing," a memorandum of 1927 stated, candidly and not surprisingly. From time to time private approaches were made to get matters back to normal. The manuscript, left behind when the French deported the German Schweitzer from Africa, had been recovered when the Frenchman Schweitzer returned: it had neither been "eaten by termites" or "stolen by a native who might have been attracted by the box," as Schweitzer had feared when writing to Dr. Baker. In 1934, Mr. Robert Schirmer, another member of the family and of the board of directors of the firm, wrote to Dr. Schweitzer during a stay in Germany, offering to visit him in Gunsbach, Schweitzer's native village in Alsace, before his return to New York to "finally settle this matter which has been dragging on since almost a quarter of a century." He also pointed out that 1935 was to be the 250th anniversary of the birth of Bach and that this would be a most appropriate occasion to complete the publication. The meeting took place, the business problems posed by the outdated, prewar contract were resolved, and any feelings which might still have been left from the days of the "Dear Sir" letter (its author had long since left the scene) were soothed. But all this did not produce a manuscript!

"I don't know when I will be able to make the final revisions," Schweitzer writes from Lambaréné in 1937. "I am at present fully occupied with philosophy." And, as a P.S.: "It is now three years since you visited me in Gunsbach. How much sadder has the state of the world since become." In 1943 there is talk of his plans to come to the United States after the war to give organ recitals. He also hopes to continue the organ edition of Bach's works for Schirmer. But in

1945, still from Lambaréné, a letter arrives, again, as were all his letters, written by hand, on onion-skin paper in perfectly straight lines, with almost never a word crossed out or inserted; everything, thought out in advance, appearing on the page unfalteringly, in beautiful, imaginative language, be it German or French. If there were several sheets to a letter, they were neatly tied together with a piece of thin, white thread. "Now, that the friendly rapports between the house and myself have been restored," he writes, "I should finish the three volumes. *Mais je ne le puis.* All my energy and time has to go to my work on philosophy which I hope to finish before I die. And all this has to be done in addition to my work in my hospital. You must understand that I cannot return to the work on the Bach edition before having consecrated myself to these other things. What can you do? Such is fate! ". . . And still later, in 1946: "My life is so full and I have so much to do. Ah, if this could have been arranged after the first war, when I was not yet engaged in other work."

So it was quite an occasion when we, at last, took our seats around the conference table in the board room, waiting for the tall, erect figure at its head to speak. To everybody's surprise he told us that he was now ready to complete the task and to design a working plan for the remaining three volumes. Nies-Berger, Alsatian by birth and American by choice, fluent in German, French, and English and steeped by tradition—his father had been the organist of one of the churches in Strasbourg where Albert Schweitzer had played the organ in his early days—and by vocation in the manifold secrets of Bach's organ world, was to take the late Widor's place in what was still to be done to finish the edition. The pre-World War I notes, spared by the termites, needed careful revisions in the light of then present-day Bach research. Most important, he told us, was a new approach to the ornaments—an extended treatise on the trills, mordents, ascending and descending appoggiaturas, and their interpretations was one of the important features still to be worked out. Again, it was to be a formidable task. It turned out that it was easy to plan on a July afternoon in New York but very difficult to execute between a hospital in Lambaréné, a Nobel Prize, and what, in addition, was daily coming his way.

Three years later—no sign even of volume 6, not to speak of 7 and 8—Dr. Schweitzer returned from Lambaréné and Edouard went from New York to meet him in Gunsbach, where the doctor was to spend the summer, to try to get something out of him. I was then traveling in Europe and when I suggested to Nies-Berger that perhaps my official presence might help to rekindle the spirit of the by now sadly historical meeting in the Schirmer board room, he wrote to say that he had spoken to the doctor and that he, the doctor, would be very glad to see a representative of his publisher and to talk to him. So we traveled, my wife Elsbeth and I, to Strasbourg for unforgettable food and a look at the St. Thomas Church, so intimately connected with Dr. Schweitzer, and from there to Colmar for a visit with the Isenheim altar and its painter, Mathis der Maler, and then on a country road on to Gunsbach which—its houses, its fields, its church—looked and felt and smelled exactly like any of the little villages on the opposite side of the Rhine where we had grown up.

At the Schweitzer house we were asked to go to the church: the doctor had been practicing for a series of records of Bach organ music since eight in the morning and had left word for us to join him. A sound truck was parked, unfittingly, in front of the old village church and ugly cables impeded the traffic of horse-drawn carts. Soon we were sitting with the world's most famous organist in the loft and watching him work with untiring concentration for many hours, interrupting his work only occasionally to sharpen the miserable remains of a pencil with his old-fashioned, huge pocket knife or explaining to us some essential features of the organ or the fundamental difference between a trill starting on the upper note and a trill ascending from below, accompanying his demonstrations with historical and analytical comment.

The wooden floor of the church had been heavily sprinkled with water to improve the acoustics. On a bench, trying to keep his feet dry, was one solitary visitor: Nies-Berger, who had been stationed in the nave of the church to check on the registrations and dynamics applied by the organist and difficult if not impossible to judge from his position on the organ bench. Nies-Berger continued to shout suggestions and criticism which the old master untiringly tried out till, at last, a piece pleased both the critic downstairs and the player on high, and work on the next piece began at once. Around half past twelve Schweitzer called out again: "How was that?" and Nies-Berger replied, happily, from below: "Just perfect." "He is hungry," Schweitzer told us, smilingly. "He wants to go to lunch."

A little later we all walked through the village. The old man, slightly stooped, his enormous, gnarled peasant hands folded behind his back, stopped frequently as people came to talk to him, patiently listening, asking questions himself, never showing the slightest sign of being tired or irritated.

There had been no mention of the appointment that I thought—foolishly, I suppose—was the main reason for my being here. He asked us to come to the house in the afternoon, but when we arrived, an unannounced horde of Belgians had descended on the village, their bus parked in front of the Schweitzer home. Schweitzer, who never permitted his doors to be closed or anyone anywhere at any time turned away, received them in his garden, spoke to everyone who wanted to speak to him, patted their children, asked to be introduced to their wives, and posed for pictures to their Belgian heart's delight. By the time they finally departed, my chance had departed with them. Nies-Berger, understanding but powerless, suggested that we come for breakfast the next day.

As we approached the house at seven-thirty, half an hour ahead of time, we heard Dr. Schweitzer practicing the piano—he had been at the little upright since six o'clock. To talk business at breakfast was unthinkable: there was a large crowd (every meal was always cooked so as to accommodate a potential invasion of unexpected but readily admitted guests), admirers, musicians, doctors, people who wanted to go to Africa and people who had come from there, family, friends. One man, when I told him that I had been waiting for two days for an appointment, laughed and said he had gone all the way from Chicago to Lambaréné to transact some literary matter with the doctor and had now been here, in Gunsbach, for two weeks and was still waiting and hoping for a proper occasion. But at the end of the breakfast session, Nies-Berger, whose soul was half-rooted in the busy spirit of New York and half in the nirvanian timelessness of Gunsbach, stood bravely up to the innocently evasive host, and that same afternoon, we had our meeting.

We discussed many details and procedures, even money, which was very difficult to discuss in front of a huge bowl of apricots that had come in from the garden and in view of the magnificent old tree, basking in sunlight, which had born them. But it all still seemed to be very vague. So, as the meeting was drawing to its end, feeling that I had to bring something home to justify the expense of a visit to the Isenheim altar and that, perhaps, after a wait of forty-two years it would not betray an unbecoming urgency, I asked what he thought his timetable for the completion of the job might be. "*Lassen Sie den Alten in Ruh* [Leave the old man alone]," he said, retiring ever so slightly.

Soon he was smiling again and came out of the house to see us to our car and to wave us good-bye on our way back to the world of deadlines, printing schedules and P & L statements.

The old man stayed behind. In his own good time he fulfilled the promise he had made to "dear master Widor." The sixth volume of the complete edition of the organ works of Bach was published in 1954. The seventh and eighth were ready when he died and were published posthumously. The files Schweitzer, Albert, and Bach, J. S., had at last been closed.

XVII

A FEW MONTHS before Ralph Hawkes, rather surprisingly and without any other pre-lunch notice than one raised eyebrow (the other still remained smilingly and reassuringly unraised), severed diplomatic relations with me one Friday afternoon, and while I was still enthusiastically and unsuspectingly in his employ, I attended the first performance of a new opera at the Brander Matthews Theater at Columbia University. It was in November 1946.

The little theater, long since bulldozed, was pleasantly situated in a quiet street within the Columbia domain in upper New York, vis-à-vis an old brownstone house where Béla Bartók had once occupied a small, dark, Columbia-sponsored studio and where he had spent many hours during the two years of his Columbia assignment, working on his scientific papers and patiently listening to recordings of folk music. The Brander Matthews Theater had a nice, quite adequate, and very workable stage, a pit which could accommodate a moderate-sized orchestra, and just enough of an auditorium to seat at an opening night about everybody in New York who was interested to hear a new opera. And everybody always came—there was scarcely a strange face in the audience. It was a relaxed, pleasant, professional gathering of people who all seemed to have checked their jealousies, envies, and hatreds at the little checkroom in the lobby—this was academic soil, and such objects had to be left outside just as cameras, walking sticks, and transistor radios have to be left behind before entering San Pietro in Vincoli.

It is difficult to recapture the atmosphere of these happy

occasions, now that everything takes place in shiny, cold musical mausoleums whose checkrooms are strictly for umbrellas and raincoats and where sentiments, unchecked, have to be taken inside.

The productions at the little opera house operated by the university were not determined or influenced by commercial considerations and restrictions. The orchestra consisted of students. The conductor was, more often than not, a member of the faculty. Most of the singers, too, were students and an occasional outsider—such a later-on famous singer as Teresa Stich-Randall, for example, took part in the world *première* of Virgil Thomson's *The Mother of Us All*—was glad to appear in these stimulating surroundings and in productions that were extensively reviewed by a friendly press and attended by an audience of professionals the like of which the participants could scarcely expect anywhere else.

After the curtain had descended on the short opera I had come to hear that November night in 1946, I hurried backstage. I was excited beyond belief. For close to ten years, since the day I had had to leave my desk as Director of Operatic Activities at Universal in Vienna, I had been spending my time learning how to sell sheet music, arranging for performances of symphonies, and trying to adjust my professional life to the Winklerian conception of an American musical world in which an opera house was to be shut if not torn down if it didn't make money. I had been missing my operatic past terribly.

American composers seemed not interested in wasting their time on a field that promised few, if any, returns for so long and hard a labor. Obviously, as long as they didn't risk failure, they could scarcely acquire the tools with which to build success. Some of the older generation—Frederick Converse, Deems Taylor, Walter Damrosch—had tried their brief luck with operas fashioned after outdated European models and produced for discouragingly short runs by the Metropolitan Opera in Gatti-Casazza's day. It had taken twenty-six years after the Metropolitan had opened in 1883 for the first American opera to make its appearance on its stage and five days, two performances, for the work to be dropped for ever. One of the fortunate composers, Horatio Parker, had won a $10,000 prize offered by the Board of Directors of the Met for the encouragement of American operas. *Mona* had four performances, and when I looked it up on the Schirmer publication card, I found a faded, humiliating "disc." penciled in the torn corner—another confirmation of one of Max Reger's eternally true if untranslatable puns: *Je preisser ein Werk gekrönt ist, umso durcher fällt es*—the higher the prize, the bigger the flop, which isn't quite as funny but just as sad.

The present generation of composers, reviewed from a seat at Brander Matthews in 1946, seemed profoundly disinterested. Aaron Copland had written brilliantly and successfully for the stage in his ballet scores for *Billy the Kid*, *Rodeo*, and *Appalachian Spring*, all of which I had been connected with from their very beginnings, all of them unforgettable—most unforgettable, perhaps, the tender sadness of *Appalachian Spring* danced with absorbed and touching intensity by Martha Graham at a wonderful *première* in Washington, a Library of Congress–Elizabeth Sprague Coolidge Foundation event, one of the nights—just as the night I was now attending at Brander Matthews—one would always remember. But Copland had only shown a sideline interest of minor significance in opera—one little work for high-school performance, written in 1937 in the aftermath of the European wave that had produced Weill's *Jasager* and Hindemith's *Let's build a city*, and a second, later attempt, strictly a *Nebenwerk*.

Louis Gruenberg's O'Neill opera *The Emperor Jones* had

been produced at the Metropolitan (with Lawrence Tibbett in the only part) and had gone from there nowhere fast. Ernest Bloch's *Macbeth* was not performed in America. And American as it had seemed to us when we produced it in Frankfurt and printed it in Vienna, (though to the composer's grief I had printed his name as Georges on the cover of the score, so much of a Parisian American he had become in my subconscious mind), George Antheil's *Transatlantic* had never made the voyage back home across the sea. And most of the prominent, most widely performed composers—William Schuman, Henry Cowell, Roy Harris, Walter Piston, Samuel Barber—a whole generation of up-and-coming writers, had never tried their hand at opera.

As I sat in the little theater and watched and listened, I remembered well that I had been told again and again that my operatic past as a music publisher was just that—past. But I felt, instinctively, that the opera I had just heard might be the thing that could put back on my desk the little sign, missed so long and so ardently—Director of Operatic Activities. The work had not been conceived for the unlimited forces, the lavish monetary resources, and the professional brilliance of the subsidized European-style opera house. It was specifically written for the limited facilities of the rapidly expanding American college theaters, universities, and workshops. I had counted an orchestra of only fourteen players in the pit. The conductor was Otto Luening, not a professional maestro, but a member of the Columbia Music Department. The work demanded a minimum of scenery and costumes, no chorus, and a cast that surely could easily be duplicated in hundreds of the new operatic establishments all over America. And the opera was written in English.

There was happy pandemonium backstage. I finally managed to corner the composer, introduce myself, and ask him whether he would let my firm, Boosey & Hawkes, publish his opera. He said he was pleased but sorry: he already had an offer from another publisher. I was very disappointed.

I shouldn't have been. A few months later, after Ralph Hawkes had raised his second and final eyebrow after lunch, and after I had consequently arrived at Schirmer's, I was asked to ascend to the directors' room where, shortly before, I had been treated to the dazzling display of my book. I was introduced to a smiling, palish, youthful-looking man with a prominent, Caesarian nose, well but casually dressed in a brown sport jacket, slacks, and elegant continental tie. He was constantly in motion and always seemed most happily harassed. It was the composer who had been pleased but sorry when I had visited him backstage at Brander Matthews and had asked for the opera he had just delivered to Schirmer's. The opera was *The Medium.* The composer was Gian Carlo Menotti.

• • •

THE WORLD of Gian Carlo Menotti—I have lived in it, off and on, for more than two decades—is full of adventure, color, surprises, charming hysterics, ups and downs. The offs and the downs are always gracefully mended and reversed with an embrace, a let's-not-talk-about-it-any-more, and a fabulous repast in a French restaurant on the upper East Side of Manhattan called *Quo Vadis?* As he arrives, breathlessly rushing in from overseas calls or a casting crisis, the composer is greeted with profuse Italian adulation, somehow surprising in a French restaurant, by the headwaiter who seems simply in love with the word *maestro*, which keeps rolling off his tongue like a richly spiced hors d'oeuvre. While his guest studies the bill of fare (he himself is always on some repulsively frugal diet), the maestro, nibbling on some terrible herb, has the telephone brought to the table to talk to his secretary, who tells him that he is already late for his next three appointments.

We had good and bad times together at the *Quo Vadis?*, at the office, in his beautiful home in Mt. Kisco, in Spoleto at the festival which he has singlehandedly created, maintained, and made after his image, and at most of his *premières*—*The Consul* in Philadelphia, *The Saint of Bleecker Street* in New York, *The Bishop of Brindisi* in Cincinnati and Vienna, *Maria Golovin* in Brussels during the World's Fair, *Martin's Lie* in the cathedral of Bristol, where we shivered through rehearsals during what was alleged to be a June in the company of a TV crew from New York and of the large staff of young people that always follow him around, bravely freezing in England and sweating in Greece.

The first of the many Menotti-ites I was to have the pleasure of meeting in these many years was a group called C Z & L. They produced *The Medium* on Broadway coupled with a curtain-raiser Menotti had added, *The Telephone.* The operas ran for almost a year—a unique event in the history of Broadway, where opera is a dirty word. Z was Efrem Zimbalist, Jr., who soon left to become a celebrated cop in Hollywood. L was a most attractive lady by the name of Edith Lutyens, who got married and, unhappily, faded from my view forever. C was one of the most charming and most unusual men ever associated with the business side of the theater, where one usually has to deal with grim, neurotic, overworked, conceited, rude, unpleasant, and nervous boors who can only be reached through a protective screen of lawyers, agencies, press agents, and secretaries, which is just as well because it is not quite as unpleasant as to talk to them directly.

If C had a lawyer, I never met him. He always answered the phone himself or, if he was away or didn't feel like answering, it just rang no matter how urgent the unconveyable message might have been. He was a very tall, blond, elegant American aristocrat, and it surprised none of his innumerable friends when, after he inherited a fairy-tale fortune, he forgot all about the theater, retired from New York, and bought himself a flock of the famous white Austrian Lippizaner horses. He flew them in special planes, with grooms, saddles, and family trees, across the Atlantic to Florida, where he trained them, riding dressage himself under the supervision of famous Austrian riders. One of the sternest and most demanding of them was Mr. John White, director of the New York City Opera, the man who once had carried matinal oranges at the Fulton Market and who looked simply magnificent, riding a $10,000 stallion through C's Tallahassee orange groves, a last, noble link between C's operatic past and equestrian present.

C was really, as such an extraordinary man should be, a double C. His name was Chandler Cowles. Chandler knew a single German sentence which, unfailingly, he would greet me with, no matter how long it had been since we had met and no matter where we met. "*Hans, hast du gut geschlaffen?*" he would cry out—in the Galleria in Milan, on the Grande Place in Brussels, in front of the embarrassed Plaza Hotel in New York. He must have heard the words from one of his many German-speaking girl friends (he had them in all denominations, but seemed to prefer foreigners from whom he could learn something), when she opened her eyes in the morning. He adapted the phrase, I guess, as a token of tender remembrance of which I was flattered to be part.

Nobody who saw CC or just met him casually could possibly have imagined that this lackadaisical, playboyish-looking man would be able to produce operas—the most uncommercial, difficult thing to produce on Broadway. He did it with a quiet, smiling efficiency, endless patience, and genuine artistic devotion. He never interfered with Menotti. He let him pick singers, designers, and conductors, and the only concession he made to the alleged idiosyncrasy of the public to opera was to call the operas he produced—*The Telephone* and *The Medium*, *The Consul*, *The Saint of Bleecker Street*—"plays with music," which, of course, fooled nobody. He had a wonderful way with Menotti, who never must be pushed or shown impatience, irritation, or—the worst—concern for money unwisely spent. When we went to Philadelphia for the final rehearsals of *The Consul*, most of the third act was not written, was not even clearly in Menotti's mind. Well-meaning people urged cancellation or predicted disaster. Others suggested Chandler play the work in two acts. Chandler was dreamily, smilingly, elegantly unconcerned. "*Hast du gut geschlaffen?*" he yelled exuberantly as he saw me worriedly enter the theater filled with desperate backers, tired coaches, the great copyist Arnold Arnstein with a crew of minor copyists and stacks of paper, ready to copy what was not written and perhaps never would be, and a composer who had also to write the libretto (Menotti writes all his libretti), stage it (Menotti stages all his *premières*) and cast it (Menotti casts all his first performances, down to the last super). *The Consul*, of course, all three acts of it, went off as planned and with a bang that still echoes throughout the international operatic scene.

A few weeks later, after we had brought *The Consul* to New York, I set out on one of the unforgettable voyages of my life. I was returning to the scene of the many operatic triumphs of my first life, trying to sell an American opera created during my second. What could have been a more unexpected, a more stimulating, a more joyous adventure?

The score of *The Consul* had not yet been printed—I had a few blueprint copies and a couple of librettos, flashy production pictures, posters, and, of course, the press notices in my valise. Wherever I went, I asked for a coach who usually had little difficulty in playing the uncomplicated music. I had a marvelous time, conducting so as to indicate the right tempi, translating, and singing—I particularly enjoyed singing Patricia Neway's aria "To this we've come," putting all her sobs and violent despair in my performance. I also was a really first-class magician. There is a passage in his song where he recites the list of celebrities for whom he has performed and as I sang with full voice "And the Queen of Belgium" for the little audience in the Royal Theater in Brussels, there was a gasp and a smile and applause—and I had made a sale. Arrangements had to be made for a French translation and I made a side trip to Antwerp to visit an agent who had been our agent for Belgium in Hertzka's time. It turned out that he was still Universal's agent and Ricordi's agent and just about everybody's agent for Belgium, and he was happy to add our name to his simply enormous list—he just could squeeze it in at the bottom of his letterhead. We had an emotional reunion—the first of many that were to follow on this sentimental trip. A French translation, he explained, was not enough for Belgium, small as it seemed to be: he also needed a Flemish translation and, as he also handled Holland, a translation in Dutch.

So French and Flemish and Dutch translators made their appearance, opera directors from Antwerp and Liège and Amsterdam listened, politely spellbound, to my performance, contracts were signed, dates were set—after twenty-five years I was back in the days of Jonny, of Schwanda, of Hertzka. Only Fräulein Mizzi was sadly missing. On to Stockholm, where Bonniers, the biggest newspaper and book publishers in Scandinavia, had arranged for me to perform—by now I really felt like the international magician in my opera—for the staff of the Royal Opera House. They promised to arrange for translations in Swedish, Finnish, Norwegian, and Danish! Then to Paris, to Milan—but it was all still on the periphery of European operatic life, which again centered in Germany. Again, as it had been before, the German subsidized theater flourished. Many of the bombed-out opera houses had been rebuilt, many were about to be reopened. I had several offers from people who wanted to handle *The Consul* and could not make up my mind.

There was an old friend in Basel, Kurt Reiss, another of my pre-American connections and a theatrical agent of repute. It was tempting to do business with a man in Switzerland: Basel's untouched solidity was in overwhelming contrast to the still unfathomable turmoil of most of the rest of the continent. But Reiss, too, could not quite make up his mind—he had partners in Germany he would have to consult. I told him that I was going on vacation and that in three weeks, on Wednesday afternoon, I would be with my wife in the Konditorei Hanselmann in St. Moritz which, as everybody knows or should know, offers the finest combination of glaciers and pastries in the world. If he would come there, let's say at four o'clock, and bring me a check for ten thousand francs, he could have *The Consul*.

He played it nicely. He came through the door at precisely four o'clock, preceded by his dog (who was at once ejected, as *Hunde* are *verboten* at Hanselmanns), took, without saying hello, a large-sized, solidly Swiss-looking check from his pocket, handed it to me, sat down, and ordered a hot chocolate with whipped cream.

He could afford it. Over the years he has paid us more than ten times the amount of his initial advance. *The Consul* was produced at almost every opera house in Germany, Switzerland, and Austria and was shown on television all over the continent, which, under the prevailing system of European tariffs and fees brought much more money than a sustaining television showing of an opera ever brought in the United States. The contract was worth a lot to all concerned, and I guess if Mr. Reiss really wanted, he could by now get his dog into Hanselmanns on a strictly commercial basis.

• • •

A YEAR BEFORE he wrote *The Consul*, Menotti had received a commission from an American television network to write an original opera for TV for them. He was to deliver it within a period of twelve months "from the date hereof" and it was "to comply in all respects with their program policies" and in particular "was not to contain obscene or off-color themes, jokes, songs, sacrilegious expressions, or any other language of doubtful propriety." They paid him half of the agreed fee, which was much less than what Mr. Reiss got for *The Consul* in Vienna and very little considering all the restrictions of doubtful propriety they had imposed on him. The second half was to be paid upon delivery of the score.

The twelve months passed and still another year went by and Menotti was busy writing and producing and directing and casting and worrying about the Flemish translation and being harassed. He just couldn't think of a TV opera, and perhaps he didn't want to, because TV executives and lawyers make him nervous as, indeed, they should or, perhaps, he could only think of an obscene or off-color one which would not have complied with their program policies. The executives and lawyers kept on calling us, and at last Menotti said I just can't think of anything and frankly they bore me to tears. Now that I have a little money—Chandler had paid his royalties for *The Consul* on Broadway like the lord he is and there was the check from Reiss and the first guilders from Amsterdam—why don't we give them back their money and tell them to—?

We delivered the message, carefully stripped of its undeliverable undercurrent, but to no avail. They didn't want their money back; they wanted a TV opera. They would wait a little longer, the executive said, but not too much longer; otherwise we have to talk to our lawyers, and you don't want that and we really want something for Christmas. Menotti asked us to tell them maybe their lawyers would write the opera, and he would be glad to stage it, and they thought it was very funny and let's see what will happen. We didn't worry too much because as there was usually a different executive on the line every time we called because Mr. Yesterday's Executive isn't with us any more, we thought maybe the next one will just forget the whole thing and Gian Carlo can spend some more time learning Swedish so he can worry about the translation of *The Medium* for the production in Goteborg.

Then, all of a sudden, toward the middle of October 1951, Menotti called. "Tell NBC," he said, "I'll have an opera for them for this Christmas."

He had gone to an exhibit of paintings at the Metropolitan Museum, all pertaining to Christmas. Among them was *The Adoration of the Magi* by Hieronymus Bosch. As he saw the painting, he remembered lying in bed as a little boy, home in Cadegliano, in Lombardy, where he was born and grew up, waiting with his younger brother to hear the song of the three kings and the trot of their camels–there is no Santa Claus in northern Italy, it is the three kings who bring the children their gifts on Epiphany. Standing before the painting, he suddenly heard the supernatural song of the three kings coming over the hills. He also remembered that, as a boy, he had been lame for some time and had been, miraculously he believed, healed "in Varese." The story, soon to be known as *Amahl and the Night Visitors*, was before his eyes.

Soon October drifted away and November came–only

fifty-four writing, casting, rehearsing days till Christmas. Menotti had gone to Princeton to audition the Columbus Boys Choir and—as always—had come up with a marvelous choice, Chet Allen, the first Amahl, by now probably a huge, bearded father of seven, but then the most sensitive, charming-looking, touchingly singing little boy. One of our copyists took the morning train every morning to Mt. Kisco, where the cook, having driven down from Menotti's house, would meet him with a few penciled pages of music. The copyist had just time to snatch the music from the cook, dash across the rails, and catch the southbound train back to New York. By the time he arrived, most of the music had been copied in ink and a messenger boarded a train for Princeton, to be met there by a driver from the Boys Choir who delivered another bit of music for next morning's rehearsal. The music was completed in early December. There was little time left for Menotti to write out the orchestral score: he called in some of his pupils and while he paced up and down the studio, calling out flutes and oboes and strings —a Rubens of music—they filled in the details.

We heard *Amahl*—the title of the work and the musically flowing name of its hero had been last-minute inspirations—a few weeks before the Christmas deadline in the dingiest, dustiest, moth-eatenest ballroom in a now defunct Eighth Avenue hotel. Toscanini was among the small number of people who had come to the rehearsal. Gian Carlo directed tirelessly in the propless emptiness of the ballroom. Somebody played the music on an old upright. Olin Downes of *The New York Times* drifted in, a few musicians, a couple of NBC executives, happily sensing *Morgenluft*, at least one Italian countess.

The morning after the first performance *Amahl* made the front page of *The New York Times*. We went uptown to the Metropolitan Museum of Art and asked them to lend us their color plates for *The Adoration of the Magi.* We were going to put the picture in seven beautiful colors, in gold and purple and grateful incense, on our score.

It seemed the least we could do for Hieronymus Bosch after what he had done for us.

XVIII

AIDA was the last of twenty-two opera librettos to be sent to the printer. What a summer it had been, what a wonderful time. But now it was all over and done with. Tomorrow morning I would drive over to the little post office in Farley, Vermont, and mail the proofs back to New York. *Basta.*

For a month I had been watching the golfers, swimmers, and horseback riders leave refreshed in the morning and return exhausted at night while I sat on a porch at a rickety bridge table, peacefully and healthily proofreading librettos with no more exercise all day than finding a wrong accent on a *più* or discovering that Lohengrin was singing Elsa's lines. Every morning I mailed another batch of oversized galleys back to Schirmer's production department, which had thoughtfully provided me with oversized envelopes recklessly stamped with much too much postage. Every morning I had to upset the postmistress of Farley, a fine woman but unaccustomed to and horrified by such consistent extravagance. It was a lovely vacation.

• • •

THE PUBLICATION of Menotti's workshop-prone operas had brought revolutionary changes in our lives. We had entered into a brand-new, sparklingly interesting sphere of activities. Schirmer's, in the distant past, had published most of the standard operas under the guidance of Albert Schweitzer's corresponding editor, the late *Lieber Herr* Baker. The scores were mostly reproductions of European editions, even those which, like *Pagliacci*, *Cavalleria rusticana* or *Hänsel und*

Gretel were still copyrighted in Europe and in most other countries of the world and could be pirated legally only in the United States. Like so many other publications that owed their existence to the peculiarities of American copyright philosophy, these illegitimate operatic children were housed in the Schirmer warehouse in bins marked with a huge red arrow, a symbol supposed to tell the order-filler that such hot merchandise was not to be sent beyond the permissive borders. The symbol was increased in size as well as in the gaudiness of its coloring after the score of *La Bohème*, legally stolen from Ricordi fifty-six years after its first publication but still their most sacred property outside of the United States for many years to come, was sent as a "New Issue" to the Ricordi store on the Via Berchet in Milan, with a nice letter asking for their continued patronage and a bill really to rub it in.

The Schirmer vocal scores of standard operas had a moderate sale to the few American opera houses which occasionally needed a few copies, to music schools or singing studios, and to libraries which, hopefully, had to replace shopworn acquisitions every five years. Translations in turn-of-the century opera-ese had been printed in most of the scores, some of them—the worst—made by *Lieber Herr* Baker himself. The translations, quite apart of all their *thou*s and *thine*s, were unsingable: they were only meant to guide the public through German, Italian, French, and Russian texts, though many were easier and much more enjoyable reading in Russian. They were not meant to be used for performances in English, an act considered a sacrilege almost never committed and not taken into consideration by the translators. The scores had ugly, depressingly drab mustard-colored covers, and when the salesmen went on their cross-country trips, they skipped the section in the order blank headed Opera Scores and hurried toward greener pastures.

All this changed overnight. Already the outward appearance of our new crop indicated new basic attitudes. Grandma Moses looked real snappy on the score of Kurt Weill's *Down in the Valley*, poorly paid as she had been. Saul Steinberg contributed one of his melancholy fantasies for *The Telephone*, and the cover of *The Medium*, whatever else one thought of it, was at least bright red. When we published Menotti's *The Saint of Bleecker Street*, Gian Carlo took a painting of a saintly-looking lady from the wall of his studio in Mt. Kisco whence she had been looking on the Croton Reservoir for many years, and we made her, at great expense, into a superbly religious-looking cover. Bosch, of course, was *hors de concours*. Soon, the salesmen stopped skipping the opera section and, almost overnight, we had an entirely new business. Hundreds of places all over America which never before had shown interest in opera wanted to produce our new properties. We were utterly unprepared. We had no mailing lists, no precedents, no experience. We had to learn everything from our new customers.

We improvised and hurriedly printed licensing agreements but we didn't have the faintest idea what to charge. The new performers had no box office or, at best, charged only a nominal admission. What do you charge if you are part of a curriculum? So we telephoned some of our prospects, trying to make *them* tell *us* what their local traffic would bear, which turned out fine because they were flattered and somehow put on their honor and offered us much more than we would have dared to ask. If they refused to play our game and insisted instead that we quote them a fee, we felt depressed all day when they retorted with a cheerfully surprised "Oh, that's quite all right," or were happy for the rest of the week when they told us that we were out of our mind.

We had to learn fast. Only a fraction of the many who

suddenly wanted to become operatic producers—it didn't take long before we dealt with several hundred of them—could afford the expense of even so small an orchestra as most of our scores called for or had the space to seat it: we had to find a musician who made us two-piano arrangements of the Menotti scores, of *Down in the Valley*, and of a few similar works that drifted in. Many of the new producers had never produced an opera before: they needed help, and we had to find another man who made us stage guides, a craft he had inherited from the old Gilbert and Sullivan days: they were scores, interleaved with blank pages on which the man indicated props, costumes, and lights, and on which he drew fancy diagrams to suggest positions and movements for soloists, chorus, and supers.

Mr. Zimmermann who, until recently, had administered the Schirmer performance department not only single-handed but strictly on a part-time basis, spending the rest of his day with chores more profitable to the management, was relieved of all extraneous duties and given an assistant and a secretary. The tiny little black book in which he had in the past recorded his meager achievements—an occasional Roy Harris Third Symphony, a once-in-a-while Schuman *American Festival Overture*, an almost never Hadley *The Culprit Fay*—was replaced by a powder-blue card system in a gray metal box and he was forced, after a hard, emotional struggle, to throw the little black book away. It was a symbolic sacrifice.

As the appetite all over the country grew, we were desperately looking for new repertory to fill the rapidly increasing demands. But few composers in America were interested in or capable of writing theatrical material suitable for the very special performance conditions prevailing in our newly discovered operatic territories. Many of them weren't attracted to the theater at all and could point to Bruckner,

Chopin, Mahler, and Brahms to prove that composers could make the grade without bothering with opera. Others aimed at more ambitious, large-scale works in the great tradition of the professional international opera theater. So it was with excited anticipation that (on a Washington's birthday, I still remember my trip through the deserted streets of New York) I went to see Leonard Bernstein to try to talk him into finishing a little one-act opera he had been working at, off and on, for quite some time. After I had entered the ancient elevator in the building on Fifty-seventh Street where he lived, I knocked at its dark wood in happy superstition: it was the same building where *Down in the Valley*, my fortunate *Morgengabe* to Schirmer's, had been spawned. My mission was bound to succeed.

But L.B., strikingly dressed in a mauve velvet jacket that would have made Richard Wagner mauve with envy, wasn't at all sure about his new opera. He was still convinced that the work "just wasn't right" and that it didn't have a satisfactory ending, and as he was unable to think of a different one he suggested instead that we play Mozart on two pianos. Spanish bullfighters, looking at us from posters covering the walls, listened elegantly unconcerned to the many wrong notes I hit while Bernstein played away laughing, singing, shouting cues whenever I got lost, and politely and exuberantly pleased when we finished together.

Later, we went back to the opera. It was called *Trouble in Tahiti*, written to Bernstein's own libretto. He played and sang and acted, crying over the sad parts—"Isn't it beautiful!"—and jerkily dancing on the piano bench when playing and singing the marvelously nonsensical words and the sophisticated music of the little Greek-chorus blues trio, and when he played and jubilantly sang the later famous aria, "Oh, what a terrible movie," it sounded then and there like a later famous aria. The work had a cast of only five singers, a small orchestra, scenery that any college workshop would be most happy to design, build, and paint, and a story that would strike a responsive chord in every unhappily married couple in America and thus was sure to enjoy great popularity. The work was a natural.

It turned out to be just that when we heard it for the first time after we had climbed through the mud to a new, very unfinished auditorium at Brandeis University. Bernstein had decided to release *Trouble in Tahiti* for its dedication. Lotte Lenya and Marc Blitzstein were also there for a try-out of some of Kurt Weill's *Three Penny* songs with Blitzstein's ingeniously fitting English lyrics. There was also some *musique concrète* on the program, an attempt by a French engineer to use as musical material everyday noises, such as the falling of a drop of water in a sink or the roar of a train in a tunnel, a coughing, rasping granddad of electronic music. I was the moderator for the occasion—Bernstein still gratefully remembered the twenty-five dollars we had paid him for his piano arrangement of *El Salón Mexico*, and here was his chance to pay me back—introducing the works, the composers and M. Pierre Schaeffer's concrete tape of his *Symphonie pour un homme seul* over a badly wired loudspeaker, and having a marvelous time.

Bernstein had been under contract with us for several years. We had published a few piano pieces, some instrumental solos dedicated to various dogs, a song or two, and his second symphony, *Age of Anxiety* with piano solo. Everybody, of course, loved the composer, but it was again an awful lot of prestige music and when he brought us a Serenade for violin solo and string orchestra based on Plato, some in the organization who perhaps weren't sufficiently steeped in Greek philosophy began to wonder. Luckily, as it soon turned out, they were told by the management to wonder silently. We published the Serenade and we were really in the red, and then he walked in one day, with the music to *West Side Story* and the age of anxiety sure was over.

Bernstein is a publisher's dream. It isn't only that almost anything he touches turns into gold. He is wonderful to work with, reliable, grateful, and appreciative as few into-gold-turners ever are and, best of all, he is almost never seen. His scores, proofs, musical directives, and wishes are delivered through a musical assistant—and his wishes are wishes, never orders, and when they sound like orders we know it is the assistant speaking and pay no attention. Daily occurrences, a man in Yokohama asking for a score, a citizen of Gelsenkirchen wanting to know where he can buy a record of *Fancy Free*, a piano teacher in Tulsa writing at length to find out whether the d flat in one of Bernstein's piano pieces shouldn't be a d natural which, it turns out, it should be—these and many similar instances of public interest in his music are painstakingly and patiently related to us by a lady of angelic efficiency who had once been his piano teacher and has now, for many years, been Bernstein's alter ego. Business of a weightier nature is conducted by two soft-spoken, fast-thinking specialists, a lawyer and a CPA, Mr. Freeman and Mr. Friedman, who, when they are announced, sound like two emissaries from *Alice in Wonderland*, but are very real and quite formidable.

Publishers as a rule loathe composers who have agents, lawyers, accountants, or secretaries, and react most sourly toward those who try to inject an intermediary between the creator and the exploiter. Nobody minds the little protective army surrounding Leonard Bernstein. Obviously, he can only be all the things he is—conductor, music director, television star, script writer, author of books and librettos, musical pedagogue, box-office magnet, composer of kaddishes and hit shows, husband, father, Jew, best-dressed man of the age, pianist, and darling of at least three continents—by organizing his life down to the last detail.

I never dealt with anyone leading so hectic a life in so leisurely a way and with such contagious relaxation. Bernstein has either no time at all or all the time in the world. Angelic Miss Coates will call in January and tell you that he will see you in his dressing room on May 23 at two-thirty and, of course, you resent such princely arrangements. But when you arrive at two-thirty four and a half months later, still resentful, you are admitted on the dot. He is overjoyed and calls you Hansl, which nobody has called you since 1912, and you love it. He is the only composer you know who, when he asks you how you are, gives you, for a split second at least, the impression that he really wants to know although you have sense enough not to tell him.

There is nobody else at the interview with the exception perhaps of a young lady in a white smock who enters silently and wordlessly begins to massage his hair—but she isn't really present and she probably *really* came from *Alice in Wonderland* and will soon disappear through the large looking glass that is so essential a part of the dressing room. Nobody interrupts, nobody phones, nobody pops his head in the door, and for twelve and a half minutes you are given the impression that you are the only thing in the world that matters to L.B. Then Miss Coates knocks gently at the door and it is time to go. You'll have another chance in two years, eleven months, and four days.

• • •

THE MOST IMPORTANT and far-reaching impact of the new operatic explosion we had been so suddenly and so happily hit by was, so it soon appeared to us, the fact that the new operas were sung in English. For the first time a genuine, workable, contemporary repertory of operas was written to

English words. Its acceptance was an extraordinary event. It showed an inevitable, inescapable trend at a time of rapidly increasing new audiences and of a sudden plentiful supply of American singers on all levels of accomplishment.

Soon the Ford Foundation, responding to the startling combination of new forces and tendencies, began to pump close to a million dollars into the creation and performance of new American operas, subsidizing composers, libretto writers, and producers. While the results in many a case showed rather convincingly that money can't buy everything, the very fact that such a movement had got under way and had taken on such very large proportions showed where the new winds were blowing. From England came the operas of Benjamin Britten. Even Stravinsky wrote his only full-length opera, *The Rake's Progress*, to an original English libretto.

This had momentous consequences. The controversy—opera in English or opera in the original language—was rapidly resolved by the practical facts of American operatic life. Nobody suggested that Tebaldi or Nilsson should sing Puccini or Wagner in English. Nobody expected Freni and Corelli to sing of anything else but *amore*, and the outcome of a poll among Metropolitan audiences to determine whether they wanted to hear *La Bohème* in Italian or in English was, of course, as easy to predict as an election in Peking. But many of the large American universities created operatic theaters of almost professional excellence and performed their entire repertory—even *Parsifal*, even *Don Carlo*, even *Pelléas et Mélisande*—in English. They did not attempt to force their singers to parrot the sound of Italian, German, or French, which never sounded like the Italian, German, or French the composers had heard when they had written the music, or to sing and act, to love and die, in words and sentences which were not, in the moment of truth, their own and which were strictly Greek to their audiences. Verdi had insisted that his operas be performed in Paris in French; Gounod was delighted to conduct a series of German *Fausts* for a series of German marks. Wagner's *Tannhäuser*, during the composer's lifetime, was performed not only in French, as everybody knows, but also in Hungarian, Italian, Russian, Dutch, Danish, Swedish, and Polish. Purists have no help from the composers. When Walter Ducloux planned to produce Richard Strauss's last opera *Der Friedenstag* at the University of Southern California, the composer's son, Franz, wrote him that the work "must definitely be performed in translation, as it could not be understood otherwise and as it also was a principle of my father [and the son underlined the words *Grundsatz meines Vaters*] that his works should always be given in the *Landessprache*, the vernacular."

Soon professional ensembles—the Santa Fe Opera, for instance, or the yearly summer event in Central City—followed the same practice and gave most of their seasons, American works and imports, in English, to the ever-increasing delight of their ever-increasing audiences. Others, the New York City Opera a typical case, added a liberal sprinkling of performances in English to their traditional Italian *Butterflys* ("There are too many Italian barbers in New York—we just can't let them down") or French *Carmens*. A cycle of five Mozart operas in which people for the first time understood the recitatives, became one of the theater's most popular hits.

To us, sitting on *Lieber Herr* Baker's forty-five unsingable standard operas, only one conclusion was to be drawn from these developments, whose potential seemed limitless: the time had come to rapidly un-Baker our operatic scores and publish them in new, singable, performable, understandable, contemporary translations.

As we embarked on the new adventure—what a wonderful business to be in, always a new departure, always a shift in the wind, always a new frontier, just when you think the world is stale and dull and all staked out—I remembered well my own operatic upbringing in Germany and Vienna. The impact of opera first experienced in your own language is long and powerful. It brings opera very close to you. It isn't something strange, forbidding, something requiring the study of a score or of a libretto or both. You don't feel inferior because you don't know what "*Finch'han dal vino*" means. "*Wie eiskalt ist dies Händchen*" were the words we knew, understood, loved, sang, hummed, lived with as part of our musical experience, not a remote, icy "*gelida manina.*" *Die Liebe von Zigeunern stammt* was a coarse, flat, silly translation of Carmen's proclamation of the sorcery of love, but for us it was the opening line of the *habanera;* we sang it and we sing it to this day coming home from the opera house. Few will ever go home from the opera house in New York and probably none in Dallas, singing to their heart's delight "*L'amour est un oiseau rebelle.*"

Coarse, flat, often silly they were, these translations. But after a generation of singers had learned them, a generation of publishers had printed them, and a generation of operagoers had memorized them, nothing could be done about them anymore. The Toreador song, for any operagoer in the vast German operatic space, began with the words "*Auf in den Kampf.*" I remember a brave attempt at the Vienna opera to introduce a new, undoubtedly much better translation. It sounded all wrong to the audience. These were not the words Bizet had written his music to. After a few performances, when *Carmen* came back, back came "*Auf in den Kampf.*"

Whatever we do today may be around for a very long time. The operatic translator deals with very fragile and terribly celebrated material: "*La donna è mobile*," "*Celeste Aida*," "*Dies Bildnis ist bezaubernd schön*," "*E lucevan le stelle.*" Every word, every syllable filled with heavy tradition. The new words have to fit the sound of the original word and the music surrounding it, they have to fit the voice and the breathing of the singer, they have to sing easily and naturally. Operatic translation is not a sideline for doctors and retired businessmen, although it is surprising how many retired doctors and businessmen send us translations, mostly with unpleasant letters deriding those we already published and followed by even more unpleasant letters after we turn them down.

The operatic translator has to be a sensitive musician. He also must find a precarious balance between writing dull, pedestrian opera-ese and being cute and make eighteenth-century operatic figures use colloquial American slang. He must be good, but not too good. He is a servant of the composer, a craftsman, not a poet in his own right. After he wrote a novel about Verdi, Franz Werfel once tried his poetic hand on new translations of some of Verdi's operas. They read beautifully on paper, melted on the tongue when they were recited in a lecture hall, had elegant rhymes, and were brimming with suggestive, poetic images. But when they were sung on the stage the words were much too big for the music. They didn't serve: they tried to usurp. They soon disappeared again and the old, familiar, inferior but serving and serviceable words were restored.

One more basic directive: we tried to avoid desk translations: everything had to be tested in the cleansing fire of the stage. *The Magic Flute* and *Così fan tutte*, two out of a dozen translations Ruth and Thomas Martin had made for us—he a musician from Vienna, she a linguist from New Jersey—came from performances at the Metropolitan. Their *Figaro* came from the City Center. *The Merry Wives* came from Ann Arbor, *The Masked Ball* from Baton Rouge, *L'Elisir d'amore* from Central City, *The Tales of Hoffmann* from Cincinnati, *The Barber of Seville* from Lake George. Quite a few came from the defunct NBC opera theater, made by a prolific writer, Joe Machlis, whom, however, we tried to avoid, as he was always in Acapulco and infuriated everybody upon his return by a simply indecent tan. Many of our Verdi translations came from the University of Southern California, where Walter Ducloux, a veritable let-me-play-the-lion-too Bottom of opera, produces, conducts, coaches, determines the repertory, and translates. Only Richard Wagner posed a special problem: there weren't very many performances of his works in English and we had to look for untested literature. Luckily I remembered a very nice man who had once visited me and had left a volume of Wagner translations he had published. He hadn't asked for anything special, just had come in to say hello and to leave his paperback "in case." Well, the case was here. We located him with great difficulty and made a deal with him. It turned out that translating Wagner was his obsession, spiritualism his vocation. He invited me frequently to seances where I was to meet Robert Schumann to talk to him about the publication of a posthumous violin concerto.

One by one the new scores made their appearance. We had found a young lady whose husband worked on the night shift in one of the news agencies, coming home for dinner at six in the morning: she had interminable, quiet, and uninterrupted nightly hours on her hands and has filled them, for many years, by pasting, strip by never-ending strip, Martin, Ducloux, and Machlis over Dr. Baker's English words. We had found a man with the surest of hands who could change ties and bows and notes and rests on our printed pages to accommodate occasional changes in the music necessitated by the new English words. We trained still another freelancer to go to work and paste up chorus parts, writing in hundreds of bars of tacet till, at last, the chorus came in for twenty lines only to disappear again till Act IV, Scene 3. We published vocal scores and chorus parts and issued licenses, and Mr. Zimmermann's metal box was soon too small. And then, just as we were running out of projects and were already nibbling, a little desperately, at Rossini's *L'Italiana in Algeri* and trying to evaluate the doubtful potential sales of a new edition of Verdi's *Macbeth*, Mr. John Gutman called from the Metropolitan Opera and asked would I please come to see him.

Apparently they had been watching our efforts with as much benevolence as the high and the mighty will ever be able to muster. John explained that the Met, for seventy-five years, had been selling librettos published by the firm of Fred Rullman. Rullman had been a ticket broker. He had obligated himself, way, way back, to buy whole blocks of tickets at the beginning of a season if, in return, he would have the concession to print the official Met libretto. He had long since departed, of course, and the affairs of the firm had been in the hands of a lawyer by the name of—honestly—George Frederic Handel. Handel, too, had now reached if not surpassed the age of Methuselah and the ancient contract was coming to an end. Would we be willing and able to produce a complete line of brand new librettos by September?

This was March. He also pointed out that all of them would have to have new translations as well as the carefully revised and corrected original text, a history of the opera, a synopsis, an index scene by scene; that they were to be printed on special paper; that each translation would have to be approved by him, Gutman, and the new cover design by the great Bing himself. There would be twenty-four operas in the repertory the next season. Two were the property of other publishers and therefore untouchable. Twenty-two would be our responsibility.

And so we went to work, consulting vocal scores and full scores, first editions and later editions, battling accents in French and Italian and umlauts in German and making an agonizing choice between da sè, Da sè, (da sè), (Da sè), da se. and Da se., all of which appeared frequently on one and the same libretto. We began shortening lengthy stage directions which were useful in a score but of no interest to the reader, wrote erudite introductions with the help of erudite junior assistants, and lifted synopses from books and magazines. The summer came, the opening of the Met was only a few months away, and at last I packed my proofs and a couple of dictionaries and went off to Lake Morley, Vermont. I had a fine summer with Ortrud, Elsa, Leonore, Dorabella, and Cio-Cio-San. Then at last, it was all over and done with. The next morning I would drive to the little post office in Farley for the last time and mail the last batch of proofs to New York. We would meet our deadline.

And then, just as I was about to seal the oversized envelope with its much too many stamps, something made me take the proofs of *Aida* out again for one more, unscheduled look. This is what I read on page 5:

AMNERIS

Yes, Radames was killed in battle.
Why are you crying?

AIDA

I'll cry to the end of time.

AMNERIS

The gods have wrought your vengeance.

AIDA

They always brought me despair and disaster.

AMNERIS

Tremble! I can read your heart!
Best regards.

"Best regards?" *Best regards!* It didn't take long to find out what had happened. Walter Ducloux, on reading the last proofs, had made a change. He sent a letter containing these passages, and ended it—and why not?—with "Best regards." To make sure that his change would be transmitted to the printer without any possible chance of a new mistake, we cut out that section of his letter and pasted it on the proof. What could be safer? But we had also cut out "Best regards" . . .

XIX

I KEPT THE PROOF and pasted it on my wall as a steady, salutary reminder of our follies and of the pitfalls waiting for us at every bend of the road. But it also seemed to sum up, nicely, what had brought me along this multi-bended road from the day I had said a hasty good-bye to Professor Honiger in Freiburg and had boarded the fateful train to Vienna, many years ago. Because Aida couldn't possibly be just any pin-up girl. No pin-up girl was ever called Aida. It could only be the embodiment, the very symbol of music. And he who isn't happily prepared to wink at her and to give her his very best regards every morning before he sits down to work on his music publishing desk, he better be a district attorney in Obergrundersheim.

• • •

THE TWENTIES, the forties, the sixties are slowly fading into musical history, waiting for its bitter, acid tests.

When I wrote my book *Menagerie in F Sharp* twenty years ago, I opened it with a visit to Symphony Hall in Boston on a Friday afternoon. Ernst Krenek, like myself a newcomer to the then safer shores of the new world, played his Piano Concerto. It was radical, atonal, aggressive music. An old lady next to me joined in the polite applause and then looked at the program. After a while she turned to her husband and said: "Conditions in Europe must be dreadful."

That was in 1938. Thirty years later, the old lady's daughter was surely again in Row F, Seat 11, where her mother and grandmother had been on Friday afternoons. On the program was a new piano concerto, this time by an

American composer. And if she had inherited not only Seat 11, Row F, but also the brilliant perception that should have put the mother among the great thinkers of our time, the daughter could have said only one thing: "Conditions in the world must be dreadful."

I must end my report.

To the eager young men who surround me I am, I suppose, a slightly frayed Hertzka myself. It is nice to hear them say, my God, what you know and how much experience you have and what we can learn from you, but I don't fool myself. I remember that we said the same things to old Mephistopheles in Vienna, but after we closed the door we said I wish the old man would stop philosophizing and telling us what to do and when he starts reminiscing I wish he'd stayed in textiles. I won't even try to tell my eager young men that we thought it was a good fortune to be in our twenties in the twenties. It doesn't mean a thing to them. They will have the good fortune to peek into the next century.

And the very last thing I will ever tell them is that we meet some of our composers in a place called Quo Vadis? when there are ten thousand restaurants in New York with simple, culinary names. They are sharp. They'll get the significance.

Maybe, one of these days I will decrumple my doctoral diploma after all and have it framed and put it on the wall next to Aida. I still have it at home in a slightly torn, bulging folder, together with my old German passport and my American citizenship papers and the New York birth certificates of my children and the little, color-framed cards announcing the birth of theirs. The diploma is in Latin, so nobody can really read it, and it won't do me much harm any more after all these years. But I will feel a little more secure when I look at the date, MCMXXIII, and won't mind so much when

I see the respectfully condescending disapproval on the eager faces of my young men and know what they will say to each other after they close the door.

Later, I will wink at Aida and wave at the old diploma, quite content to go to lunch all by myself after I have asked one of my eager young men: "Would you like to join me?" and he has looked at his eager calendar and said "So sorry."

INDEX

INDEX

INDEX

A NOTE ABOUT THE AUTHOR

Hans Walter Heinsheimer was born in Karlsruhe, Germany, in 1900. After university studies in Heidelberg, Munich, and Freiburg, he became (1923–38) Director of Operatic Activities for Universal Edition, the great Vienna music publishing house. Later (1938–47) he was Director of Symphonic and Operatic Music for Boosey & Hawkes, New York. Since 1947 he has been Director of Publications for G. Schirmer. He is the author of two earlier books: *Menagerie in F Sharp* (1947) and *Fanfare for Two Pigeons* (1952), and has contributed articles to *Holiday*, *The Metropolitan Opera Program*, *Opera News*, *Reader's Digest*, and *Saturday Review*. Mr. Heinsheimer and his wife, who have two married children, live in New York.

A NOTE ON THE TYPE

The text of this book was set on the Linotype in Janson, a recutting made direct from type cast from matrices long thought to have been made by the Dutchman Anton Janson, who was a practicing type founder in Leipzig during the years 1668-87. However, it has been conclusively demonstrated that these types are actually the work of Nicholas Kis (1650-1702), a Hungarian, who most probably learned his trade from the master Dutch type founder Kirk Voskens. The type is an excellent example of the influential and sturdy Dutch types that prevailed in England up to the time William Caslon developed his own incomparable designs from these Dutch faces.

The book was designed by Anita Karl.
It was composed, printed, and bound
by The Haddon Craftsmen, Inc.,
Scranton, Pennsylvania